THE BEGINNINGS
OF BUDDHISM

THE

BEGINNINGS OF
BUDDHISM

by KŌGEN MIZUNO

translated by
Richard L. Gage

KŌSEI PUBLISHING CO.   *Tokyo*

Gautma Buddha - Teachings

This book was originally published in Japanese under the title *Bukkyō no Genten*.

The device used on the title page and chapter-opening pages is the Sanskrit character meaning "Tathāgata Shakyamuni," an epithet of the historical Buddha.

Edited by Ralph Friedrich. Cover design and layout of illustrations by Nobu Miyazaki. Book design and typography by Rebecca M. Davis. The text of this book is set in monotype Baskerville with handset Lidiant for display.

First English edition, 1980
Fifth printing, 1992

Published by Kōsei Publishing Co., Kōsei Building, 2-7-1 Wada, Sugi-nami-ku, Tokyo 166. Copyright © 1974, 1980 by Kōsei Publishing Co.; all rights reserved. Printed in Japan.

LCC 81-127127   ISBN 4-333-00383-0

Contents

Preface   ix
     A Note on Names and Spellings, *x*

1. The Indian Background   3
     The Culture of Ancient India, *3*   Indian Philosophy at the Time of Shakyamuni's Birth, *5*

2. Shakyamuni: From Birth to the Great Departure   9
     Political Conditions in the India of Shakyamuni's Time, *9* The Year and Day of Shakyamuni's Birth, *11*   Birth and Life in the Palace, *14*   The Great Departure, *17*

3. Discipline and Enlightenment   20
     Meeting with the King of Magadha, *20*   Meditation Practices, *22*   Ascetic Austerities, *24*   Enlightenment, *26*

4. The First Sermon and the Beginning of the Teaching Mission   28
     After Enlightenment, *28*   Departing to Teach, *31*   The First Sermon, *33*

5. Yasa and Teaching by Due Course   36
The Four Friends of Yasa, *39* Initial Enlightenment
Through Intellectual Comprehension or Through Faith, *41*

6. The Four Noble Truths and the Principle of
Healing   43
Suffering and Its Cause, *47* Suffering Eliminated and the
Way to Eliminate It, *51* The Eightfold Noble Path, *54*

7. The Growth of the Buddhist Order   59
Early Missionary Activities, *59* The Journey to Uruvela,
60 The Heart of Benevolence, *64* Entry into Rajagaha,
65 The Conversion of the Two Great Disciples, *68* The
Two Great Disciples and Maha-Kashyapa, *87*

8. The Visit to Kapilavatthu   90
The Conversion of Suddhodana and the Shakyas, *90* Rea-
sons for Turning to Religion and Growth Thereafter, *93*
The Conversion of Upali, *97*

9. Clergy and Laity   99
Abandoning Secular Life as a Custom, *99* Characteristics
and Value of the Order, *103* The Sangha, or the Order, *105*

10. From Magadha to Anga   109
Shakyamuni's Reputation, *109* The Conversion of Pukkusati, *112* The Conversion of Sona, *114*

11. Buddhism and Jainism   120
Early Buddhism and Jainism, *120* Jainism and Buddhism in
Magadha, *122* Jainism in the Lands of the Shakyas and the
Vajjis, *126*

12. Reacting to Outside Criticism and Praise   130

13. Buddhism in Kosala   135

The Founding of the Jetavana Monastery, *135* Early Buddhism in Kosala, *139* Legends Born About This Time, *142* From the Land of the Bhaggas to Kosambi, *145*

14. The Law of the Buddha and the Law of the
    World   148
    True Men of Religion, *148* The Law of the World and the Law of the Universe, *151*

15. Oneness of Theory and Practice   157

16. Supernatural Powers   163
    Shakyamuni's Supernatural Powers, *167* Prohibition of the Use of Supernatural Powers, *169*

17. The Great Decease   173
    Moral Conduct and the Mirror of the Law, *176* The Rainy Season and the Buddha's Illness, *179* The Four Great Teachings and the Final Meal, *181* The Twin *Sala* Trees, *185* The First Council, *189*

18. A Buddhist Guide for Living   192

Glossary   200

Index   214

Map   12

Photographs   69

Preface

In the eighteen chapters of this book, I give an account of basic Buddhism, centered on the life of Shakyamuni, the historical Buddha, and the primitive teachings of his time. The book is not an ordered, doctrinal presentation but a blend of what I have to say about the teachings and of material concerning the life of Shakyamuni taken from the oldest and most reliable sources. Though I did not intend to write a detailed biography, I have made use of the historical evidence considered most correct.

The oldest extant Buddhist classics—the Agama sutras and the Vinaya-pitaka—were not written as biographies of Shakyamuni and contain only a fragmentary exposition of his words, actions, teachings, and discussion. These works, which cover a period of more than forty years, deal less with the life of Shakyamuni than with correct revelations of his teachings and, although not compiled with the intention of producing scholarly, historically factual records, contain fairly detailed accounts of the first two or three years of activity after Shakyamuni attained enlightenment and of the events of the period of about a year surrounding his entrance into nirvana.

The writing of biographies of Shakyamuni did not begin until several centuries after his death. There are about ten kinds of such biographies, all of which show him as a superhuman being for whom nothing was impossible. They reveal his greatness but fail to give a picture of his true humanity and go too far in the effort to create a powerful impression.

Attempts on the part of later writers to make Shakyamuni seem supernatural led Western scholars to assume that he had never existed as an actual human being but was a fiction invented on the basis of ancient Indian sun myths. In order to obtain an impression of Shakyamuni as a living human being and to understand his true greatness, it is essential to rely on the unembellished accounts found in the oldest historical sources. Though fragmentary and incomplete, this material gives a clearer, more vital picture than accounts compiled in later periods.

A true picture of Shakyamuni and the religion he founded is of maximum importance today for the following reasons. Shakyamuni is ranked as one of the four great sages of the world, together with Socrates, Jesus Christ, and Confucius. Buddhism itself ranks with Islam and Christianity as one of the world's three great religions. People of learning and culture in both the East and the West who attempt to interpret the issue impartially agree that, of the four great sages, Shakyamuni had the most harmonious and outstanding personality. Furthermore, cultural leaders throughout the world insist that, in terms of rationality and of inspiring peace and a spirit of generosity, either Buddhism or something similar to it is the ideal kind of religion for the future of all mankind.

A Note on Names and Spellings Western scholars generally employ the word Buddha—which means the Enlightened One —as the name of the historical Shakyamuni in the same sense in which Jesus Christ is a name. There are two reasons for this prevailing Western usage. First, occidental scholars learned about Buddhism initially from such places as Sri Lanka (Ceylon), Burma, and Thailand, countries where Southern (or Theravada) Buddhism is practiced and where the word Buddha is in fact often used to mean Shakyamuni. Second, people in the West recognize only Shakyamuni as a Buddha and consider the two appellations synonymous. On this point, they are misinformed. Recognizing other Buddhas of the past and the future, Southern Buddhism makes a distinction by referring to Shakyamuni as Gotama Buddha, Gotama being a surname of the Shakya clan into which Shakyamuni was born. In his own time, Shakyamuni was referred to by people of other religions as Samana Gotama, which means Gotama the ascetic. Consequently, there is substantiation for the Southern Buddhist tradition of employing this name.

The teachings of Northern (or Mahayana) Buddhism differ in many respects from those of Southern Buddhism. One point of discrepancy is the Northern belief that, in addition to the many Buddhas in the three realms of past, present, and future of the world in which we live—the world subject to transmigrations—in the worlds of the ten directions of space (eight points of the compass and the nadir and zenith), there are innumerable other Buddhas. All of these Buddhas are categorized according to time, space, and the basic natures of the Buddhas themselves. Since there are many Buddhas in Southern Buddhism and many more in Northern Buddhism, to refer to Shakyamuni simply as the Buddha invites confusion. The problem is solved, however, if one of the more exact names of the founder of the religion is used. In this book, the name Shakyamuni (Sage of the Shakya Clan) is generally employed, and the term Buddha is restricted to those instances in which stress should be placed on the sense "the Enlightened One."

In relation to the spelling of names and terms derived from original Pali and Sanskrit sources, it should be noted that these are given in the form in which they are most familiar to Western readers. Thus, for example, the Sanskrit "Kāśyapa" and the Pali "Kassapa" are rendered as "Kashyapa" and the Sanskrit "Śāriputra" and the Pali "Sāriputta" become "Shariputra." Diacritical marks are not used, and the interests and convenience of the general reader have been given preference over strict scholarly accuracy. Pali and Sanskrit spellings are included in the glossary.

THE BEGINNINGS
OF BUDDHISM

I. The Indian Background

The Culture of Ancient India   Great and heroic people alter the times and world in which they live, but we cannot appreciate how they do this unless we understand their environments and backgrounds. For this reason, it is impossible to have a clear understanding of Buddhism unless one takes into consideration the cultural, philosophical, and religious background of the India of about two thousand five hundred years ago.

In the main, the culture of ancient India was produced by the Aryan people, who, crossing from central Asia and through northern Iran, invaded northwestern India and conquered the indigenous Dravidians around 1500 B.C. The Dravidians survive today in the Tamil people of the Deccan region of southern India. The Aryans, who are related to the Iranians and to the peoples of Europe, used the name Aryan, which means noble, to indicate their conviction of superiority in comparison with the indigenous people.

Upon entering India, the Aryans found it necessary to call on the assistance of their gods, who were deifications of such natural phenomena as the air, the heavens, and the earth, to assist them in battling with the local population and overcoming the extreme severities of the climate. The hymns they composed to help them in worship are what are known as the Vedas—the earliest portion, or four metrical hymnals—which, still extant after three thousand years, are treasured and deeply revered by the Hindus. The early age of Aryan history is called the Vedic period after these hymnals.

After the Vedic period, the Aryans defeated their enemies the Dravidians and either forced them into the south or enslaved them. They came to enjoy an age of peace and leisure, during which they produced the Brahmanas, or commentaries on sacred rituals, and established and rigidified a caste system in which position and occupation were fixed by birth. The castes were as follows: Brahmans (priests), Kshatriyas (warriors and members of the ruling class), Vaishyas (farmers, shepherds, and people of commerce), and Sudras (slaves). The Brahmans, occupying the highest social position, were responsible for religious rituals and prayers and for education. They were practically gods on earth. The Kshatriyas, who protected and governed the land, were taught by the Brahmans, whose instructions they were constrained to obey. The Vaishyas, who were controlled and protected by the Kshatriyas, accounted for the mass of the population and engaged in production and commerce. All of these three castes were of Aryan blood, though only the Brahmans were pure. The other castes were mixed. The slave caste consisted of the conquered Dravidians. Not recognized as fully human, they were worked like cattle and treated as mere property. They were not permitted to profess faith in the Vedic religion. According to Brahmanic teachings, distinctions were drawn on the basis of both race and caste; and when the upper orders were in danger or trouble, it was thought perfectly permissible for them to take life or property or otherwise violate the rights of the lower orders. The same acts of good and evil received different rewards and punishments depending on the caste of the person committing them, and prayers were thought truly effective in making people happy only when conducted in the prescribed Brahman way by Brahman priests.

When the request a person made of the gods was large, he was expected to make great offerings. The greater the request, the greater the offering in property and in such livestock as goats, sheep, and horses. The offerings became the property of the Brahman priests, who specified what should be presented to the gods and what merit should be attached to each kind of gift. In doing this, of course, they fattened their own purses. In short, their undertaking was less a true religion than a kind of commercial deal employing the gods.

In cases of especially large-scale requests, not only animals but also human beings were sacrificed. In such self-centered willingness to sacrifice the lives of animals and even of human beings for the sake of personal happiness, compassionate or loving care, respect for life, and human equality were completely lacking; and this lack was the major fault of the formalized Brahmanic religion.

Indian Philosophy at the Time of Shakyamuni's Birth Two or three centuries before the birth of Shakyamuni, the center of Indian culture moved from the upper reaches of the Indus River southeastward to the upper and then to the middle reaches of the Ganges. It was in this new cultural heartland that Shakyamuni lived and taught.

From the time preceding his birth, a number of powerful kings had struggled for supremacy in this area. As the political power of the ruling clans gradually grew stronger, the new land developed to become rich in agriculture, animal husbandry, and production. Weaving and dyeing, pottery making, woodcraft, bamboo craft, work in ivory, and metalwork flourished, as did trade in the articles produced. Large cities grew up in places strategically located for land and water transport. In urban centers, accumulation of produce and wealth gave rise to the growth of a class of rich merchants. Concurrent with these developments, the kings and ordinary people of the newly prospering regions came to exercise actual political and economic authority, while the Brahmans were relegated to a position in which they did nothing but conduct religious ceremonies, offer prayers, and rely on the people actually in power for protection.

As politics and economics developed along these lines, human thinking grew in sophistication. People became aware of themselves; and those who were sensitive to such matters found it impossible to believe that human happiness, unhappiness, and fate in general depended on such things as ceremonies and gods. They came to see that not an outside force but the good and bad acts and the efforts of the individual exercised decisive influence. This gave rise to a belief in the law of cause and effect and of karma, or the results of actions, according to which theories a good cause produces a good effect and an evil cause an evil effect. Though it was the philosophy of the Upanishads—late Vedic treatises dealing with man in relation to the universe—that supported this new Brahman doctrine, it seems that the doctrine itself was first voiced by the ruling class and was taken over by the Brahman class later. Finally it became a common feature of all Indian religion and philosophy.

Another distinctive feature of the Upanishadic philosophy is the belief that the individual self (atman) is of the same nature as, and one with, the universal Self (Brahman). According to this doctrine, as long as the human being remains under the control of the laws of karma (results of actions) and of cause and effect, he is bound to an unending cycle of transmigrations and can never know true happiness. In order to find such happiness, it is necessary to break the cycle of transmigrations, shatter the bonds of karma, and attain the ideal realm in which atman and Brahman unite. To achieve this, systems of asceticism and meditation were evolved, though nothing has come down to us to indicate that any of the Upanishadic philosophers actually attained the ideal realm.

Buddhism too adopted the Upanishadic philosophy. For instance, it teaches the doctrines of karma, transmigration, and cause and effect in the three worlds (past, present, and future) of sentient beings and the idea that, in the world of transmigration, evil karma and unhappiness must be eliminated. But Buddhism goes further to teach that, as long as good karma and the happiness caused by it are controlled by transmigration, they cannot be absolute and that only when a being has entered the tranquil realm of nirvana, where the bonds of transmigration and karma no longer exist, can he attain the ideal. Buddhism is like other later Indian religions in that its ideal is escape from the cycle of transmigration.

But the teachings of the Upanishads, regarded as secret, were passed only from Brahman teacher to student and were not for general consumption. Such secrecy inspired members of the royal

clans and the ordinary citizenry who did not have access to Upanishadic wisdom but nonetheless wanted to solve the great problems
of human existence to abandon secular life and go in search of
enlightenment on their own. In contrast with orthodox members of
the Brahman caste who went in search of wisdom, seekers from all
of the other castes—except the slave Sudras—were called *samanas*,
which means monk or ascetic. As I have already mentioned, Shakyamuni was one of these *samanas*. Unorthodox *samanas* did not rely
on Brahmanic teachings but established their own theories.

By about the time of Shakyamuni, there were already many
such unorthodox seekers of truth, not a small number of whom
claimed to have found enlightenment and headed large groups of
disciples and believers. The six heretical, or non-Buddhist, teachers
mentioned in Buddhist writings are outstanding examples of the
type. Among these men there was a variety of philosophical approaches: nihilists who denied father and mother, good and evil,
cause and effect, and karma; materialists who claimed that nothing
had actual existence but the elements that compose flesh and who
therefore rejected both spirits and good and evil karma; fatalists
who held that the conditions in which the elements were combined at birth determined personality and fate or that, since good
and evil past karma dictated life, actions and efforts in this world
could not alter the preordained situation; and skeptics who, seeing
that all people argued in favor of their own versions of the truth,
insisted that so many truths could not exist and therefore doubted
the very existence of truth itself and refused to make any judgments
on the issue of good and evil.

In spite of their numerous conflicting doctrines and teachings, the
samanas are said to have won respect among ordinary people for the
comparatively serious way in which they lived and for their fasting
and ascetic practices. But much of their actual practice was irrational. Some of them superstitiously claimed that covering the body
with dust or dirt or living like a dog or an elephant guaranteed
liberation in the coming world, that all guilt could be cleansed
away by bathing in a holy river, or that directions and dates dictated human fate.

Shakyamuni was born into an age of such spiritual and philosophical confusion. He observed all of this, experienced some of it directly, and, always with a critical attitude, selected what was worthwhile. He then discovered a new, independent theory and a way of putting it into practice. On the basis of these discoveries he founded Buddhism.

2. Shakyamuni: From Birth to the Great Departure

Political Conditions
in the India of
Shakyamuni's Time In the sixth or fifth century B.C., Shakyamuni was born a prince in a small state extending from what is now southern Nepal to the northern border of India. At this time, India was divided politically into sixteen major states, all of which were engaged in a bloody survival-of-the-fittest struggle for supremacy. Highly unstable political conditions were reflected in the inability of the people at large to achieve unity among various orthodox and unorthodox religious and philosophical views. Some awaited the coming of the great wheel-rolling king (*chakravarti-raja*), who would rule the world, not by armed force but by virtue, whereas others longed for the appearance of a great teacher, or Buddha, who would bring man spiritual salvation.

The state of the Shakya tribe, into which Shakyamuni was born, was not one of the sixteen major states. Located in the foothills of the Himalayas, remote from political centers, it enjoyed calm in the midst of general warfare. But since it was subordinate to the great kingdom of Kosala directly to the southeast, it was not entirely independent. It is believed that numbers of small states came into being in India several centuries before the birth of Shakyamuni. In the early stages, most of them were what might be called aris-

9

tocratic republics run by means of a system according to which all members of the tribe occupying and controlling the particular land area ruled together. A state in India during this period was designated not by the name of the land on which the people lived but by the name of the ruling tribe—that is, the tribe constituted the nation, and the nation was referred to by the name of the tribe. The country of the Shakyas was a council-system republic ruled by the aristocratic class of the Shakya tribe. There were other similar aristocratic republican states—for instance, the Malla and Vajji states to the southeast of the Shakyas. But since they were weak, such states were gradually conquered by the autocratic monarchies around them.

Among all the states of India at that time, the four greatest were the autocratic monarchies of Kosala, Magadha, Vansa, and Avanti. They had already annexed some of their neighboring sixteen major states: Kosala annexed Kasi, Magadha annexed Anga, Vansa annexed Cheti, and Avanti annexed Assaka. And not long after the death of Shakyamuni, Magadha was to rule the entire region around the middle reaches of the Ganges by conquering the Vajjis, neighbors on the north; the Mallas, still farther north; and the formerly mighty Kosala.

Though not directly under its control, the Shakya state was in the field of power of Kosala and is sometimes referred to as the Shakya of Kosala. Since the Shakyas had moved to the region at the foothills of the Himalayas from the central part of India several generations before the birth of Shakyamuni, they were already an established royal clan, though the area they controlled was small. Because they were remote and had little contact with the central powers, they had no need of the four kinds of fighting forces common in India at the time: infantry, cavalry, chariot-mounted warriors, and elephant-mounted warriors. In the late years of Shakyamuni's life, the Shakya state was swallowed up by Kosala.

At the time of Shakyamuni's birth, his father Suddhodana had been elected king of the state. The five hundred families of the Shakya clan that are thought to have made up the tribe owned all towns, villages, and fortresses. As the most outstanding family in the tribe, the Gotama, Shakyamuni's family, owned the fortified town of Kapilavatthu, which was centrally located and which they made their capital.

The Year and Day of Shakyamuni's Birth   There are no historical records about the year and day of the birth of Shakyamuni, and there can be no accurate way of ascertaining the date now. Nor is this surprising, since dates in ancient Indian history are usually impossible, or at least highly difficult, to pinpoint. One of the most certain dates in this period, however, is that of the reign of the third-century-B.C. emperor, Asoka, who can be placed with some certainty because, in the edicts that he had carved in stone, mention is made of five Greek kings whose dates are known in Western history.

There are two Buddhist traditions about the relation between the date of Shakyamuni's death and the ascension to the throne of Emperor Asoka. The Southern Buddhists hold that Asoka acceded to the throne 218 years after the death of Shakyamuni; the Northern Buddhists say that 116 years separate the two events. Though there is roughly a century between the two dates, both Northern and Southern Buddhists agree that Shakyamuni lived for eighty years. Therefore, according to the Southern Buddhist reckoning, he lived between 560 and 480 B.C. and, according to the Northern Buddhist reckoning, between 460 and 380 B.C. Though the former interpretation is more widely held, the latter is not without supporters. Such countries as Sri Lanka, Burma, and Thailand, which follow the Southern Buddhist tradition, claim that Shakyamuni lived eighty years and died in either 544 or 543 B.C. and date the foundation of their nations from whichever of the dates they assume to be correct.

There is no documentary evidence clearly establishing the day on which Shakyamuni was born. Japanese and Chinese Buddhists, following texts on the life of Shakyamuni translated into Chinese from Sanskrit—for example the Buddhacharita—celebrate April 8 as his birthday and hold ceremonies in which sweet tea is poured over a statue representing him as a newborn infant. (The tradition arises from a legend that Shakyamuni was washed with warm and cool waters at birth.) Since the late nineteenth century, in Japan,

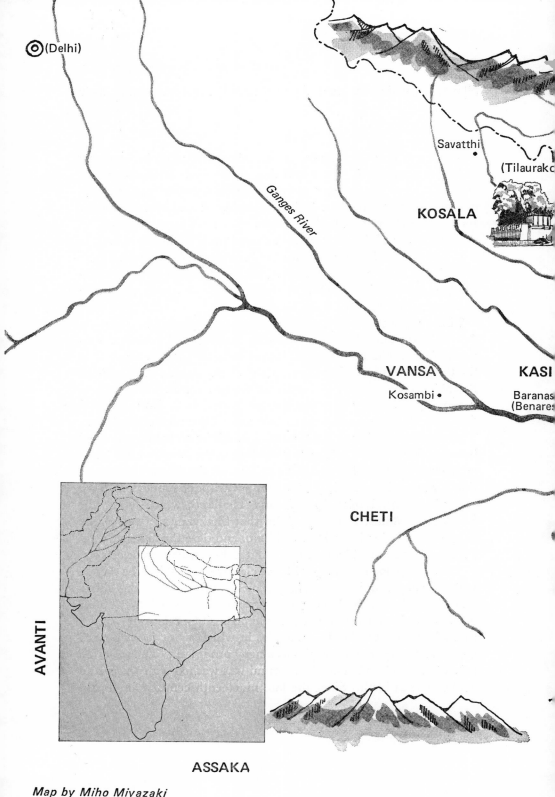

(Delhi)

Ganges River

Savatthi

(Tilaurako

KOSALA

VANSA

KASI

Kosambi

Baranas
(Benares

CHETI

AVANTI

ASSAKA

Map by Miho Miyazaki

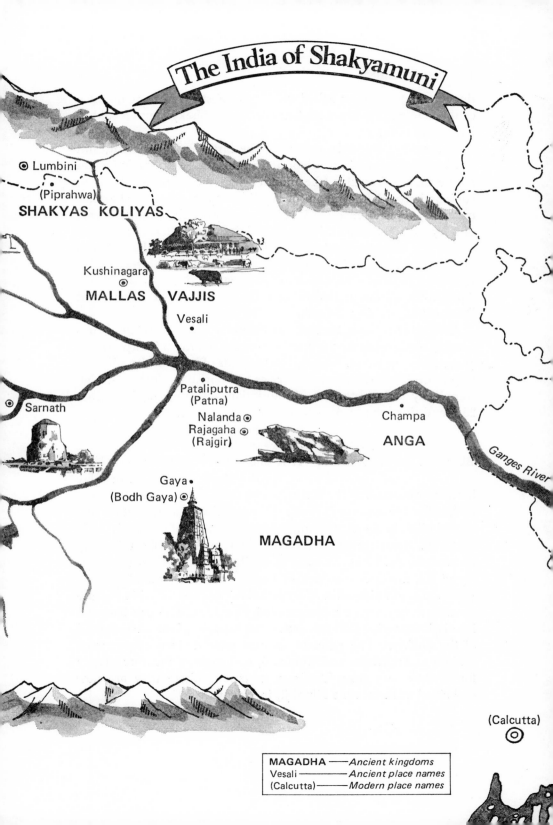

The India of Shakyamuni

Lumbini
(Piprahwa)
SHAKYAS KOLIYAS

Kushinagara
MALLAS VAJJIS

Vesali

Sarnath

Pataliputra
(Patna)
Nalanda
Rajagaha
(Rajgir)

Champa
ANGA

Gaya
(Bodh Gaya)

MAGADHA

Ganges River

(Calcutta)

MAGADHA	— *Ancient kingdoms*
Vesali	— *Ancient place names*
(Calcutta)	— *Modern place names*

this ceremony has been called the Flower Festival in remembrance of the flower-filled Lumbini Garden, where Shakyamuni is said to have been born.

In Southern Buddhist countries, the birth, enlightenment, and death of Shakyamuni are celebrated on the same day: the full moon in the month Vesakha (the month when the star Vesakha is in conjunction with the moon, or April-May according to the solar calendar). The full moon of Vesakha usually occurs in the early part of May. Southern Buddhists call the joint celebration of the three events the Vesakha Festival, and in recent years similar celebrations have been held by some Japanese. In general, however, Chinese and Japanese Buddhists assign separate dates to the three: April 8, the birthday; December 8, the day of enlightenment; and February 15, the day of death.

Absence of reliable ancient documentary evidence makes it impossible to say whether the Northern or the Southern interpretation of the dates is correct. Nonetheless, as parts of long local traditions, they both deserve as much respect as the Christian custom—which completely lacks historical substantiation—of assigning December 25 the distinction of being the birthday of Jesus Christ.

Birth and Life in the Palace   It is said that Shakyamuni was born in the Lumbini Garden, which lay between the states of the Shakyas and the Koliyas. Over two centuries after Shakyamuni's death, Emperor Asoka set up a stone memorial pillar in the garden and reduced the taxes of people living in that area. Since the pillar survives today, it is possible to identify the site exactly. Furthermore, it is possible to know where the country of the Shakyas was located because an urn revered by that tribe and containing relics of Shakyamuni was unearthed in the late nineteenth century at a place called Piprahwa. The urn bears an inscription proving that this area is the location of the ancient land of the Shakyas. The relics in the urn were divided among such nations as Sri Lanka and Thailand, and some of them ultimately found their way from Thailand to Japan, where they are now enshrined in the temple Nittai-ji, in Nagoya.

As was customary in her time, Maya, the mother of Shakyamuni, wished to give birth to her child in her own family home, which was located in Devadaha, the capital of Koliya. As a princess of the royal house of that state, she was related by family ties to the Gotamas. (The kings of the two states were brothers, and the families intermarried. Indeed, Yasodhara, who was to become the bride of Shakyamuni, was a princess of the Koliya royal house.)

On the way to Devadaha, Maya stopped to rest in the Lumbini Garden, where she admired the riot of flowers. When she raised her right arm to pluck a flowering branch from an *asoka* tree, she felt initial labor pains. Without further preparations, she gave birth under the tree. Legend has it that the *nagas* (dragon-kings) provided warm and cool water for Shakyamuni's first bath. This probably means that water, heated and unheated, from a nearby pond was used.

Another Buddhist legend says that immediately after birth the infant took seven steps and said, "I alone am honored, in heaven and on earth." There is no ancient documentary evidence for this tradition. The oldest records claim that, on his way to Benares after his enlightenment, Shakyamuni made this statement to Upaka, a young believer of another religion.

Since he had long awaited a child, King Suddhodana and everyone else in the palace were overjoyed at the birth of a son. The king immediately called a famous seer named Asita, who stated that, if he remained at home, the child would become the wheel-rolling king and that, if he left home, he would become the great teacher, the Buddha.

Highly satisfied, the king gave his son the name Siddhattha, which means "he who has accomplished his aim." Perhaps it seems odd to give a name like this to a newborn child, but the act is related to the Indian and Buddhist belief that former lives of discipline and achievement are prerequisite to true innate greatness. A person can accomplish his aim only if he has lives of good deeds and good karma behind him. Shakyamuni had lived a long series of former lives in which he had done good and received the merits of his actions, and these lives served as the cause of his being born in this world. In this sense, he had achieved his aim.

Life in this world is never unadulterated happiness. In the midst
of joy at the birth of the infant Siddhattha came sorrow when, on
the seventh day after her delivery, Maya died. It is impossible to say
whether she perished because the child came late in life or because
she gave birth out of doors without adequate preparations.

Fortunately for the child, his mother's younger sister, Mahapajapati, was on hand to act in the capacity of foster mother. Spir-
itually and materially, the prince grew up secure in the love and
compassion of his father and Mahapajapati and in the respect of all
around him. But, as he gained understanding, the intelligent prince
was sometimes grieved. He did not have a true mother. Furthermore, the political position of the Shakyas, who were subordinate
to Kosala, was most uncertain. Both of these factors must have inspired great uneasiness in him.

Once again according to legend, when he was fourteen or fifteen,
the young prince had an experience that revealed to him the all-
pervasiveness of the cruel struggle in the worlds of animals and
human beings. At the annual agricultural festival, during which
five hundred oxen were used to plow the fields, he saw insects turned
up with the soil. Small birds flew down to pick up the insects
in their beaks, only to be seized in their turn by larger, predatory
birds.

In intellectual and physical studies, the prince was outstanding
because of innate excellence. Putting faith in the forecast of the
seer Asita, his father expected much from his son and made him
crown prince and heir apparent. But this did not please the young
man, who steadily grew increasingly thoughtful and sad.

To cheer him, his worried father and foster mother built three
palaces, one for cold weather, one for hot weather, and one for the
rainy season. They appointed many beautiful court ladies to wait
on him and arranged banquets with dancing and music. Furthermore, they encouraged him to marry the lovely princess Yasodhara.
For a while, the prince lived a settled life, about which he later
reminisced:

"I was very weak and frail in my youth. In my father's house
were ponds here and there where they planted red, white, and yellow lotuses and water lilies for my pleasure. I used nothing but fine

incense from Kasi. My turbans, robes, underclothes, and outer clothes were of fine, light Kasi silk. Day and night, when I walked through the grounds, someone held a white umbrella over my head to protect me from the heat, the cold, the rain, and falling dust. Three palaces were built for me: one for the hot weather, one for the cold weather, and one for the rainy season. During the four months of the rainy season, I lived in the palace built for such weather, enjoying music played only by beautiful women, and I never went out. In ordinary houses, servants and workers are fed scrap rice and sour gruel, but in my father's house even the servants and workers were given white rice and meat."

The Great Departure   According to late Buddhist traditions, the prince's father, hoping to give his son pleasure, arranged four trips outside the capital city, one through each of its four gates. On three occasions, the prince encountered distressing sights: an aging person, an ill person, a corpse. Finally, on the last trip, he met a calm, serene ascetic monk, and this inspired in him a longing to lead the same kind of life. The story of these trips may not be historical fact, but it shows the deepening concern that the prince felt for the ineluctable, sorrowful fate of all mankind. The trips through the four gates symbolize the state of mind about which Shakyamuni later spoke in the following way:

"Though I was young and was living a life of luxury, I was often obsessed with the thought that many people pay no heed to the aging, illness, and death of others. They consider the affairs of outsiders none of their business and, failing to apply the experiences of others to themselves, refuse to realize that they too must grow old, fall ill, and die. But I did relate the aging, illness, and death of others to myself, and this caused me to suffer and be ashamed and to abandon pride in vigorous youth, health, and life."

Numerous Buddhist classics mention similar reflective thought on the part of Shakyamuni during his life in his father's house and show that, even in his young years, he was exceptionally sensitive to the anguish and fear of old age, illness, and death.

From what has been said so far, it is clear that the mind of the young prince turned, not to colorful, superficial economics and politics, but to a constant search for eternal truth. This can be explained partly by his innately speculative nature. Personal elements, like sorrow at the loss of his mother and the political instability of the Shakyas, of whom he was supposed to become the king, played a part in developing his outlook. But this was not all. Aware of the sorrowful fate of human beings and other living things—that is, aware that all must grow old, become sick, and die—and of the constant struggle and war for survival of the strong at the expense of the weak, he must have longed to find a realm free of suffering and insecurity. His interest was concentrated on this search, the most immediate aspect of which was the resolution of his own personal anxiety and suffering.

This lofty desire and an awareness of the nature of the basic human problem blinded the prince to worldly glory and desire and led him to follow the custom of his time by leaving home and devoting himself to the search for a solution to human unhappiness and for spiritual peace.

The birth of his son Rahula made it easier for him to leave. In the India of his day, providing an heir to carry on the family line was a major duty toward one's ancestors. To abandon home, even for the sake of pursuing enlightenment, without furnishing an heir was considered undutiful. Though natural affection may have hindered him, the birth of his son provided the occasion for Shakyamuni's departure, since he had fulfilled his duty to his father and his wife. There is a tradition that he left his father's home at the age of nineteen, but the oldest and most reliable documents give twenty-nine as his age at the time.

It was an accepted concept then that a person could not pursue the way to ideal truth in an ordinary family setting. Though the prince studied diligently and devoted himself to philosophical reflection while living with his family and surrounded by court ladies, his very environment made earnest discipline and profound thought impossible. Paying no heed to the weeping pleas of father, foster mother, wife, and child, in the middle of the night, accompanied by a retainer named Channa and mounted on his favorite horse,

Kanthaka, the young prince departed. By dawn, the small group reached the boundary. After crossing the Anoma River, the prince instructed Channa to return with Kanthaka. Then, changing his rich attire for coarse clothes in symbol of becoming a *samana* in search of enlightenment, he went his way southward to Magadha.

3. Discipline and Enlightenment

Meeting with the King of Magadha Before leaving his family to embark on a journey of religious discipline, Shakyamuni must have made thorough preparations. He probably thought at once of the two major kingdoms of Kosala and Magadha as suitable places for training because, as centers of new cultures, both were rich in philosophers and men of religion. Savatthi, the capital of Kosala, might have seemed attractive because of its large numbers of orthodox and unorthodox monks, but there were drawbacks that would prevent Shakyamuni from training there in full peace of mind. First, the Shakya state was subordinate to the kingdom of Kosala. Second, Savatthi was not far from his home country. His father and foster mother, who certainly were not delighted by his departure, could easily send emissaries there to summon him back.

He decided therefore to go to Magadha, to the capital city Rajagaha, where he was soon begging as a mendicant. One day Bimbisara, king of Magadha, happened to see him from the palace. Shakyamuni conducted himself with an extraordinary nobility and dignity that caught the king's attention.

Bimbisara, still under thirty at the time (he and Pasenadi, king of Kosala, were the same age as Shakyamuni) was vigorous and ambitious to increase the power of his state and expand its territories. Eagerly seeking a counselor who might be his right-hand assistant in his undertakings, when he saw the young mendicant near his palace, he thought that he had found just the right person. He immediately sent some of his retainers to inquire about the young man.

Having finished some hours of begging, Shakyamuni went to Mount Pandava to the west of the capital, where he sat under a tree and began to take out the food he had received. The retainers reported this to the king, who, accompanied by a group of his ministers, set out at once to go to Shakyamuni, who was resting after his meal. They exchanged greetings, and the king asked Shakyamuni a number of questions. Ancient texts describe this meeting in the following way.

Prince Gotama, who was handsome of appearance, went to Magadha, to the city of Rajagaha, surrounded by mountains, to beg for food. King Bimbisara, who was in a high tower, saw him and said to his ministers, "Observe this man. His appearance is elegant; his body is large and noble. His way of walking is perfect; his eyes are trained one fathom in front of him. He is correctly aware and, keeping his eyes turned down, seems to be of a truly noble lineage. Send messengers to find out where this monk is going and where he lives."

And the messengers of the king followed the prince.

Preserving the five senses properly, correctly aware, and wise, going from house to house begging, when he had acquired the amount of food he needed, the young sage stopped begging and went out of the city to Mount Pandava, where he intended to live. When they saw him approach this place of residence, all of the messengers of the king except one remained. This one returned to the city to report to the king.

"O King, the monk sits like a tiger or an ox or like a lion, in a cave at the foot of Mount Pandava."

When he heard the messenger's words, the king mounted a beautiful vehicle and hurried to the foot of Mount Pandava. Having gone as far as he could in the vehicle, he dismounted and walked the rest of the way to Shakyamuni's cave, where he sat down.

After friendly greetings, the king said, "You are young and in the prime of your vigor. You are blessed with good appearance and seem to come from a proper royal tribe. I will give you all the wealth you want. I will put at your command bright battalions of my best troops, including elephant troops. Where were you born?"

"O King, near the foot of the Himalayas, long in the domain of Kosala, is a noble tribe famous for wealth and valor. The clan, known as Relatives of the Sun, is called Shakya. O King, I have left my family and do not have any earthly desires. They are too often binding. In escape from them is peace. I am turned in the direction of abstinence and purification for the sake of finding the way. This is my only goal. I wish for nothing else."

The prince flatly refused the king's offer, and Bimbisara could only say, "When you reach your goal and find enlightenment, teach me at once and bring me salvation." Shakyamuni promised to do what the king asked, and the two parted.

Meditation Practices   Refusing the offer of King Bimbisara, Shakyamuni began to search for someone with whom to study in the vicinity of the city. The two major disciplines for the sake of enlightenment were meditation and ascetic austerities. According to the meditation system, a person sat in the cross-legged position and attained a state of spiritual unification, free from all random and distracting thoughts. In this state, the mind, which is as clear as a mirror and as calm as an undisturbed body of water, can act with complete freedom. Miraculous, mystical abilities were attributed to practitioners of such meditation, which, known as Yoga, had been a central aspect of orthodox religious training from well before the time of Shakyamuni and is still practiced in many parts of the world today.

Meditation may have had a very humble origin. In a land as hot as India, sitting in the shade of a tree is an excellent way to cool off. While relaxing in this way, some people no doubt gradually came to reflect on the world and human life and reached a state in which contact and fusion between the human mind and divinities were thought possible. Upanishadic philosophy taught a dichotomy between the material and the spiritual. According to this teaching, Yoga is a good method for freeing the spirit from the bonds of material things and from the flesh. By the time of Shakyamuni, meditation had already been studied and explained in detail. In Magadha lived two recluse religious ascetics who had left their homes to practice disciplines in the open countryside and who were especially famous for their achievements. Shakyamuni practiced meditation under both of them.

The first of these two men was Alara-Kalama. Having reached the extremely high state of meditative concentration in which nothing existed for him, he had many disciples, to whom he taught that the attaining of such a state was the ideal. Entering the trance state of nonthinking in such concentration is difficult for ordinary human beings. Among Alara-Kalama's hundreds of disciples, no one else had succeeded in it. Of course, the ability to do so depends on the level of the individual's training. But it also depends on the innate characteristics of the person: some people find it much easier than others. A meditative person from birth, Shakyamuni developed the habit of entering such states early in youth.

I have already described the spring agricultural festival at which the sight of birds killing insects only to be killed themselves by larger, predatory birds caused Shakyamuni to reflect on the harsh kill-or-be-killed condition pervading all life. At that time, he fell naturally into a profound meditation and attained a state of mental unification impossible to ordinary people. It is said that his body began to glow with a bright light that eliminated shadows cast by trees and other objects. Tradition has it that his father the king and his ministers were so surprised at this wonder that they all worshiped the prince.

The story indicates the excellence in meditation with which Shakyamuni was born, and this ability enabled him to attain, very early in training, the state that Alara-Kalama considered ideal. The meditative concentration that Shakyamuni experienced at the agricultural festival in his early youth was related to the so-called world of form. The state taught by Alara-Kalama was that of a much higher formless world where matter no longer exists. Nonetheless, already having experienced the one, Shakyamuni did not find it difficult to attain the other.

Alara-Kalama and his other disciples were startled at the speed with which Shakyamuni reached the level of his teacher. The older recluse was happy because he hoped that Shakyamuni would help him with his work. But Shakyamuni found that even attaining this high state did not ease his mental anxieties. Although, as long as he was in the state of concentration, nothing troubled him, once concentration was broken, he returned to the mental state of worry and suffering. From his standpoint, true liberation from the bonds of illusion and suffering could be attained only by reaching a state of absolute, unmitigated tranquillity. Finding that this kind of meditation was not the ideal he sought, Shakyamuni left to study with another recluse, even though Alara-Kalama tried to keep him by his side.

His second teacher, Uddaka-Ramaputta, had reached a still higher state at which neither thought nor non-thought existed. With the experience he had gained from Alara-Kalama, Shakyamuni was able to reach this state, considered the highest possible in this kind of meditation, very quickly. Uddaka-Ramaputta acknowledged his success and was very happy. Because he was growing old, he too was eager for someone to help him with his many disciples. Once again, however, Shakyamuni refused, for he found that even this state of concentration did not satisfy his demands. He left to continue his search for the true way.

Ascetic Austerities   Having attained the same level of concentration in meditation as his two famous teachers and having learned that these achievements did not solve the problems of human life, Shakyamuni decided to practice asceticism.

Ascetic practices were common, especially among the *samanas* before the time of Shakyamuni, and are widely followed even today in India. Exposure of the body to the broiling Indian sun was one method. In its extreme form, the regimen involved the Five Heats: the blazing sun above and four fires, one in each of the four cardinal directions, around the naked body of the ascetic. Another rigorous method was to stare at the sun all day, moving to follow it in its course through the heavens. The blazing light and the heat of the sun ultimately blinded persons who persisted in this ordeal. In some instances, men stood on one foot with one hand raised above their heads for long periods or lay on thorns or sharp nails. Others ate only one grain of rice a day or one grain a week. Still others tormented themselves by eating nothing for as long as from one to three months.

The reason for such practices is explained by the relation between the body and the spirit. The ascetic believes that human suffering is caused by the bondage of the spirit to the flesh. As long as this bondage continues, the spirit is unable to be free. Suffering can only be relieved by releasing the spirit from the bonds imposed by the flesh and by material things. Though pure and capable of ideal actions in its pristine condition, the spirit is hampered by the physical and the material. The goal of ascetic practices is to weaken the power of the physical body over the spirit. But since the spirit cannot be absolutely free as long as the body exists, death and the destruction of the body are the ultimate conclusions of such practices. Jainism considers discipline of this kind an ideal. Of the eleven outstanding disciples of the founder of Jainism, nine starved to death in fasting and are said to have attained ultimate freedom. Both Sankhya and Yoga, which teach meditation practices, hold that ultimate liberation can come only after death.

But man requires freedom from suffering and sorrow in this life, in this world, where he inevitably remains a compound of both the spirit and the body. Nothing can be known of the life of disembodied spirits or of life after the death of the physical body. Even if such life exists, it is unrelated to man in this world. Whatever ideal realm may exist after this life, it can probably do nothing to ease present sufferings and anxieties.

Seeking earnestly for the attainment of the ideal under the actual conditions of the real world, Shakyamuni, who had already learned that meditation did not lead to his goal, decided to try ascetic austerities. He adopted the standpoint that it is impossible to know whether a thing can or cannot be done until one tries.

He therefore traveled to a forest where other ascetics gathered and began a course of training in a wide variety of austerities that was to last for six years. He was extremely thorough and did difficult things that no one before him had done. When rumors of these austerities, including even a rumor that Shakyamuni had died, reached the ears of his father, King Suddhodana, he sent five men to care for his son. But, upon reaching the place where Shakyamuni was, these men decided to abandon the secular life and to take up ascetic training themselves. The things that Shakyamuni did were so sincere that they felt he must be on the verge of enlightenment. But when he realized that his six years of suffering had failed to produce the effect he wanted and had done no more than torment his body, Shakyamuni gave up austerities.

Virtually nothing but skin and bones, he was so weak and emaciated that, clinging to tree roots, he could barely pull himself from a river where he had washed away the accumulated grime of long asceticism. A young woman from a nearby village brought him some rice boiled in milk. He ate it and gradually recovered his strength.

His five followers thought that his willingness to bathe and accept food meant that he had failed in his search for enlightenment. Convinced that there was no longer any need to study with him, they decided to continue on their own. As they could not return to the land of the Shakyas, they set out for Migadaya, Deer Park, near Benares, where many Brahmans underwent religious disciplines.

Enlightenment Because he had proved that neither meditation nor ascetic austerities enabled one to attain the ideal, Shakyamuni saw that no other method that existed at the time could lead to his goal. In reflecting on this, the prince developed three comparisons: transferring light ignited with a fire stick to waterlogged fresh wood, transferring light ignited with a fire stick to ordinary fresh wood, and igniting fire with a fire stick on dry wood. Waterlogged and fresh wood symbolize the heart saturated with desires and worldly attachments. Dry wood symbolizes a heart in which there is no longer desire or attachment to worldly things. The act of igniting fire by means of a fire stick represents diligent effort. The most assiduous effort in ascetic austerities cannot bring enlightenment to a heart saturated with desires and attachments, just as fire struck by means of the fire stick at the cost of great effort cannot be transferred to waterlogged or fresh wood. But since fire can be struck readily by diligent effort with the fire stick on dry wood, so a heart that has already been drained of desires and attachments by equally diligent spiritual effort can attain the ideal goal.

When he understood this, Shakyamuni saw that both meditation practice and ascetic austerities were mistaken. After recovering his physical strength, he prepared a seat with soft grass under an *assattha,* or bo, tree not far from the town of Gaya and, making a vow not to rise until he attained enlightenment, even if it meant death, sat in meditation.*

In the first hours of the night of his enlightenment (the hours from six till ten), he attained wisdom about all past things. In the middle hours (from ten until two in the morning), he attained wisdom about all future things. Then in the final hours (from two until six in the morning), he was freed of all bondage and attained wisdom without illusion. He became a Buddha. And this was the starting point of Buddhism.

*The place where Shakyamuni attained enlightenment has come to be called Bodh Gaya, and the bo tree is also called the Bodhi (wisdom) tree in indication of the enlightenment of the Buddha. Today various historical relics, a great stupa, and a bo tree—said to be the fourth planted there since the enlightenment—attract many visitors and pilgrims.

4. The First Sermon and the Beginning of the Teaching Mission

After Enlightenment For several weeks following his enlightenment, Shakyamuni remained meditating and thinking in the vicinity of the same bo tree. For the first of those weeks, seated in the meditation position, he reflected on and rejoiced in his enlightenment, the nature of which can be briefly explained as understanding of the Law of Causation, an unprecedented doctrine and a major element of Buddhism. Briefly, the doctrine states that all things have a direct or primary cause; that when this cause comes into contact with an opportunity or condition (secondary cause), the result appears as an effect; and that this effect leaves traces behind it. It pertains to the operations of all phenomena and is to be distinguished from the law of cause and effect, which deals with the individual. The difference between the two is discussed later in this book (see page 96).

During the time he lived in his father's house and during his later period of discipline, Shakyamuni had studied all the theories of philosophy then current in India and had undergone all the practical religious regimens of his day. But he had proved them to be both theoretically and practically imperfect. Many of the philosophies of that time dealt with an ontology unrelated to faith and the practice of religious teachings. Their fundamental concern was with something comparable to metaphysics in Western philosophy and involved the soul or self (atman in Buddhist terms). The element setting Buddhism apart from the stream of Indian philosophy in general is its doctrine of non-self, or anatman, and its rejection of the idea of an eternal, immutable entity that can be called the real soul or the real substance. The basic tenet of the Buddhist position is this: there is no need to be concerned with solving questions about the existence or nonexistence of things unrelated to faith or religious practices. Instead, we must concentrate only on the world of phenomena—the world in which we live and suffer, the world where we seek liberation from suffering. Since this world of phenomena and of birth, destruction, and change is related to faith and religious practices, we must observe and deal with it correctly.

In Shakyamuni's time, there were various religious and philosophical theories concerning the phenomenal world and matters of faith and practical religion. Some of these theories doubted or rejected the idea of causal relations. Others, while recognizing causal relations, either held that the connection between cause and effect was indefinite or interpreted as basic causes things that were not basic causes. Moreover, the methods advocated by the followers of such philosophies for the attainment of the ideal state left much to be desired. In some cases, they held up as ideals for human beings things that could not be recognized as such. Even when the ideals they set were correct, the methods for their attainment were mistaken, insufficiently effective, or otherwise imperfect.

The Law of Causation, which is perfectly sound from the rational, ethical, and religious viewpoints and which has a universal validity enabling it to withstand any criticism, was formulated as a result of examination and criticism of all the other imperfect and irrational systems in India in Shakyamuni's time. The Law of Causation teaches both the theoretical and practical application of the idea that there is no immortal, immutable self or soul.

The Law had never been taught in India before. It is the characteristic that sets Buddhism apart from other philosophies and religions. But though he discovered it, Shakyamuni did not create it.

This Law is an absolute truth—recognizable as true by all peoples, in all places, and at all times—existing eternally independent of the appearance in the world of a Tathagata (a term for a Buddha, Tathagata means one who has come the full Way, who has reached the truth and come to declare it). Shakyamuni merely discovered and taught the Law.

During his weeks of meditation under the bo tree, three matters occupied Shakyamuni. First, he experienced the joy of liberation. Second, he reflected further on the content of his enlightenment and gave it doctrinal organization. Third, he devoted thought to ways of teaching what he had discovered to the people of the world.

Since the Law of Causation is difficult to understand, Shakyamuni suspected that people blinded by desires and pleasures would not comprehend it even if he taught it. No matter how he might struggle to impart its meaning, the world probably would not accept what he had to say, and his efforts would be wasted. In such a case, he thought it would be better not to attempt to teach at all.

According to ancient writings, at this time, Brahma, the highest of the Hindu gods, appeared to Shakyamuni and said that if he, the World-honored One, failed to teach his truth, the world would become even more degraded and dark than it already was. If he would devise a method of teaching, however, in spite of the difficulty of his message, some people would understand. Brahma pleaded with Shakyamuni to condescend to carry his truth and salvation to the world. This story, which has come to be known as the Pleading of Brahma, is, like the stories of demons assailing Shakyamuni before and after his enlightenment, a narrative representation of the hesitations, doubts, and complex feelings that he must have experienced.

As an outcome of the Pleading of Brahma, Shakyamuni decided to teach the truth to which he had been enlightened. And when he had arrived at a method of making his message as easy to understand as possible, he concluded his weeks of meditation and began his teaching. He was physically prepared to set forth on this mission because, during his meditation, he had recovered his vigor by eating the nourishing food given him by two brother merchants who were leading a caravan through the vicinity.

Departing to Teach   Shakyamuni next gave thought to the kind of people who would be most likely to understand what he had to teach and decided that the two recluses, Uddaka-Ramaputta and Alara-Kalama would be most suitable learners. But when he inquired about them, he learned that both had died. Then he thought of the five ascetics who had served him and shared his hardships during his six years of rigorous discipline. Since they would be next most suitable learners, he set out for Benares, where they were at the time.

On his way he met Upaka, a young man of another religion, who noted that Shakyamuni was more serene and noble than ordinary people and that he had a solemn majesty about him. Upaka asked, "Whom did you follow in becoming a monk? Who is your teacher?" Shakyamuni replied, "I am the absolute victor. I am absolutely wise. I have been enlightened to the truth and am liberated. I have no teacher. In heaven and on earth, I am the most worthy of honor." Since the opportunity was not yet ripe, the young man merely said, "I dare say that is true" but did not ask for the teaching. Later, however, he was to accept the Buddhist teaching and become a holy man.

Begging as he traveled, Shakyamuni finally reached Benares. From a distance, the five ascetics saw him coming and agreed among themselves to treat him coolly: "Here comes that fallen ascetic Gotama. We need not greet him in a kindly way. If he wants to sit here, he can do as he likes."

But in spite of their agreement, when Shakyamuni drew near, they were unable to remain still. One of them rose to greet him. One took the clothing he carried and his begging bowl. Another made a seat for him. Another fetched water to wash his feet. Still another prepared a footrest and brought a cloth to dry his feet. Nonetheless, because they despised him in their hearts, they treated him as an equal and called him friend, which was considered rude to a person of Shakyamuni's enlightened state.

Shakyamuni said to the five ascetics, "O brothers, you must not use that form of address to a Tathagata. I am a Buddha. I have attained the highest enlightenment and have been freed of the cycle of birth, death, and transmigration. I will teach you. All you need do is listen. And if you put what I teach into practice, you too can finally be enlightened in this world." But they did not believe his words: "Friend Gotama, you could not attain enlightenment by undergoing severe ascetic practices. How did you manage to become enlightened by abandoning your efforts and living a life of luxury?"

Then Shakyamuni said, "O brothers, I did not abandon my efforts. I did not enter a life of luxury. I am a Buddha. I have attained the highest enlightenment. I am a Tathagata who has transcended the cycle of birth, death, and transmigration. I will teach you. All you need do is listen. And if you put my teaching into practice, you too can finally attain enlightenment in this world." But once again the five ascetics did not believe him.

The same dialogue was repeated a third time, and on the last occasion the Buddha said, "O brothers, have I ever taught you with this kind of confidence and authority before?" "No," they answered. And, seeing that his attitude was different and that he had both commanding dignity and confidence, for the first time they were prepared to listen to what Shakyamuni had to say.

"O brothers, there are two extremes that must be avoided. One of them is living a life of passion. This is by no means holy. It does nothing for the sake of achieving the ideal of enlightenment. The other extreme to be avoided is devotion to ascetic practices that punish the body. This is nothing but empty suffering and does nothing for the sake of attaining the ideal of enlightenment. I have departed from these two extremes and, by having the Eye of the Law opened, have discovered the Middle Path leading to nirvana and liberation. Putting this into practice, I attained the highest enlightenment."

Since they had mistakenly assumed that Shakyamuni, unable to go on with ascetic practices, had abandoned his efforts and given himself over to a life of worldly pleasure, Shakyamuni taught the five ascetics that both sensuality and asceticism fail to lead to enlightenment. He then told them that the Middle Path between the extremes was the right way and that it comprised the Eightfold Noble Path of the Four Noble Truths, with which the following section is concerned.

In listening to a sermon a person must abandon preconceived ideas and approach the matter with an open, frank mind if he is to understand and accept. The five ascetics first admitted that they had been mistaken about Shakyamuni and then listened to his teachings.

The First Sermon   After explaining the doctrine of the Middle Path, Shakyamuni presented the Four Noble Truths. His first sermon is contained in the Sutra of the First Rolling of the Wheel of the Law. The comparison inherent in this title is with the *chakravarti-raja,* or wheel-rolling king, who is supposed to govern the whole world by rolling a wheel. In a similar fashion, the Buddha guides and saves mankind by rolling the Wheel of the Law. All of the sermons of Shakyamuni are referred to as Rolling the Wheel of the Law.

The contents of the first sermon are the teaching of the Middle Path, the Four Noble Truths, and the twelve stages through which Shakyamuni attained enlightenment.

The Four Noble Truths are explained as follows:

"O brothers, this is the Noble Truth of Suffering. Birth is suffering; old age is suffering; illness is suffering; death is suffering; meeting people one hates is suffering; parting from people one loves is suffering; failing to get what one wants is suffering. In other words, all five aggregates of the body and mind, which have attachments to things and to people, and of the environment are suffering. This is the Noble Truth of Suffering.

"O brothers, this is the Noble Truth of the Cause of Suffering. Craving—for sensual pleasure, continued existence, and annihilation; for happiness in all places, accompanied by joy and covetousness—which leads to rebirth, is the basic cause and reason for suffering. And this is the Noble Truth of the Cause of Suffering.

"O brothers, this is the Noble Truth of the Extinction of Suffering. The Noble Truth of the Extinction of Suffering is the total elimination of craving, abandoning it entirely, being liberated from it, and no longer having any attachments.

"O brothers, this is the Noble Truth of the Path to the Extinction of Suffering. The Eightfold Noble Path—right view, right thinking, right speech, right action, right living, right effort, right memory, and right meditation—is the Noble Truth of the Path to the Extinction of Suffering.''

Shakyamuni then explained the twelve stages by means of which he attained the highest enlightenment. He divided each of the Four Noble Truths into three stages of attainment. In the first stage, he acquired theoretical understanding of the Four Noble Truths as they are. In the second stage, he put his theoretical knowledge into practice. Doing this involves a correct understanding of the nature of suffering, the extinction of the causes of suffering, the application of the ways in which those causes are eliminated, and traveling the full Path. As one continues practical application in connection with the Four Noble Truths, theory and practice come to agree entirely, and one arrives at the third stage, where all the practical aims have been fulfilled. At this point, one is ready for the highest enlightenment.

Shakyamuni explained that only when he had completed these three stages was he sufficiently convinced of being a supremely enlightened Buddha to announce his nature publicly. Only then had he achieved perfect liberation, and only then had he escaped from the cycle of birth, death, and transmigration.

It is said that on hearing this sermon the five ascetics reached the first stage of enlightenment because they understood theoretically what Shakyamuni said. They had reached the stage that is called the Eye of the Law—that is, the Eye of Wisdom in relation to Buddhist truth. A person who has attained this level will never be confused about his faith or be tempted by other faiths. He will be firm in immovable conviction. This is initial enlightenment, and a person who has attained it is a holy man of the first rank.

When the five ascetics had arrived at this level, Shakyamuni taught them the doctrine of non-self according to which the five aggregates—the things that compose our minds, bodies, and environments—in short, ourselves and everything around us—are transient and soulless. Since this is a major Buddhist tenet, I shall discuss it in greater detail later.

The five ascetics came to comprehend the principle of these basic teachings and then began their practical application in the second phase of moving toward enlightenment. It is said that at the conclusion of this stage, they became *arhats*, or people who have attained enlightenment through their own strenuous efforts.

5. Yasa and Teaching by Due Course

In Shakyamuni's day the city of Benares was an important trade and commercial center inhabited by many wealthy merchants. One of these merchants had a son named Yasa, who lived, completely free of want, in handsome circumstances with a beautiful wife and with everything that might seem to make his lot enviable. But, seeing only emptiness and misery in his life of luxury and sensual pleasures, Yasa had lost all hope for the future. Fleeing from what was to him only futility, once at midnight he slipped from his home and walked to the outskirts of the city in search of mental peace.

Unaware of the presence of Shakyamuni, who had been out of doors meditating in Deer Park since early morning, Yasa drew near, crying out that he was in great anguish. Shakyamuni called to him by name and, telling him that there was no more sorrow or pain in this place, instructed him to sit down and added that he would teach the Law to him. Surprised to be called by name, the young man removed his gilt slippers and, after making a respectful greeting, sat down near Shakyamuni.

It was Shakyamuni's custom to adjust the difficulty of his teaching to the needs and capacities of his audience. (In Buddhist literature this is called teaching by due course.) In the case of Yasa, Shakyamuni began by teaching a triple doctrine of the law of cause and effect and karma, which was widely accepted as correct in the India of that day. The three parts of the triple doctrine were those of giving alms to the poor and to men of religion; abstaining from destroying life, stealing, lying, and wrong sexual activity; and the assurance of rebirth in a happy state in heaven if one led a life of almsgiving and observation of these moral precepts. In other words, this set of doctrines taught that a good act produces a good effect. It also taught that a bad act produces a bad effect. It taught, for example, that a person who was stingy and gave no alms and who destroyed life, stole, lied, or acted in other immoral ways was sure to be reborn in hell or in the regions of hungry spirits or of animals.

Although these theories of good producing a good effect and evil producing an evil effect are not necessarily those of Buddhism alone, understanding them is a prerequisite to understanding and accepting the Buddhist faith. A person who fails to comprehend the law of karma or who rejects the law of cause and effect cannot possibly accept the correct doctrines of Buddhism.

After explaining to Yasa the triple doctrine of benefits for good works and the law of cause and effect inherent in them, Shakyamuni pointed out that, whereas there was much evil in a life of sensual pleasure, a life apart from selfish desires was both pure and serene. With this, the mind of Yasa was purified, and he rejoicingly accepted Shakyamuni's teachings. His receptiveness has been compared to that of a piece of bleached cloth, which readily accepts the dyer's colors.

When Shakyamuni realized that the mind of Yasa had become like white cloth, he instructed him in the characteristic teaching of Buddhism—that is, the Four Noble Truths of suffering, its causes, its extinction, and the way in which such extinction can be effected. Eager to learn, Yasa quickly understood the Four Noble Truths correctly, and, acquiring the Eye of the Law, he became a holy man of the first degree.

In the morning, when it was discovered at Yasa's home that he was missing, great consternation arose. Messengers were sent in all directions to look for him, and his father himself traced his son's path to Deer Park. Arriving there, he followed the tracks of his son's gilt slippers to the place where Shakyamuni was.

Shakyamuni made Yasa temporarily invisible. When the young man's father arrived and asked if Yasa had been there, Shakyamuni told him to sit down quietly, since he would probably find his son in a short while. Shakyamuni then followed the same progressive series of teachings that he had given Yasa: the triple doctrine of almsgiving to the poor and to holy people, of abiding by moral precepts, and of the promise that good acts would be rewarded by rebirth in a blessed state, and then the Four Noble Truths. Having heard this sermon by Shakyamuni, the rich merchant, like his son, acquired the Eye of the Law and accepted the Buddhist view of the world and of human life. He rejoiced in this attainment and became a lay member of the Buddhist faith for the rest of his life.

Listening for the second time to this sermon, Yasa actually experienced the truth, attained the highest enlightenment, and became an *arhat*. As I have already said, the Eye of the Law, the theoretical understanding of the truth of the Buddha's teachings, is the first stage toward ultimate enlightenment, which is attained only after this truth has been perfected in practice. In other words, when the theories are actually experienced and theory and practice become one, the seeker after truth reaches the stage of highest enlightenment.

Shakyamuni then revealed Yasa to his father, who at once told his son that his mother was greatly worried by his absence. He went on to warn the young man that he should do nothing to bring about his mother's death. But because he himself had acquired the Eye of the Law, he immediately realized that it was fitting for his son, who was now an *arhat,* to leave home for the life of religion. He thereupon entreated Shakyamuni to guide Yasa in the religious life and asked the two of them to come to his house to dine.

On the following day, Yasa, now a Buddhist monk, went with Shakyamuni to his own home for the promised offering of food, and there Shakyamuni used the method of teaching in due order to enable both Yasa's mother and his wife to acquire the Eye of the Law. Together with Yasa's father, they vowed to abide by the five precepts—to abstain from destruction of life, stealing, wrong sexual activity, lying, and intoxicants—and to take refuge in the Three Treasures: the Buddha, the Law, and the Order. And thus they became devoted lay Buddhists for the remainder of their lives.

The Four Friends of Yasa   Living in Benares were four close friends of Yasa, all sons of wealthy and famous merchant families. When these young men heard that Yasa had left his home to lead the religious life, they decided that if such a wise person as their friend had taken this step, the teaching he vowed to follow must be wonderful. They resolved to call on Yasa in Deer Park. When they did, their friend took them before Shakyamuni with a plea that he instruct them. Following the same course of graduated teaching, Shakyamuni enabled the four to acquire the Eye of the Law. They then requested to be allowed to follow him. Upon receiving permission, they became monks and later attained the enlightenment of *arhats*.

In addition to these four young men, Yasa had fifty other friends who were members of the families of wealthy merchants. It seems likely that the children of commercial families of this kind all knew each other well. At the time, Benares was the capital of Kasi. But Kasi, having been conquered by Kosala, was in the twilight days of its prosperity and was never again to be independent. Perhaps this state of affairs caused the young sons of the merchant families to lose hope for the future and to take no pleasure in the glories of the secular world. At any rate, when they learned that Yasa, who occupied a leading position among them, and his four close friends had left their homes for a life of religion, they too visited Shakyamuni. As an outcome of his teachings, they decided to leave their homes and to become monks. It is said that they, too, ultimately became *arhats*.

By this time, not long after Shakyamuni's enlightenment, there was a total of sixty-one *arhats*: Shakyamuni himself, the five ascetics whom he taught first, Yasa, Yasa's four close friends, and the fifty other friends from Benares. Because all of them were endowed with what is called the three types of superior wisdom and the six powers of saving sentient beings—perfect freedom of activity, ears capable of hearing everything, insight into the minds of others, remembrance of one's former existences, eyes capable of seeing everything, and perfect freedom (the last three of these six powers constitute the three types of superior wisdom)—they were able to guide and teach other people in the correct way. Indeed, the very word *arhat* means more than self-perfection alone and implies guidance and salvation for human society.

While still meditating under the bo tree, Shakyamuni had given thought to ways of teaching his message. Now that he had a group of sixty *arhats* capable of helping in his teaching mission, it was only natural that he should put them to use. He told them that since they had attained the highest enlightenment and emancipation from the bonds of the world, they should go into various regions to teach the superlative truths and the way to put them into practical use for the sake of the peace and happiness of mankind. He added that there were many people who, though subject to very little confusion and passion, still suffered in the realm of transmigration only because they had not heard the precious teaching. Such people would find liberation if the correct way were only shown to them. He then said that he himself would go to the village of Sena in Uruvela and that the others should go where they wished, as long as they went one by one. They were instructed to guide and teach as many people as possible. This was the beginning of the teaching mission of the disciples of the Buddha.

The many religions that existed in India both before and after Buddhism taught personal discipline and liberation alone. Almost none of them gave thought to instructing others or society in general or to the creation of an ideal realm in the actual world. Initially, Shakyamuni left his father's home and undertook the life of religious discipline for the realization of his own personal ideal. But when he had developed a correct view of the world and of man through observations of the nature of human life and the universe, he saw that human beings do not live in isolation. The fate of each person, intimately connected with the flow from past to present and from present to future, is further intimately connected with the fates of the people around him, with society, and with the natural environment. For this reason, individual happiness cannot result from the improvement of the individual alone. Shakyamuni realized that, because of the Law of Causation, such happiness can only result from simultaneous improvement in society and the environment. From this standpoint, he naturally adopted the policy of saving and teaching others. This characteristic attitude sets Buddhism apart from other Indian religions and philosophies and explains its spread beyond India to the rest of the world.

Initial Enlightenment Through Intellectual Comprehension or Through Faith   As I have said, the Eye of the Law, or initial enlightenment, is obtained when a person hears and comprehends the teaching of the Four Noble Truths. Such was the case with the five ascetics whom Shakyamuni taught first and with Yasa, his parents, his wife, and his friends. A person with the Eye of the Law sees life and the world in the Buddhist way and can never again fall into superstitions or false beliefs or be tempted by other religions or philosophies. He has reached the state that is called nonretrogression. Those who have reached this state are certain to attain the highest level of enlightenment.

In the Buddhist scriptures, discussion of the Eye of the Law is invariably accompanied by mention of the doctrine that whatever is subject to the condition of origination is subject also to the condition of cessation. This is a simplified expression of the Law of Causation to the effect that suffering, for example, which must have a cause, can be eliminated by the removal of that cause. The Eye of the Law is the pure and spotless eye that perceives the veracity of the Law of Causation.

The Eye of the Law is an intellectual understanding of the Truth arrived at through an intellectual process. But, by nature, some people are stronger in terms of emotions and willpower than they are intellectually. Such people are said to be able to attain enlightenment by means of emotion and will. In short, there are two ways to become enlightened: intellectually through the truth of the Law—and obviously the attainment of the Eye of the Law—and through faith and deliberate intention.

Enlightenment by means of faith involves complete trust in the Buddha, the Law, and the Order—the Three Treasures—and observation of the holy precepts. Of course, fundamentally, a person cannot be a Buddhist at all without this trust. But it is especially important that such trust be unshakable in persons who strive to attain enlightenment by faith alone. Those who came into direct contact with Shakyamuni were no doubt easily moved to unconditional faith by his greatness. Others, who had been instructed by members of the Order, had probably been moved to trust as a consequence of the greatness of the Buddha and the wonderful nature of the Law.

A person who has openly expressed his reverence for the Buddha, the Law, and the Order is bound to abide by the five precepts: not to take life, not to take what is not given, not to indulge in wrong sexual activity, not to tell lies, and not to drink intoxicants. When faith has been firmly established, observance of these precepts becomes absolute. Such faith is said to be as fixed and indestructible as adamant and to represent initial enlightenment on the way to the highest enlightenment by means of the path of faith. It is a state of nonretrogression comparable to that of the person who has attained the Eye of the Law.

6. The Four Noble Truths
and the Principle of Healing

According to ancient Buddhist writings, at about the time of his enlightenment under the bo tree, Shakyamuni reflected on the Law of Causation. Since this law is extremely difficult, to enable ordinary people to understand it he organized his teachings in the form of the Four Noble Truths, which are a clarified version of the Law of Causation. Whereas the Law itself is for the understanding of people of outstanding wisdom, the Truths were devised for the sake of teaching ordinary human beings. In the cases of the five ascetics, Yasa, his parents, his wife, and the young rich men of Benares, Shakyamuni employed the teaching of the Four Noble Truths to lead to an understanding of the Buddhist interpretation of the world and human life and thus to enable these people to attain initial enlightenment.

The Four Noble Truths were taught on the basis of a principle of healing spiritual suffering and misery that is similar to the principles that doctors follow in curing illnesses of the body. To effect a cure, a doctor must first accurately diagnose the illness. If his diagnosis is incorrect or insufficient, a complete cure will probably be impossible. For instance, pain in the stomach can be caused by various ailments. If the doctor diagnoses incorrectly and, acting on the basis of that diagnosis, warms the patient's body when

43

it should be cooled, or vice versa, he will not only fail to cure but will also probably aggravate the situation. Accurate diagnoses spell the difference between good doctors and quacks. This is the first stage of therapy.

The next requirement for treatment is a correct understanding of the cause of the illness. Of course, if the diagnosis is incorrect, it is impossible to understand the cause. On the other hand, a correct diagnosis does not always guarantee correct interpretation of the cause. Illnesses caused by external wounds, overeating, overdrinking, overwork, bacteria, or other factors all demand different kinds of therapy. This is the second stage.

To understand the nature and cause of the trouble, the doctor needs fundamental knowledge and experience concerning the organism in its sound, well state—that is, knowledge about good health. Health is usually judged on the basis of such things as facial color, temperature, respiratory rate, pulse, blood pressure, and so on according to standards for the patient's sex and age. But in more intensive examinations more exacting, higher standards of judgment make it possible to uncover abnormalities even in people who seem perfectly healthy. The more exacting the ideal standards on which health is judged, the more clearly are maladies and their causes seen and the wider the range of treatment that can be applied. This is the third stage.

The final stage of therapy is to apply the treatment judged best in each case on the basis of knowledge, experience, and judgment gained from the first three stages. All methods, direct and indirect, are used that will cure the illness and restore sound health. Among the direct methods are medication, injections, operations, and other mechanical or physical treatment. Indirect methods for curing and for restoring good health include such things as heat or cooling treatments, rest, walks or exercise, diets, bathing, and so on. If the method employed is the proper one, the patient will gradually be freed of negative physical aspects, and positive ones will accrue to him, restoring good health.

Just as there are four stages of therapy for physical illness, so there are four stages in the process of relieving suffering and misery that are illnesses of the spirit. Those stages are set forth in the Four Noble Truths.

Shakyamuni, a great physician of the spirit with abundant wisdom and experience, conformed his treatment—teaching of the Law—to the illness of the individual. The nature of his teaching method is to offer different doctrines according to the spiritual and intellectual capacities of the audience, just as a doctor adjusts therapy to the needs of the patient.

The first of the Four Noble Truths (the Truth of Suffering) states that all existence is suffering. The nature of the state of suffering must be accurately understood. No matter whether the individual diagnoses his own suffering or that of others, suffering itself must be clearly seen for what it is. It is wrong to interpret as a normal state something that is actually suffering or to suffer when there is no cause to do so. In other words, the first requirement is to see things accurately and completely, neither in a distorted way, as through colored glasses, nor partially, as through clouded glasses. In order to allow people to see things correctly, before teaching the Four Noble Truths, Shakyamuni employed the gradual teaching method that I have already described. This method enabled his followers to accept the Law of Causation and to understand causation correctly.

The second of the Four Noble Truths (the Truth of Cause) postulates that illusion and desire are the cause of suffering. Since there is no suffering without a cause, it is essential to determine whether that cause is the outcome of internal or external elements or a combination of both. If the cause is understood, by eliminating it one eliminates the suffering itself.

The third of the Four Noble Truths (the Truth of Extinction) deals with the ideal condition in which suffering has been totally extinguished. This is the standard against which to judge suffering and nonsuffering. Although only a person who has reached this state can understand it completely, correct awareness of ideals and even scant familiarity with the Four Noble Truths gives a certain amount of knowledge about it. Without such knowledge, it is impossible to recognize suffering as suffering, to know that elimination of the cause of suffering removes the suffering itself, or to put into practice the means of achieving such an elimination.

The fourth of the Four Noble Truths (the Truth of the Path) sets forth the means of eliminating suffering step by step. Doctors use either direct or indirect methods to cure illness. The direct methods attack the symptoms. The indirect methods restore general bodily health. Similarly, the fourth of the Four Noble Truths prescribes indirect and direct methods. Either the desires and attachments causing suffering are directly eliminated, or a state or environment in which such desires and attachments and the suffering they entail do not occur is produced. The Eightfold Noble Path contains all the direct and indirect methods needed to remove suffering and to build a perfect personality in physical and spiritual terms. Developing such a personality—that of a Buddha or an *arhat*—resembles physical therapy aiming both to cure the present sickness and to create a sound, healthy body in which sickness does not occur. The comparison with the healing principle shows how rationally organized the doctrine of the Four Noble Truths is. It further shows the identity between these Truths and the research attitude of such fields of learning as modern natural science.

Scientific investigation adopts a two-stage method. In the first stage, laws are formulated about the operations of the phenomena under investigation (natural science for natural phenomena, the humanities for phenomena of human culture and civilization, and the social sciences for social phenomena). In other words, the first step in scientific investigation is discovering the Law of Causation in the world of phenomena. This is identical with the Buddhist method of acquiring a correct view of the world and of human life as operations of the Law of Causation. Understanding the actual world as suffering arising from desires and attachments in the terms of the Four Noble Truths corresponds with the first stage of scientific investigation.

The second stage is the application of the Law of Causation. Creation of conditions and states of affairs that human beings consider ideal is a matter of applied research. All the conveniences of civilization and the products of culture have resulted from the application of scientific laws. Putting to use laws of phenomena in spiritual culture, politics, and economics for the sake of the improvement of humanity would probably result in the creation of an ideal culture and society. Viewed in this light, the teaching of the Four Noble Truths—in a wider sense, of the Law of Causation—is in line not only with medical science but also with all of the other sciences. It is amazing that Shakyamuni evolved these teachings, which distinguish Buddhism from all other religions and philosophies, as long as two thousand five hundred years ago. The teachings prove the universal applicability, truth, and rational nature of the doctrinal theories of Buddhism.

Suffering and Its Cause   I have already shown that the doctrine of the Four Noble Truths is explained in the first sermon Shakyamuni ever delivered and that it is contained in the sutra called The First Rolling of the Wheel of the Law. For further elucidation of this doctrine, I shall base my discussion on material found in the sutra known as the Discourse on the Analysis of the Truths.

In The First Rolling of the Wheel of the Law it is said that birth is suffering, old age is suffering, illness is suffering, death is suffering, contact with those one hates is suffering, separation from those one loves is suffering, failure to satisfy one's desires is suffering, and clinging to the five aggregates that compose the minds and bodies of all sentient beings is suffering. The above-mentioned sufferings of birth, old age, illness, and death are called the four sufferings, and when the other four (meeting those one hates, parting from those one loves, not being able to satisfy one's desires, and clinging to the five aggregates) are added to these, the list is known as the eight sufferings.

Birth (more exactly, conception) is suffering because it is the entry point into the world of suffering and transmigration. Viewed in this light, the suffering of birth is one with the suffering of being alive in this world.

The first Noble Truth sets forth three kinds of suffering: physically perceived suffering, psychological suffering resulting from the failure to fulfill desires or expectations, and the suffering of being bound to the series of transmigrations (*samsara*) in a world where total absence of pain and complete tranquillity do not exist.

The last of the eight sufferings—the five aggregates—means attachment to form (physical things), perception (operation of the perception of pleasure and pain), mental conceptions and ideas (the operation of conceptions and symbols), volition (the operation of various mental processes including that of volition), and consciousness (the operation of conscious judgment and of consciousness itself). This set of aggregates refers to all phenomena, both internal to the sentient being and external in the form of environment. Since clinging to them binds the sentient being to the world of transmigration with its inherent miseries, the suffering of the five aggregates can be said to correspond to that of the world of transmigration.

Though the eight kinds of sufferings include physical suffering and suffering resulting from being in the world of transmigration, the majority of them belong in the second category: psychological sufferings resulting from failure to fulfill desires or expectations. It is true that old age, illness, and death involve much that is physically perceptible—for instance, the intolerable pain often accompanying illness and the physical suffering of the last hours prior to death. Nonetheless, the major meaning of suffering is the psychological misery caused by old age, illness, and death.

In the case of illness, worse than actual physical pain are the psychological pains caused by forebodings about the frustrating effects illness will have on work and plans; possible loss of financial security, position, honor, and authority; desperation; the financial plight of the family; and many other unfortunate things that the person has not experienced before. Old age undeniably brings the misery of loss of physical freedom, but much more serious are worry and anxiety about the future.

Death is an instantaneous event. Any suffering it involves is necessarily of short duration. The true suffering of death takes the psychological form of anxiety about what will happen to one and to one's family and fear of the unknown. Such fears can be only idle speculation.

Sufferings caused by union with the disagreeable, separation from the pleasant and beloved, and unfulfillment of desires are purely psychological. It can be said that most psychological suffering is the outcome of failure to obtain something that was desired or hoped for. Much of the unhappiness and misery in human life falls into this category.

The physical suffering experienced by human beings and other animals is objective. In contrast, psychological suffering is largely subjective. Furthermore, the same state of affairs can inspire either pleasure or sorrow, depending on the mental attitude of the person experiencing it. Personality and time produce differences in the degrees of pleasure or sorrow felt. Religions strive to do away with suffering and sorrow by altering mental attitudes and views of the world and life. In dealing only with subjective, psychological joy and sorrow, religions attempt to eliminate misery by reversal of attitudes or even by a kind of mental paralysis. On these grounds, communists attack religions as opiates of the people. But as long as the religion is a correct one, far from paralyzing the mind or clouding the reason, it revises incorrect interpretations of what is sorrow and, by providing a correct view of the world and of life, leads to sound judgments and actions. By altering subjective mental attitudes, a true religion finally brings about improvements in the body, mind, and surrounding environment. A religion that does such things can hardly be described as an opiate.

The doctrine of the Four Noble Truths begins by altering mental attitudes and inspiring a correct subjective interpretation of the world and of life and ultimately leads to alterations in objective matters: improvements in the mind, body, and environment and the perfection of the personality.

The major elements of the eight sufferings set forth in the first of the Four Noble Truths are psychological in nature. Moreover, many of them result from mistakenly interpreting as suffering something that is actually not suffering or from exaggerating minor sufferings. When the mistaken interpretation is pointed out and corrected, suffering is immediately either eliminated or greatly reduced. Pointing out the causes of mistaken interpretations of suffering is the purpose of the second Noble Truth.

The Sutra of the First Rolling of the Wheel of the Law teaches that the causes of the eight kinds of psychological misery are three cravings: for gratification of the desires, for continued existence, and for annihilation. These cravings are described as thirsts—that is, they are unreasonable, passionate desires like that felt by a person dying for want of water. Unlike the love of God taught by Christianity or love as compassion taught by the Buddhists, these cravings are lusts that should be eliminated. The source of such thirst is blindness and delusion concerning the true nature of existence, the world, and humanity. Since ignorance and mistaken desire are the causes of suffering, eliminating them eliminates suffering itself.

The first of the three cravings—gratification of desires or craving for sensual pleasure—may bring temporary delight but, if pursued without cease, leads inevitably to sorrow, pain, and sometimes to loss of health. The number of conflicts and tragedies that have occurred in the world because of the desire for sensual pleasure is not small. An instinctive drive, the craving for sensual pleasure should be used only for the sake of the propagation of the race and the maintenance of the individual. It can often introduce a sense of beauty and happiness into life. But an ignorant, violent thirst for pleasure must be eliminated or purified into selfless love. This love, still further purified, becomes the spirit of compassion.

In the time of Shakyamuni, there were people who believed that hedonistic pursuit of the pleasure of the moment was the greatest human happiness and the highest human ideal. In his initial sermon, Shakyamuni told the five ascetics that, on the basis of his own experiences and thought, he had seen that a life of sensual pleasure does not lead to holiness and is useless in the attainment of ideal human aims. This is part of the Buddha's teaching that extremes of sensuality and physical mortification must be avoided for the sake of the Middle Path leading to the ideal.

The second craving, the craving for continued existence, is a burning desire for a happy and permanent life. This desire is based on the belief that, since the present world is filled with suffering, one must regard it as insignificant and valueless and must hope and dream of rebirth in a paradise of happiness in the coming world. The last desire, the desire for annihilation, is a thirst for nothingness. It is a nihilistic approach insisting that, because everything in ordinary existence leads to pain, the only way out is to renounce existence entirely. There were people in Shakyamuni's time who followed this philosophy too. Both the craving for existence and the craving for annihilation are foolish attempts to escape from reality and refusals to see the facts of the world and of human life as they are. Buddhism rejects this philosophy, like sensualism and asceticism, as extreme.

Suffering Eliminated and the Way to Eliminate It The third Noble Truth sets forth a state in which the cravings—the thirsts that hinder the attainment of the ideal—have been totally eliminated. In Buddhist terms, this state is called nirvana. The proper way for a Buddhist to live and behave is not only to seek the attainment of this ideal state for himself but also to strive to help other people and all of society to attain it too.

But it is not easy for the individual to reach the goal. It is consequently much more difficult to teach and lead others to it. Nonetheless, understanding the Four Noble Truths and living a life of faith practiced according to them enable the individual to understand and provide limited experience with the state in which cravings have been completely extinguished. As I have explained, for a doctor to diagnose a sickness correctly and know its causes, he must obtain knowledge and experience of the healthy physical condition and use them as standards for judgment. The greater his experience and knowledge of the sound state, the more exhaustive and accurate his diagnoses. Similarly, the third Noble Truth is a standard for the other three: the deeper one's experience and knowledge of it, the deeper and more correct one's understanding of the others.

Little is said in the Buddhist canonical texts to explain the state in which the causes of suffering have been eliminated, since, by nature, this is not an intellectual matter but something that must be comprehended through actual experience. Still, before one can experience this state correctly, one must have outside, intellectual, and theoretical knowledge. Such knowledge intensifies understanding of the other Noble Truths. Gradually, as one becomes more intensely and deeply aware of the meaning of the extinction of the causes of suffering, the nature of the sufferings standing in the way of the attainment of the ideal and the faults and passions causing them become more apparent. One realizes the importance of the causes of suffering and becomes determined to take proper steps to remove them. These steps are explained in concrete terms in the last of the Four Noble Truths.

In his first sermon, Shakyamuni explained the importance of the Middle Path between sensuality and asceticism. This Middle Path to the attainment of the goal of liberation, which is the fourth Noble Truth, is called the Eightfold Noble Path. It is the most rational method for eliminating the causes of suffering.

In treating illness, in addition to therapy directed immediately against the symptoms, doctors sometimes prescribe regimens related to diet, sleep, and exercise designed to create a generally healthy body capable of resisting illness. Something similar applies to treating spiritual disorders. Of course, it is essential to remove ignorance and cravings that directly bring about the lusts causing suffering. But it is also necessary to eliminate all other conditions that make it easy for suffering to develop and to produce spiritual good health and resistance against the further occurrence of suffering.

To this end, training in eight aspects of human behavior is provided in the Eightfold Noble Path. The system inherent in this path is intended not only to eliminate temporary suffering but also to create a perfectly healthy character in which suffering will not arise under any circumstances. Buddhist training and enlightenment employ present suffering as the occasion to institute a course leading ultimately to the perfection of the character.

The Noble Path is described as Eightfold, but this does not mean that its eight elements are isolated from each other. They are indivisibly connected and act cooperatively as a unit. The original Pali name of the Path means the holy way comprised of eight parts. The *way* is in the singular, though it consists in eight elements: right view, right thinking, right speech, right action, right living, right effort, right memory, and right meditation.

Though some people claim that the order in which they are listed here is the one in which these goals should be attained, others say that, since all eight exist simultaneously, there is no question of precedence among them. These two opposed views extend to all kinds of Buddhist training, but I should like to summarize the matter by discussing the three types of learning that embrace all Buddhist doctrines and practices.

These three types of learning are precepts, concentration, and wisdom. Precepts (or morality) are for the sake of correctly training mind and body and establishing correct physical and mental habits. Concentration, or meditation, is for the sake of spiritual unification after the mind and body have been properly trained. It produces a state in which the mind is as clear as a mirror and as still as the surface of an undisturbed body of water. Correct wisdom, reached when this kind of spiritual unification has been attained, makes possible correct judgments and suitable actions. In the light of this progression, the order for training and attainment in the three types of learning is this: precepts, concentration, and wisdom.

But, since the three types of learning correspond to three aspects of the human spirit—intellect (wisdom), emotion (concentration), and volition (precepts)—and since all three of these exist simultaneously as parts of the human spirit, the three kinds of learning, too, are not independent of each other but form a unity. From this viewpoint, there is no question of precedence among them. Nonetheless, for the sake of attainment of the states toward which the three kinds of learning are directed, the order precepts, concentration, and wisdom is reasonable.

The eight aspects of the Eightfold Noble Path can be fitted into the threefold division of all Buddhist learning in a number of different ways. For instance, some advocate this categorization: right view and right thinking—wisdom; right speech, right action, and right living—precepts; right effort—belonging to all three types; right memory and right meditation—concentration.

If the Eightfold Noble Path is practiced in this way, in terms of the three kinds of learning, the following order is established: wisdom, precepts, and concentration. But this order does not agree with the one that I have already said is reasonable.

Still, in the light of the experiences of *arhats* who have attained the highest degree of development and of beginners along the Path, it can be shown that this second progression too is reasonable. *Arhats* are said to advance beyond the Eightfold Noble Path finally to attain right wisdom before their total liberation. For them, then, the progression is wisdom, precepts, concentration, and again wisdom. Since the initial wisdom attained by an inexperienced person is less actual wisdom than faith based on teachings heard from more experienced people, the true progression then is faith, precepts, concentration, and wisdom. Still, like the eight aspects of the Noble Path itself, the three types of learning are simultaneously coexistent.

The Eightfold Noble Path   Sutra annotations explain the Eightfold Noble Path in two ways: secular for the purposes of daily life and Buddhist for enlightened sages. Since the Path leads to enlightenment, it is undeniably Buddhist. At the same time, it is secular because it pertains to daily life and can serve in the creation of ideal conditions for all human affairs. The explanations presented below—a combination of the Buddhist and secular interpretations—are derived from material in commentaries on the sutras.

1. Right view. In the secular interpretation, this means a correct understanding of the law of cause and effect, of karma, and of the karmic rewards and retributions meted out in the three worlds of the past, present, and future for good and evil. In everyday affairs, it is highly important to understand cause and effect and to think rationally. In the Buddhist interpretation right view means understanding the Four Noble Truths, the Law of Causation, and the correct Buddhist interpretations of the world and human life.

Right view is the opposite of all the heresies that run counter to correct Buddhist interpretations. In the narrow sense, heresies either doubt or reject the law of karma. This is considered the greatest of all obstacles, for a person who holds such heretical views would under no circumstances desire to be admitted to the Buddhist following. In the wider sense, heresies—the opposites of right view—include mistaken views: failure to realize that all things are impermanent and that nothing has an ego and the resultant belief in a real individuality and the things belonging to it; holding extreme views, such as the all-encompassing belief that all is immutable or the nihilistic belief that nothing exists; being attached to practices and observances that are irrational and superstitious and that, while admitting the law of cause and effect, misinterpret the relations between the two or that advocate incorrect training methods as correct ones. As long as these kinds of heresies persist, it is impossible to eliminate ignorance and lust.

The minute a person understands the Law of Causation and the correct Buddhist view of the world and human life, his mind is set moving in the right direction. Consequently, in the affairs of the world as well as in Buddhist discipline, the important thing is to orient the mind correctly and to institute a correct plan. Once a proper basic policy has been adopted and put into action, progress along the Path becomes easy. This is the purpose of right view.

Beginners, however, must rely on others to point out right view, since they lack both proof and experience. They can do nothing but believe what their leaders tell them, and for this reason their right view should be called right faith.

2. Right thinking. In the Buddhist and the secular senses, this means thinking without desire, anger, or will to harm. In other words, it is thinking removed from covetousness, wrath, and foolishness. When, as a result of right view, the mind is correctly oriented, thinking in all instances is free of egoism and the emotions characterizing it. Right view produces the will and determination to think right. This will and determination manifest themselves in right speech, right action, and right living.

3. Right speech. Right speech means refraining from lying, malice, a double tongue, careless language, and fruitless chatter. In practical terms, all of these kinds of speech impede efficiency; in Buddhist terms, they stand in the way of training along the Path. Avoiding them and telling only the truth, praising and encouraging others properly, speaking to arbitrate for the sake of accord, and talking in a way that serves in the attainment of the ideal are what is meant by right speech. As I have said, right speech derives from well-intentioned, right thinking. It generates reserve energy giving rise to good habits. All actions leave a reserve of energy that becomes habits for further action. Accumulation of such habits forms

the personality. Both habit and personality play an immense role in everyday life. Because it includes the element of correct speech habits, this aspect of the Eightfold Noble Path belongs in the precepts category of Buddhist learning. The same thing is true of right action and right living.

4. Right action. Right action means abstaining from deliberate killing, from stealing, and from wrong sexual activities. In other words, right action entails love and protection for living things, generous almsgiving, expounding the Law, and proper marital relations. They too are the outcome of will and determination produced by right thinking and include the reserve energy for the creation of habitual right actions.

5. Right living. Right living is obtaining food, clothing, and housing by proper means. This entails being faithful in one's work and living seriously without resort to shady methods, like gambling, for a living. But it further includes an orderly way of life in which hours for sleep; kinds, quantities, and numbers of meals; hours for work, study, rest, exercise, and entertainment are all properly regulated to suit individual needs. A controlled life that keeps a person in good health and enables him to work more efficiently is highly important, no matter what the environment. It can help determine success or failure.

6. Right effort. Right effort is described as of four kinds: (1) Striving to prevent evil from arising. (2) Striving to abandon evil that has arisen. (3) Striving to produce good. (4) Striving to increase good that has been produced. These actions toward evil and good pertain to more than considerations of morality. Evil is anything that runs counter to the ideal, and good is anything that agrees with the ideal in politics, economics, and health on either the individual or the society-wide basis.

In terms of health, these four kinds of right effort can be reworded as follows: (1) Striving not to develop bad health habits—like overeating, overdrinking, and disorderly living—if they have not already been developed. (2) Striving to eliminate such bad habits if they have been developed. (3) Striving to develop good health habits if they have not already been developed. (4) Striving to increase the good health habits that have been developed. Efforts in these directions will improve health without fail. Furthermore, efforts of a similar kind in any field ensure a gradual approach to the ideal. For this reason, right effort is a part of all three kinds of Buddhist learning: precepts, or morality; meditation, or concentration; and wisdom. This aspect of the Eightfold Noble Path can be called courage, since courage is essential to spiritual development.

7. Right memory. This has the double meaning of retaining in recall things one has experienced and of evoking and remanifesting these things. Commentaries on the sutras set forth four insights on which right memory works: the body, the emotions, the mind, and the world—that is, the entire physical and mental environment. In the Buddhist sense, right memory means constantly bearing in mind the four insights: that the world is transient, that the body is impure, that perception leads to suffering, and that the mind is impermanent. In secular terms, right memory means being always careful, clearheaded, and attentive. Slight lack of attention is frequently the cause of serious accidents or fires. Though carelessness in itself is a small, scarcely criminal matter, since it often leads to such things as airplane crashes, collisions of trains or ships, and serious fires; results in tremendous financial loss; and causes death and injury, it can be considered many times more grave than murder or robbery.

8. Right meditation. Right meditation leads to spiritual unification, mental tranquillity, and the attainment of the state in which thought and concepts no longer exist.

Commentaries on the sutras explain four stages of meditation, all leading to high states of spiritual unification impossible for ordinary people in everyday life. Meditation was widely practiced in India before the time of Buddhism. Shakyamuni himself mastered it while in his father's home and during his period of spiritual discipline, and Buddhism can be said to have made use of four stages of meditation that had already been taught in India.

Aside from the specialized concentration involved in these four stages of meditation, spiritual unification is very important in daily affairs like thinking, reading, writing, and making talks before audiences. Without it, one is unable to adopt a cool, calm attitude; and objective thought and speedy, appropriate action are impossible.

Correct meditation is necessary to the acquisition of correct wisdom and to putting that wisdom to effective use. As I have already mentioned, right meditation leads to the paramount stages of right wisdom and right liberation. Through meditation under the bo tree, Shakyamuni attained enlightenment and acquired mystic powers. Though there are many kinds and stages of meditation, discussion of them is too specialized for a book of this scope.

7. The Growth of the Buddhist Order

Early Missionary Activities One day, after spending the three-month rainy season in Benares, Shakyamuni turned to his disciples and said, "You and I have been delivered from the fetters of the world and have attained the highest enlightenment. For the sake of the peace and happiness of the people of the world, wander in all regions, preaching the doctrine that is glorious in the beginning, glorious in the middle, and glorious in the end, and reveal the clear and perfect Law of faith and practice. There are some people who suffer from practically no illusions. If they do not hear the true teachings, they will continue to invite suffering in the realm of transmigration. If they hear the true teaching, however, they will be liberated from the fetters of illusion. I shall go to the village of Sena. You go into various regions, as you like, but let no two of you go together. Teach and guide as many people as possible." And this was the initiation of the missionary activities of the Buddhist Order.

From the time of Shakyamuni, the Buddhist Order has had three functions that are considered essential. For Buddhism to develop ideally, as it should, all three of these functions must be fulfilled.

First, the members of the Order must strive to perfect themselves in faith and practice. They must have correct faith and must understand the Buddhist view of the world and of humanity. In addition, striving for unity of both theory and practice of faith, they must discipline themselves and strive for liberation from illusions and hindrances.

The second function is the salvation and purification of all society. Before they can work to lead and save others, members of the Order must strive to attain self-perfection. Nonetheless, it is important that even people who have not perfected themselves guide others in Buddhist training to the best of their abilities for the sake of peace and happiness. This is expressed in the nature of the bodhisattva, who, though not yet a Buddha, assists others in attaining buddhahood.

The third function is the eternal preservation of the Law. Far from being inferior, Buddhism is recognized as one of the most outstanding of the world's religions and philosophies. But even an outstanding teaching might as well not exist if there is no one to teach it and demonstrate its excellence. To carry out its missionary role, an order must transmit a correct teaching in a correct way. If there is a break in the transmission, even a correct teaching can be lost. Preventing such an occurrence is the purpose of the third function of the Order, which is expressed in the maxim: "May the righteous Law of the Buddha last forever!"

As long as the Order continues to fulfill these three functions—as it has whenever Buddhism has flourished in a flourishing region— Buddhism cannot fail. Shakyamuni initiated the Order to carry out precisely these three functions.

The Journey to Uruvela   After sending his sixty disciples to various regions, Shakyamuni himself set out for Magadha, which was at that time a newly flourishing kingdom. If the Order were able to grow there, it would mean a great step forward. It is unlikely, however, that Shakyamuni had deliberate intentions of merely increasing the size or scope of his group. He acted solely out of a great compassion inspiring him to bring his unique teaching to as many people as possible.

On his way from Benares to Uruvela in Magadha, Shakyamuni

entered a quiet forest and began seated meditation. At that time, thirty young men of royal blood, all but one with their young wives, were enjoying themselves in the woods. One of the young men was unmarried, and a harlot had been procured for him. As the others were lost in their amusements, the harlot stole their gold, silver, and jewels and ran away. When they saw what had happened, the young men and women hastened in search of her. Coming upon Shakyamuni seated in a grove, they asked if he had seen the woman. He replied by asking why they were looking for her. After hearing their reason, he asked, "Which is more important, to seek that woman or to seek yourselves?" They answered that seeking themselves was more important. Whereupon Shakyamuni said, "Sit there, and I will teach you the Law whereby to seek yourselves." They then listened to his sermon.

Following his usual custom, Shakyamuni taught first the triple doctrine of almsgiving to the poor and holy people, abiding by the moral precepts, and the assurance that good acts are rewarded by rebirth in a blessed state. From this he gradually moved to the Four Noble Truths. Upon hearing his words, the young men came to understand the true nature of human life throughout the world and attained the pure and spotless Eye of the Law. They requested to be allowed to abandon the secular world and were accepted as members of the Order.

Continuing on his way, Shakyamuni entered the kingdom of Magadha and turned toward Uruvela, the place where he had passed six years in religious austerities. (The bo tree under which he had attained enlightenment was in this vicinity.)

Living in the region were three brothers of a Brahman family by the name of Kashyapa. Ascetics who wore their hair matted, they believed that they could find the ideal realm by serving the god of fire and by carrying out ceremonies in his honor. All three of them were in their seventies or eighties and had large followings: the eldest, Uruvilva-Kashyapa, had five hundred disciples; the second, Nadi-Kashyapa, three hundred; and the youngest, Gaya-Kashyapa, two hundred. With their total following of one thousand people, they were the most highly respected and influential religious leaders in Magadha.

Although Shakyamuni had probably heard of these men when he was undergoing religious disciplines at an earlier time, it is likely that, eager in the search of a new ideal, he found the old concept of liberation through serving the god of fire totally worthless. As a Buddha, however, he must have thought that converting these leaders to Buddhism would be the way to win the absolute trust of the king and the people and thus to convert the entire kingdom. He turned first to the conversion of Uruvilva, the eldest.

Uruvilva-Kashyapa was a stubborn old man so convinced that he was preeminent in religion throughout the land that there was no reason to expect him to lend an ear to theories. Shakyamuni went to the hermitage where he lived and said, "If it is not disagreeable to you, I should like to spend a night in the room where your sacred fire is kept." Uruvilva said that it was not disagreeable but that a very dangerous snake lived in that room. "I hope he does you no harm," he said. Shakyamuni answered that no matter how savage the snake, it was unlikely to harm him and that he greatly desired to stay in the room. This conversation was repeated three times, and finally Uruvilva said, "Use the room as you like."

Shakyamuni entered the room and sat in meditation. Surely enough, the malevolent snake came out and tried several times to attack him. But because he had a great heart of compassion for all sentient beings and felt no animosity toward the snake, Shakyamuni subdued it with benevolence and love. Entering the state of meditation known as the heart of benevolence, he calmed the fierce serpent, reduced it to a small, harmless creature, and went calmly on with his meditation throughout a peaceful night.

Unaware that Shakyamuni was a Buddha and believing him to be only a *samana,* or monk, on the following morning, Uruvilva-Kashyapa felt certain that the young *samana* had been killed by the fierce snake. But when he looked into the room where the sacred fire was kept, he was surprised to see that the snake had been exorcised. While respecting Shakyamuni's great powers, however, Uruvilva remained convinced that he himself was the first man of religion in the country and that the younger man could not be as holy as he. According to Buddhist tradition, Shakyamuni performed many wonders in order to convince this stubborn Brahman of his greatness. Finally, Uruvilva bowed before his mighty personality and powers in the Law. It was one of Shakyamuni's methods to use manifestations of his mystical powers to convert people who refused to be convinced by theoretical teachings and doctrines.

After being shown the various wondrous spiritual powers of the young *samana*, Uruvilva-Kashyapa realized his own inferiority and asked to be taught and to be allowed to become one of Shakyamuni's followers. Shakyamuni counseled him: "As a teacher of five hundred disciples, you must not act rashly. First discuss the matter with them and then do what is suitable." Uruvilva went to his disciples and said, "I am going to become a follower of the Great Samana. Each of you may do as he likes." The disciples all followed Uruvilva in becoming members of the Buddhist Order. They shaved their heads and beards and threw their old ceremonial implements into a river.

The two remaining Kashyapa brothers lived along the lower reaches of this same river. When they saw the ceremonial implements floating downstream, they were greatly surprised. After investigating the situation and learning the cause of the occurrence, they too became followers of Shakyamuni. In other words, in a very short while, the Order expanded by one thousand new members. No doubt all of the new converts heard the teaching of the Four Noble Truths and came to understand the Buddhist view of the world and humanity.

Then Shakyamuni, with the thousand monks, turned again toward Rajagaha, the capital of Magadha. But along the way they stopped at a volcanic mountain called Gayasisa. In the evening, seeing fire glowing from the mountain, Shakyamuni preached what is called the Sermon on Burning. All human perceptions, sensations, thoughts, and the actions based on them are burning—more violently than the external fire of the mountain—with the flames of such poisons as covetousness, anger, and ignorance. Because of this burning, human beings suffer. But, correctly realizing the cause of the burning and doing away with the sensations, perceptions, ideas, and actions will extinguish the three poisons—covetousness, anger, and ignorance—and thus remove the cause of suffering. By means of correct knowledge and experience, it is possible to be liberated from all fetters and to reach the ideal realm. The one thousand monks who heard this teaching attained enlightenment and became *arhats*. This sermon, suggested by fire issuing from a volcano, taught the former believers in the fire god that the true way is not to worship but to extinguish fire. Deeper reflection on their former errors assisted them in finding the true way to enlightenment.

The Heart of Benevolence   Though it is a slight digression, I should like to offer a few words of explanation about the heart of benevolence, the state of concentration in meditation that Shakyamuni used to subdue the fierce serpent in the sacred-fire room of Uruvilva-Kashyapa. This state, which can be attained by anyone, refers to the benevolence that is one of the four infinite virtues—benevolence, compassion, giving happiness, and impartiality—and means constant compassion and kindness for all beings, not just for those that are dear but also for unrelated beings and even enemies against whom one might otherwise entertain bitterness.

According to Buddhist classics, eleven categories of merit attach to the practicing of the heart of benevolence. These categories are: peaceful sleep; peaceful awakening; no bad dreams; constantly clear, bright facial complexion; love from other people; love from nonhuman beings; protection of the gods; imperviousness to fire, wounds from blades, and poison; free entry into the concentration stage of meditation; at death, freedom from confusion (death comes as easily as sleep); after death, even if enlightenment has not been attained, at least the privilege of rebirth in a happy state of the Brahma heaven.

A person who is constantly compassionate toward all human and nonhuman beings exudes all-inclusive warmth. Such a person does not fight with others or entertain grudges and hatreds. For that reason, he has no need to be afraid. His mind is always at rest; therefore he sleeps well, is never troubled by bad dreams, and wakes refreshed in the morning.

Because he gets adequate sleep and does not need to worry, such a person has a perpetually wholesome and clear complexion, which inspires good will in the people and animals with whom he comes into contact. Most of us have a sixth sense enabling us to tell at a glance whether a person is or is not trustworthy. Animals like dogs, cats, and even birds have intuitive senses even more highly developed than ours and make judgments of human beings on the basis of their eyes. A dog will bark only at people who he thinks deserve to be treated warily—that is, only when he is frightened or mistrustful. Naturally a person who is beloved of both sentient and nonsentient beings enjoys the protection of the gods. He is always mentally peaceful and calm and meets all dangers coolly. Such calm disarms people who might attempt to harm him. This is what is meant by being impervious to fire, blades, and poison. The Buddhist classics contain many instances of people who have been saved from injury by this characteristic.

Because his mind is always calm, it is easy for the person with the heart of benevolence to enter the concentration stage of meditation. This same calm protects him from perplexity, suffering, and mental confusion when death is near and enables him to die with the peacefulness of falling asleep. The heart of benevolence can be a way of attaining enlightenment and of escaping from the cycle of transmigrations of birth and death. But even if this does not happen, the person with the heart of benevolence is certain to be born in a happy state of the Brahma heaven.

Anyone can have the heart of benevolence. And if everyone did, the world would be an infinitely happier, brighter, and more peaceful place.

Entry into Rajagaha   Together with the three Kashyapa brothers and the one thousand new monks, Shakyamuni traveled to Rajagaha, the capital of Magadha. As the greatest men of religion in the land, the three brothers enjoyed the maximum respect of the king, his ministers, and the general citizenry.

It will be recalled that shortly after he left his father's home for the life of religious discipline, Shakyamuni encountered King Bimbisara in the city of Rajagaha. At that time, the king asked him to return to the secular life and assist in managing affairs of state.

Citing the pursuit of his ideal as his reason, Shakyamuni refused. The king then requested that when Shakyamuni had attained his ideal, he should return and teach him the truth he had discovered. Shakyamuni gave his word, and it was probably to fulfill this promise that he returned to Rajagaha.

When he heard that the young *samana* Gotama had become a Buddha with a glorious reputation and was at a nearby shrine with a great following, the king, with a large train of ministers, retainers, and ordinary citizens, went to meet him. Ancient tradition says that he was accompanied by twelve myriads (twelve thousand or possibly twelve hundred). Even if this is an exaggeration, the crowd may have numbered in the thousands. Although the king knew what a great person Shakyamuni was, the people in general did not. Since the Kashyapa brothers were not only venerable in age but also the recognized first men of religion in the land, the people thought that the young *samana* must have become the disciple of the old Brahmans. Still, it seemed strange to them that the Kashyapas and their followers had cut their matted hair off entirely.

Shakyamuni, who realized the doubts in the minds of the people, said, "Uruvilva-Kashyapa, why have you abandoned the fire god?" Stepping forward and laying his head in worship at Shakyamuni's feet, Uruvilva replied, "The World-honored One is my master, and I am his disciple."

At last, the people saw that Shakyamuni had made these three famous men his disciples. Nonetheless, in the light of the age of the Kashyapa brothers and the fame and respect they commanded, this turn of events must have been difficult to accept. The totality with which the Kashyapas submitted and entrusted themselves to him without thought of their own pride or reputation or the opinions of the world suggests how great a person Shakyamuni was.

For the king and the multitude, Shakyamuni preached in his usual gradual way from the triple doctrine of almsgiving, precepts, and reward for good actions to the Four Noble Truths. Deeply moved, all those present attained the pure and spotless Eye of the Law and came to understand the Buddhist interpretation of the world and of humanity.

The king rejoiced most at the sermon and said, "When I was

crown prince, I had five wishes. The first was to be crowned king of the country. That wish was quickly fulfilled. My second wish was that the absolute and holy Buddha would come to our territory. The third was that I could serve the Buddha. The fourth was that I might hear a sermon from the Buddha. And the fifth was that I might be enlightened by his teachings. I could not be happier than I am, now that all five wishes have been fulfilled."

Among all the monarchs of the major kingdoms in India of his time, Bimbisara was the most cultivated and outstanding. It is possible to know this from the Buddhist classics that contain sermons addressed by Shakyamuni to him and colloquies between him and Shakyamuni. Consequently, he probably actually entertained the five wishes he mentioned.

King Bimbisara entrusted himself to the Buddha, the Law, and the Order and vowed to be a Buddhist follower for the rest of his life. He then requested that Shakyamuni and his followers attend a meal that he was going to prepare for them on the following day. As was a custom in India then, Shakyamuni expressed his assent by remaining silent.

Throughout the night, Bimbisara had his people make preparations. On the following day, he sent a messenger to invite Shakyamuni and his thousand followers. At the meal, the king himself served Shakyamuni. Perhaps in recognition of his greatness and in token of absolute allegiance, the king and the others who had become believers knelt and worshiped the World-honored One. Nothing of the kind was ever done for other men of religion. Indeed, even Brahmans, no matter how outstanding, were not allowed to do so much as carry on reciprocal conversations with kings.

After the meal, Shakyamuni once again preached a sermon for the king. Then Bimbisara, who was now devoted to the faith, donated, as a place of residence for the Order, a bamboo grove that he owned in the outskirts of the city. Shakyamuni accepted the offer, and this place was to become the Bamboo Grove Monastery, the first monastery of the Buddhist Order.

Though called a monastery, originally the grove had no residential buildings. In the time of Shakyamuni, the members of the Order wandered from place to place as mendicants without permanent abode. In the monastery, the main building was used for sermons and ceremonies. Aside from time of illness, all the members of the Order lived out of doors, where they sat upon stones under trees.

Nonetheless, the Bamboo Grove Monastery was important as a base of operations. The kind of location considered ideal for such monasteries was neither too far away from nor too close to cities. If the city were too far away, mendicant begging trips would be inconvenient; if it were too close, the noise would distract from meditation and thought. A separation of from two to three kilometers was thought suitable and was maintained in all monasteries established after the Bamboo Grove.

The Conversion of the Two Great Disciples   It was probably about six months after the dispatching of the sixty disciples at Benares that Shakyamuni arrived in Rajagaha. It must have taken some time to convert the thirty young men and the three Kashyapa brothers and their followers at Uruvela.

Before the arrival of Shakyamuni, Assaji, one of the five ascetics from Benares, had already reached Rajagaha. He wore his robes properly, held himself well, and had a controlled countenance. His general calm and composure as he begged in the city and his awe-inspiring solemnity were enough to attract attention, especially since a restrained attitude of this kind was rarely encountered in representatives of other religions.

One of the people impressed by Assaji's appearance was Shariputra, who, born into a Brahman family living near Rajagaha, was to become the highest and wisest of the Buddha's disciples. Both his mother and father were outstanding scholars and philosophers. Beginning to study Vedic learning with a Brahman teacher at the age of six or seven, Shariputra had mastered the Rig-veda, the Sama-veda, the Yajur-veda, and other orthodox Vedic doctrines by the time he was seventeen or eighteen. But, at a turning point in his life, he found himself facing a philosophical crisis. This crisis occurred one day during a bustling festival. Part of the noisy crowd, he and his close friend Maudgalyayana suddenly realized the futil-

Lumbini Garden where Shakyamuni was born. He is said to have been bathed at birth in water from the pond.

A portion of Asoka's edict, which states that because this site is the birthplace of the Buddha Asoka worshiped here, caused this pillar to be erected, and exempted the village of Lumbini from taxation.

A modern memorial and the edict pillar erected in the third century B.C. by Emperor Asoka.

The great stupa at Bodh Gaya, where Shakyamuni attained enlightenment.

Shakyamuni attained enlightenment under a bo tree like this one.

An image of the Buddha faces the Diamond Seat, which is said to mark the spot where the Buddha meditated until attaining enlightenment.

Deer Park at Sarnath, where Shakyamuni preached his first sermon after he attained enlightenment. The commemorative Dhamekh Stupa is said to have been built originally at the order of Emperor Asoka.

The edict on this pillar, erected near the Dhamekh Stupa by Asoka, consists of injunctions to the monks and nuns of the monastery at Sarnath.

◀ The remains of the monastery at Sarnath.

The Bimbisara Road climbs all the way to the summit of Vulture Peak.
The road leading to Vulture Peak at Rajgir was built by King Bimbisara.

The name of Vulture Peak is said to derive from the fact that it is shaped like a vulture and also that many vultures are supposed to have lived on the mountain.

It is said that Shakyamuni meditated in this cave at the summit of Vulture Peak.

The remains of Savatthi, the capital of the ancient kingdom of Kosala.

The remains of the house of the Savatthi merchant Sudatta, who purchased the land for the Jetavana Monastery by covering it with gold.

The Jetavana Monastery, near Savatthi, was presented to the Buddhist Order by Sudatta and Prince Jeta.

The largest Buddhist monastery, Nalanda, a monastic university, flourished from the fifth century A.D. through the twelfth century as a major center of Buddhist learning.

Jūkichi Suzuki／Shunjūsha Publishing Co.

The inscription on a sheet of copper discovered in the cylindrical Nirvana Stupa (behind the mound in the foreground) in 1911 states that this is the site in Kushinagara where Shakyamuni died.

◀ *The area of Kushinagara where Shakyamuni preached his last sermon.*

The mound built on the site of Shakyamuni's cremation.

Present-day Tilaurakota, in Nepal, one of the sites said to be the ancient city Kapilavatthu, the capital of the country of the Shakyas.

The other site said to be Kapilavatthu is present-day Piprahwa, in India, where William C. Peppe discovered the urn containing the Buddha's relics.

The site at Piprahwa where the urn containing the Buddha's relics was found.

*The urn from Piprahwa that contained the Buddha's relics. The inscription reads:
"This is the urn of the relics of the Bhagavat, the Buddha of the Shakya tribe, that
is enshrined (by honorable brothers and sisters, wives and children)."*

ity of everything around them and deeply felt the inconstancy of the world. In addition, they realized that Vedic learning was powerless to do anything to cure spiritual emptiness.

They visited many famous philosophers and men of religion in the hope of discovering the way to truth but were unable to find a teacher who satisfied their needs. For want of anyone better, they went to Sanjaya, one of the so-called six great non-Buddhist teachers of the time, and asked him to teach them.

Sanjaya, who lived and taught his two hundred and fifty disciples in a place near Rajagaha, was a skeptic who argued that there is no absolute truth in the world and that, even if such truth did exist, it would be undiscoverable. Each of the various thinkers of the time held his own version of the truth as paramount, optimum, and absolute. But Sanjaya insisted that none of them was trustworthy. If all these philosophers were right, there would be many incompatible truths confusing the very nature of truth. Sanjaya therefore adopted the viewpoint that the existence of absolute truth was dubious.

Later, when they became dissatisfied with such skepticism and convinced that there must be a better doctrine, Shariputra and Maudgalyayana set out again in search of a good teacher. They promised that if one of them should encounter an outstanding doctrine, he would immediately inform the other and that the two of them would go to the teacher together.

It was about this time that Shariputra saw Assaji and became immediately convinced that this must be the man he had been seeking. Assaji finished begging and went to the outskirts of the city. Shariputra followed him and, when Assaji's meal was over, approached, greeted the man, and said, "Your countenance is serene, your complexion is pure and bright. To follow whom did you abandon the world? Whose teaching do you follow?" Assaji replied, "There is a great *samana* of the Shakya clan. I left the world to follow this World-honored One. I follow his teaching."

"What is the nature of your master's teaching?"

"I have been a member of the Order for only a short while and cannot adequately explain my master's teaching."

"Explain just the main points simply to me, please."

Then Assaji explained the basic elements of Buddhism in the following stanza:

> All things are produced by causation.
> The Tathagata has explained the causes
> And the way to eliminate them.
> This is the teaching of the Great Samana.

Since he was already great in wisdom and had wandered long in the study of philosophy, from this simple stanza alone, Shariputra understood the Law of Causation is the main element of the Buddha's teachings. Enlightened to the fact that this was a wonderful doctrine unlike anything he had ever heard before, he decided that its teacher was the man he must follow. It is said that on the basis of no more than this stanza Shariputra understood the Buddhist view of the world and mankind and attained the pure and spotless Eye of the Law. (This stanza was to become famous as the Stanza on Production by Causation.) Enraptured by what he had heard, Shariputra at once left Assaji and hurried to the place where Maudgalyayana was.

Maudgalyayana saw his friend approaching and said, "Your countenance is serene; your complexion is pure and bright. Have you attained enlightenment?" Then Shariputra related everything that he had just experienced, and Maudgalyayana, too, at once attained the Eye of the Law from hearing the Stanza on Production by Causation. In his great enthusiasm, he said that this teaching was truly wonderful and something that one could not encounter in many thousands of *kalpas* (eons).

Instead of going directly to Shakyamuni, the two decided that, since Sanjaya had entrusted the guidance of his two hundred and fifty disciples to them, they must tell these men what had happened and allow them to do as they saw fit. But the disciples all said that, if such a wonderful World-honored One existed, they wanted to be taken to him.

Shariputra and Maudgalyayana explained the situation to Sanjaya and bade him farewell. Sanjaya tried three times to stop them, but they refused and took the two hundred and fifty disciples with them to Shakyamuni, who had already arrived in Rajagaha, had converted the king and the people, and was living at the Bamboo Grove Monastery. When he saw them coming from afar, Shakyamuni prophesied to the monks around him: "These two will become my greatest disciples."

Shariputra and Maudgalyayana requested to be allowed to abandon the secular world to follow Shakyamuni as members of the Order. They and the two hundred and fifty men they had brought with them were accepted.

Ancient Buddhist classics teach that at this time Shakyamuni had a total of 1,250 disciples. This means the thousand who came with the Kashyapa brothers and the two hundred and fifty who came with Shariputra and Maudgalyayana. In fact, about one year after his enlightenment, he had more than 1,300 disciples. In addition, followers from famous families in Magadha were constantly asking to be admitted to the Order. This caused many people to criticize Buddhism for taking children from parents and depriving wives of their husbands. Whatever the exact numbers, it is certain that the Order was growing and that there were probably several times as many lay believers as members.

The Two Great Disciples and Maha-Kashyapa One week after becoming a member of the Order, Maudgalyayana attained the highest enlightenment. In two weeks, Shariputra attained it. Once after he had left the secular world to follow Shakyamuni, Maudgalyayana was meditating in a certain village. But since he was unaccustomed to such practices, he frequently became sleepy. Seeing this and knowing that falling asleep would not lead to enlightenment, Shakyamuni kindly explained to Maudgalyayana a variety of ways to combat drowsiness. He said that, when nothing else worked and sleepiness persisted, Maudgalyayana should lie down to sleep for a while and then resume meditation.

Shakyamuni further instructed Maudgalyayana that in begging he must never be proud of his own family background or education. He must always be calm and humble and avoid causing ordinary householders to quarrel or entertain dissatisfaction. Shakyamuni then taught that, while knowing and observing things accurately, he must not form attachments and must manage himself with confidence. Putting these teachings to practical application, Maudgalyayana attained enlightenment and became an *arhat*. Because of the special mystical powers with which he is said to have been endowed, he is usually referred to as Maha-Maudgalyayana, or Great Maudgalyayana.

About two weeks after Shariputra had joined the Order, his uncle—whose nickname was the Long-nailed Itinerant Ascetic— came to investigate whether Shakyamuni, for whom Shariputra and Maudgalyayana had abandoned Sanjaya, was indeed an outstanding teacher. The younger brother of Shariputra's mother—by whom he had been defeated in discussions in earlier years—the uncle had traveled southward, studying philosophy and engaging in religious disciplines. He earned his nickname by never cutting his fingernails. Like Sanjaya, he was a skeptic.

When his uncle arrived, Shariputra was standing behind Shakyamuni, fanning him. The uncle turned to Shakyamuni and said, "I am a skeptic and cannot recognize any conclusive doctrine."

Shakyamuni replied, "Do you, who say you cannot recognize any conclusive doctrine, recognize your own conclusive doctrine?" The uncle did not know what to say. If he recognized his own theory, he would be self-contradictory in that his own skepticism could not be applied to what he himself advocated. On the other hand, if he said that his own standpoint was dubious, he would no longer have any reason for maintaining it. As Greek philosophy later pointed out, this weakness is inherent in all skepticism, and Shakyamuni posed his question because he knew this.

For the sake of the thwarted uncle, Shakyamuni explained that philosophies considering the world and the self to be eternal entities, philosophies considering the world and the self perishable and reducible to nothing, philosophies that are an eclectic blend of these two approaches, and skeptical philosophies rejecting both are all mistaken ways of thinking arising from attachment to transient entities. He then explained the Law of Causation and the need to abandon attachments to such entities and to see the world and human life as they truly are. The long-nailed uncle, realizing his error for the first time, experienced the opening of the eye of truth and attained the pure and spotless Eye of the Law. Shariputra, who had been listening, was liberated from all illusions and hindrances and attained the enlightenment of an *arhat*. Shariputra's younger brothers Upatissa, Upasena, Mahachunda, and Revata and his sisters Chala and Upachala all became *arhats*. In the Buddhist classics are many sermons related to them and many of their teachings and stanzas.

Shariputra and Maudgalyayana were Shakyamuni's two greatest disciples. Indeed it was said that Shariputra would be the next to roll the Wheel of the Law. But both of them died about a year before Shakyamuni. Maha-Kashyapa became the person to unify the Order and to occupy the position of chief elder. He was Shakyamuni's most trusted disciple and was allowed to share the spot on which Shakyamuni sat. It is thought that he joined the Order shortly after Shariputra and Maudgalyayana.

Maha-Kashyapa, too, was born of a Brahman family in the vicinity of Rajagaha and received an orthodox education. As a fine young man, he was married to Bhaddakapilani, a girl of good family. But, weary of the secular life, the two of them resolved that their marriage would be in name only. They would strive to reach an ideal spiritual state together. After discussing the matter, they agreed to abandon the world entirely and become ascetics. But they were unable to find a teacher who lived up to their ideals.

Once, accidentally hearing of the appearance of a Buddha, Maha-Kashyapa decided that just such a Buddha must become his master. He first met Shakyamuni at a shrine midway between Rajagaha and Nalanda. After immediately receiving various instructions, he enthusiastically put them into practice and, on the eighth day, became an *arhat*. Apparently older than Shakyamuni, he led a serious and stern life and became first in the practice of ascetic precepts that are known by the name *dhuta*. Since several of the disciples of Shakyamuni, including the famous three brothers, had the name Kashyapa, the title *maha*, or great, is prefixed in the name of Maha-Kashyapa to distinguish him from the others.

8. The Visit to Kapilavatthu

The Conversion of Suddhodana and the Shakyas Rumors that Shakyamuni had become a Buddha in Magadha and that he had surrounded himself with a large number of followers and disciples, including King Bimbisara himself, reached the ears of Suddhodana, king of the Shakyas and Shakyamuni's own father. When he heard these things, Suddhodana decided to request Shakyamuni to visit his native country and explain his teachings to the Shakya tribe. It seems entirely likely that both the father and the foster mother who had raised him longed to see once again the child from whom they had been separated for years and who had become a Buddha and a religious leader of the kind rarely encountered in the world.

Suddhodana sent Udayin, a friend from the time when Shakyamuni was a prince, to invite him to come to the capital at Kapilavatthu. It is said, however, that upon hearing the preaching of the Buddha, Udayin was so deeply moved that he at once joined the Order and, becoming lost in religious training, completely forgot the mission on which he had been sent by the king. Later, when he recalled his errand and presented the king's request, Shakyamuni consented to make the visit.

Proud of their ancient and excellent lineage, the Shakyas were a stubbornly haughty people. For this reason, neither the king himself nor the elders of the tribe paid truly sincere respect or homage to Shakyamuni when he arrived with his great train of disciples. Indeed, his father was humiliated that his son should lower the dignity of the aristocracy by his shabby appearance and his practice of begging food from the houses of the ordinary people. He said, "I wish you would refrain from actions that bring disgrace on our house. Although you are rich enough to feed hundreds or even thousands of followers without difficulty, you persist in begging food from the ordinary people."

Shakyamuni replied, "Mendicancy has long been a correct custom of our line."

To this the king responded, "There have been no beggars among our line, the descendants of King Ikshvaku!"

"I was not speaking of the lineages of worldly kings but of the line of the Buddhas," answered Shakyamuni. Neither the king nor the tribe in general, all of whom placed great value on worldly glory, found Shakyamuni's attitude pleasing.

Realizing that verbal discussions would not win the admiration of such people, Shakyamuni used his mystical powers to work a number of miracles, which at last caused even the obstinate Shakyas to bow their heads before his might and worship him. Thereafter, he employed his customary method of gradual instruction—beginning, as usual, with the triple doctrine of almsgiving to the poor and holy people, abiding by the moral precepts, and the assurance that good acts are rewarded by rebirth in a blessed state, and then moving to the Four Noble Truths. As a result, the Shakyas came to have a degree of understanding of the Buddha's teachings.

Shakyamuni and his followers spent the night at a garden called Nigrodha, or the Banyan Grove, on the outskirts of Kapilavatthu. On the following day, the wedding ceremony of Nanda, Shakyamuni's younger half brother, was to take place.

After Shakyamuni left the palace for the life of religion, the royal family took great pleasure in the upbringing of Shakyamuni's own son, Rahula, and of Nanda. When Nanda turned twenty, he acceded to the position of crown prince and would, it was believed, someday succeed to the throne of the aging Suddhodana. Simultaneous with the ceremony to mark his becoming crown prince, he was to marry Sundari, the most beautiful girl in the kingdom. As the wedding was about to take place, Shakyamuni went to beg food at the new home of these two young people. Nanda himself filled the beggar's bowl with food. But when he went to the house entrance to return it, the Buddha was nowhere to be seen. Nanda thereupon prepared to go in search of him. When she heard Nanda's footsteps, Sundari realized that he was going to find Shakyamuni and said, "Please come home before my makeup dries."

But, having followed Shakyamuni to the Nigrodha Garden, Nanda peremptorily had his head shaved and abandoned the ordinary world for the life of religion. Because he joined the Order in this sudden, careless way, however, he did not have the true heart of faith. All he could think of was Sundari, whom he had left behind. He could not turn his thoughts to religious training. Although he waited for a chance to run away and join his beloved, no opportunity presented itself. He could take no part in the joys or the disciplines of the other members of the Order. Sundari was always on his mind, and he is even said to have made a picture of her for consolation.

All of this finally reached the ears of Shakyamuni, who used his mystical powers to transport himself and Nanda to the Himalayas. In a part of the mountains where there had been a fire sat a wounded, burned female monkey. Shakyamuni asked Nanda, "Who is more beautiful, this monkey or Sundari?"

"There can be no comparison between Sundari's beauty and this wretched female monkey."

Then Shakyamuni took him still higher in the Himalayas to the abode of the Thirty-three Devas. There he saw five hundred nymphs of unworldly loveliness playing and amusing themselves. They were all unmarried, and no men were in the place.

Shakyamuni asked, "Who is more beautiful, Sundari or these nymphs?"

"Just as there can be no comparison between the female monkey and Sundari, so there can be none between Sundari and these nymphs."

"Then shall I see to it that these nymphs become yours?"

"If you would do that, I would devote myself entirely to religious training."

Thereafter Nanda forgot Sundari and, thinking only of the nymphs who would someday be his, gave himself over to religious discipline. The other members of the Order were at first moved by the change in Nanda's attitude. But when they learned that it had come about as a consequence of his desire to be reborn in heaven and possess the beautiful women, they regarded him as a hireling. They felt that devotion to religious training because of a wish to possess women was identical to working for money or to engaging in disciplines for the sake of profit. And that is not the way to conduct true Buddhist discipline.

Nanda found it hard to put up with the contempt he saw in the eyes of the people around him. But, after reflecting that the fault was his and that the shame was only his due, for the first time he experienced the true spirit of religion and began to dedicate himself to serious discipline along with the other members of the Order. In this way, he attained the enlightenment of an *arhat* and, it is said, requested the Buddha to dissolve the agreement they had made about the nymphs.

Reasons for Turning to Religion and Growth Thereafter

The story of Nanda's conversion has special interest because it reveals motivations for turning to religion and alterations that can occur in those motivations with the passing of time. At this point I should like to make a few comments about the emergence and growth of the true spirit of religious faith.

Nanda had no reason to be dissatisfied with his life. Raised in the love of both parents and the wealth and blessings of a good house, he was unconcerned about other things. He had the enviable appearance of a young noble. He was youthful and in good health. In addition, he was to marry the most beautiful woman in the nation and was the heir apparent to the throne of his father the king. In other words, he had nothing to complain about and therefore felt no desire for the spirit of religious faith.

Under ordinary conditions, human beings turn to religion when they suffer from illness, poverty, unhappy love affairs, domestic problems, or trouble at work. When they are free of dissatisfactions and suffering and in good mental and physical condition, they do not seek help from religion. Lack of interest in religion is probably an indication that most people are more or less content with their way of life. Even those with reason to worry cover up by means of such things as sports, amusements, drink, or women. Indeed, much of the dissatisfaction and suffering of the world is solved and eliminated by nonreligious means. Furthermore, with advances in learning and technology, people fall ill less frequently, and even when they do become ill, treatment and chances of recovery are much better than they once were. This lengthens the ordinary human life expectancy. Furthermore, social advances and the institution of social-security systems have reduced general poverty by raising the ordinary standard of living and making daily life more comfortable.

Still, in spite of advances in scientific technology and increasing convenience in daily life, illness persists, and not all illness can be successfully cured. No matter how great the aggregation of scientific learning available, people continue to become ill. Just as in the past, they continue to suffer and die from sicknesses that are either difficult or impossible to cure.

In terms of economics, too, not all problems have been solved. Crises and excess competition still work hardships and cause many small and medium enterprises to fail. Continuing inflation creates instability in spite of higher living standards. Anxiety brought about by instability is probably one of the causes of the brutality and atrocious crimes that are alarmingly common today.

How can such anxiety be relieved? Obviously the passing pleasures to which many people resort are ineffectual. When he was a prince, Shakyamuni led a life of comfort and freedom from hardship. Nonetheless, he was so assailed by anxiety that he left his home and family in the hope of finding an answer to his problem. Though at the time of his conversion Nanda seemed to be at the pinnacle of happiness, Shakyamuni saw that he was walking on thin ice and in imminent danger. He therefore forced Nanda to leave the secular world so that he could understand the great truths that all things are impermanent and that nothing has an ego.

Understanding these truths is a way for people who do not suffer from poverty, illness, or other distress to see the nature of the world as it really is and thereby to discover the need for religious faith. Although illness and poverty can be eliminated by nonreligious means, religion is the only way to deal with the shifting instability that, unseen, lies at the heart of the true nature of the world.

People today are cruel; they unconcernedly commit heinous crimes. The number of young people involved in evil acts is growing. But have we evolved pertinent programs to counter these trends? Probably many wicked acts are perpetrated by people ignorant of the law of cause and effect and of the true nature of the world governed by it.

To teach the law of cause and effect to Nanda, Shakyamuni employed the female monkey and the nymphs to point out the need to intimately link present action and future consequence. Many of the people—especially the young people—who do evil do not regard their actions as evil and may even lack clear understanding of the distinction between good and bad. It is true that, while aware of it, some people ignore the wrong they do. They refuse to recognize the validity of cause and effect because they do not realize that their wickedness must inevitably bring retribution. In short, ignorance of the principle of cause and effect sometimes incites people to evil actions.

Before dealing with the Four Noble Truths, Buddhism teaches the everyday common-sense law that a good cause produces a good effect, a bad cause a bad effect; and both kinds of causes, suitable rewards and retributions. Even small acts of good and small acts of evil unrelated to other acts of good and evil do not disappear without a trace. Instead, each is stored up to form the intellect, personality, customary behavior, and physical makeup of the individual committing them. They become part of the personality, which they daily alter in the direction of good or bad. Acts of good and evil are intimately related to the individual's happiness and fate. All human beings must understand that everything in this world is related according to the inflexible law of cause and effect.

Wide popular understanding of the truth of this law would probably drastically reduce the number of crimes and misdemeanors committed in society, though it cannot be denied that the willful ignoring of the law by leaders and people in high places encourages criminality among the general masses.

The law of cause and effect pertains to the operations of all phenomena in the universe—not just to good and evil. It is taught in relation to what is called the Law of Causation, but there is a difference between the two. The law of cause and effect deals with the individual in terms of a temporal chain extending from past into present and then into the future. The Law of Causation, however, deals not merely with the individual but also with spatial and temporal relations among individuals and everything in their environment: family, local society, school, regional society, national society, international society, the natural environment, politics, economy, culture, spiritual fields, natural phenomena, and so on. An accurate interpretation of the world and of human life, this law is extremely extensive. It is the basis on which Buddhism teaches the impossibility of true happiness for an individual without development in the direction of happiness for all the other people in that individual's environment.

Nanda undertook religious training for the sake of being born in heaven, where he would possess the beautiful women, because, relying on the law of cause and effect, he did not understand the wider Law of Causation. The people around him despised him because he sought only his own egoistic ends and ignored concord and the total development and perfection of others. After serious reflection, however, Nanda came to understand the Law of Causation.

Such understanding prompts awareness of the need to strive for the perfection of one's own personality and of all society. If society as a whole improves and develops, the happiness of the individual will be guaranteed. If society is happy, the individual and all of his fellows will be happy. This is the meaning of true happiness and of the realization of the ideal Buddhist realm. Buddhist training is for the sake of realizing such a realm. When Nanda came to see this, he began training on the basis of the Law of Causation. This enabled him to attain the enlightenment of an *arhat*.

In summary, then, as long as human beings are relatively content with their way of life, they feel no need for religious faith. They turn to deities and Buddhas for aid in time of illness, poverty, trouble, or other suffering. Faith of this kind is egoistic in that it is directed toward the elimination of the actual suffering of the involved individual. But as the person advances in faith and has the opportunity to observe coolly his own fate and the nature of the society around him, he grows from an understanding of the law of cause and effect alone to an understanding of the wider Law of Causation. This, in turn, gradually brings about alterations in his ideals and values. A true comprehension of basic Buddhist doctrines—the Law of Causation and the Seal of the Three Laws: that all things are impermanent, that nothing has an ego, and that nirvana is quiescence— changes a self-oriented faith into a faith taking into consideration other people and all sentient beings. Faith then leads from solving issues of common, ordinary suffering to a higher faith. This is the meaning of growth in religious faith.

The Conversion of Upali   Gradually the proud Shakyas came to understand the greatness of Shakyamuni and the value of Buddhism. Although not during his first visit but some years later, ultimately, in houses with two sons, invariably one son abandoned secular life to follow the excellent teachings of Shakyamuni. Anuruddha, Bhaddiya, Devadatta, and Ananda, all outstanding in one way or another among Shakyamuni's disciples, joined the Order under such circumstances.

At the time when these noble young Shakyas entered the Order a man of the lowest social caste, named Upali, also joined. Upali had been a slave and barber to the Shakya clan before he entered the Order. He cut the hair of the aristocratic Ananda, Anuruddha, Devadatta, Bhaddiya, and Kimbila when they became monks. They gave him the fine raiment and ornaments that they were wearing, but he too decided to join the Order and asked the Buddha for permission. Shakyamuni took this opportunity to correct the pride of the group of young Shakyas by admitting the slave Upali and administering ordination to him first. Since the date of admission bestowed seniority on members of the Order, Shakya-muni intended to cultivate humility in the young aristocrats by giving place of precedence over them to a person who had once been their slave. From this time onward, Upali developed great interest in the ordinances and precepts of the Order and became more knowledgeable in them than any of the other members.

Shakyamuni actually had two purposes in ordaining Upali first. He wanted to correct the pride of the Shakya nobles, and he wanted to show that within the Order worldly considerations of position, class, and occupation were of no significance. All members were the same, according to the basic Buddhist tenet that all human personalities must be recognized on an equal footing. In Buddhism, it is not a person's birth, lineage, or occupation that determines his value but his spiritual attitudes and his actions.

The Brahmanical religion was taught only to the top classes of society. In contrast, Buddhism is directed to people of all classes and even teaches compassion and salvation for nonhuman animals and all sentient creatures. Indeed, instead of emphasizing the upper classes, who are freer of suffering, Buddhism directs more attention to the greater needs of people in the lower social orders. For this reason, its teachings are generally couched in the ordinary language of the common people for greater understanding. Disciples teaching in various regions were strictly ordered to avoid Sanskrit, a language understood only by the educated upper classes. Characteristics like these illustrate the mass-orientation of Buddhism and the importance it places on the personality of the individual.

Furthermore, the rational nature of such of its basic tenets as the Seal of the Three Laws, the Law of Causation, and the Four Noble Truths makes Buddhism a correct, just, and suitable religion for all ages, regions, and races. Rationality, morality, and religious nature are all expressed in the word "Law," which itself represents Buddhism in its ideal form.

9. Clergy and Laity

Abandoning Secular Life as a Custom I have already shown how, within two or three years after the enlightenment of Shakyamuni, Buddhism had developed considerably, especially in and around the city of Magadha. Soon it spread northward along the Ganges, and when Shakyamuni visited his native country, a large number of the Shakyas were converted. In spite of the objections of his parents, Shakyamuni's half brother Nanda left his family to join the Order, as did Shakyamuni's own son Rahula. Later, one by one, other members of the five hundred families of the Shakya clan followed suit. Many outstanding young men from Magadha and its environs found the teachings of the Buddha attractive, believed them, and left home to join the Order without parental permission. This caused families to suffer so much that they raised a bitter cry of criticism to the effect that the *samana* Gotama was robbing mothers and fathers of their children and wives of their husbands and was in this way causing family lines of inheritance to be broken. At this point, Shakyamuni established the ruling that a person must have parental permission to join the Order.

If everyone abandoned the secular life and became a monk, the productivity of society would cease, and daily economic life would become impossible. Furthermore, since members of the Order were required to remain celibate, no offspring would be born, and the human race would ultimately be threatened with extinction. Perhaps out of concern over issues of this kind, Shakyamuni never advocated the life of the Order for all people. In fact, since the person who has devoted himself to the religious life exclusively is nonproductive, a producing laity is essential for the economic support of the clergy. In other words, the clergy presumes the laity, and life for the clergy without the laity is inconceivable.

India is a hot land where clothing and shelter pose less serious problems than they do in colder climates. Moreover, though occasional droughts still cause famines, in Shakyamuni's time, grains and fruits were easily raised. In other words, the essential needs of life could be readily satisfied. For this reason, as long as two or three centuries before the time of Shakyamuni, the custom of leaving home and the secular life for a life of philosophical and religious discipline was already established. It began first with the orthodox Brahmans and then spread to the unorthodox *samanas*. The existence of this custom was the basis on which Shakyamuni himself left his father's home. I should now like to turn to a discussion of the significance and value of this custom, but before doing so I must give some attention to its origin.

Perhaps the custom arose during the period of the Upanishads (about 700 B.C.) or in the period of the religious texts known as the Forest Treatises (Aranyaka), but it is certain that it is closely related to the four stages into which ancient Indian thought divided first the lives of all members of the Brahman caste and later of members of the ruling Kshatriya and mercantile Vaishya castes as well.

The first of the four stages of life was that of the student (*brahmacharin*). From the age of seven or eight, a young boy left his parents' home and went to the home of a Brahman instructor, with whom he lived and studied the Vedas and subsidiary subjects. Since the full course of learning was supposed to require twelve years, the boy would remain with his teacher until about the age of twenty. Throughout this time, he helped with household chores, begged his own food, and lived a strictly celibate life. This period might be called a time of character development. Some terms and practices related to it have found their way into Buddhist practice. For instance, the word *brahma-chariya*, which means both the studentship period and the life of purity and celibacy enforced during it, is used in primitive Buddhist terminology to mean training and discipline in the pure life and the way of the Buddha. Another influence from the Brahman studentship system is the custom of begging for food.

If extended to its fullest length, the studentship period could last for forty-eight years—that is, twelve years to master each of the four Vedas (Rig-veda, Sama-veda, Yajur-veda, and Atharva-veda). It would then take until beyond the age of fifty, or nearly all of a man's normal life. People who went the full way in this course of study correspond to Buddhist monks who live a life of total purity.

The second of the four stages was that of the householder (*grihastha*). At the age of about twenty, having completed a twelve-year studentship stage, the ordinary young man returned to his family home, married, and began wedded life. While busying himself with his own occupation, the householder was expected to protect his health, have children to ensure the continuance of the family line, correctly and enthusiastically revere the gods and his forebears, serve his parents and teacher, give alms and show compassion to mendicant students and people of religion, and observe the laws and moral codes of society. The triple doctrine of almsgiving to the poor and holy people, abiding by the moral precepts, and the assurance that good acts will be rewarded by rebirth in a blessed state taught to Buddhist lay believers may be thought to correspond to the duties imposed on the Brahman householder. In other words, the householder resembles the Buddhist lay believer, although the Buddhist lay believer who has acquired the correct Buddhist views of the world and human life and has attained a degree of enlightenment is on a much higher spiritual level than the ordinary Brahman householder.

The third of the four stages is that of the hermit (*vanaprastha*). When the householder had completed his domestic duties, when his heirs had passed through the studentship stage and were fully grown, and when he himself had reached the age of fifty or so and had gray hair, he would resign his family responsibilities and retire to live a secluded life, most often a life of disciplines conducted in forests.

Ancient Indian philosophy propounded four ideals for mankind: love of pleasure (*kama*), material gain (*artha*), morality and religion (*dharma*), and devotion to spiritual pursuits (*moksha*). The young man is devoted to *kama*, the man in the prime of life to *artha*, and the old man to *moksha*. Righteous duty, or *dharma*, is considered necessary in all the stages of life. When a man who had completed his duties as householder was about to enter the third, or hermit, stage of life, he was considered to have already given up love of pleasure and desire for material gain and to be ready to emphasize religious understanding.

Leaving his home and going into the forests, he would lead a perfectly natural life, eating the grains and fruits he found there, making clothes for himself from bark and skins, and allowing his hair and nails to grow. Nonetheless, he was expected to continue venerating the gods and his forebears, studying the Vedas, and engaging in meditative speculation and other disciplines. Indeed, the basic significance of this stage of life was the giving of oneself to religious practice and to ceremonies, philosophical speculation, and religious experience. Since silence was considered most conducive to effectiveness in their way of life, men in the hermit stage were known as *muni* (silent sages). The same word *muni* in its Buddhist application—specifically in the name Shakyamuni—derives from the Brahman usage.

The fourth and final stage is that of the homeless wanderer, or *samnyasin*, who would completely renounce all worldly ties in the pursuit of spiritual liberation. When study and discipline in the forest were over and all the problems of human life solved, the man no longer needed to learn. Walking with the aid of a staff, he left the forest and returned to the world of human life to beg and live a life of constant wandering from place to place. Three names were applied to such men: homeless wanderer (*samnyasin*), one who begs (*bhikkhu*), and one who undergoes austerities (*samana*). The words *bhikkhu* and *samana* later came to be associated with the unorthodox religious sects and ultimately were used exclusively by them.

The last two stages are those of a person who has truly abandoned secular life. It seems that few Brahmans ever completed the full four stages. It was uncommon for an old Brahman to leave home and begin a life of lone religious discipline. The custom of abandoning secular life was much more widespread among the Buddhists and members of the other unorthodox sects.

This discussion shows that leaving home for the religious life was not an uncommon occurrence in ancient India. Two things that make this understandable are the relative ease with which food and clothing could be obtained in the Indian climate and the readiness of the general public to give food and clothing to men of religion. It was therefore not odd that many people left home upon hearing the teachings of Shakyamuni.

Characteristics and Value of the Order   The person who was surrounded by family and domestic life had much to worry him. Pressed by work and the need to support his household, such a person was thought incapable of devoting himself wholly to philosophical study, religious practice, and spiritual cultivation. The householder condition was thought to preclude the possibility of total devotion, for which a man was supposed to isolate himself from all worldly things and depart from his family. On the basis of this belief, Shakyamuni himself and the followers converted after his enlightenment left their homes.

In short, the Buddhists, like the Brahmans and the other *samana* sects, left ordinary secular life for the sake of enlightenment and special experiences of wisdom resulting from total devotion to practical religious action and discipline impossible for people living as ordinary householders.

Primitive Buddhist beliefs insist that whether or not a person abandons secular life determines the degree to which he can become enlightened. There are four such degrees or stages—known as the four merits: entrance into the stream of sanctification (*sotapanna*), the state in which the person will be born once again into this world (*sakadagamin*), the state in which no return to this world is necessary (*anagamin*), and the state of perfect enlightenment (*ar-*

hat). According to primitive Buddhism, the first three stages of enlightenment are possible for a person leading the ordinary life of a householder. The highest enlightenment, that of the *arhat,* on the other hand, was felt to require separation from home and family. It was believed that a person who, in previous existences, had amassed sufficient good karma and merit and who was endowed with outstanding gifts could attain *arhat* enlightenment even as a householder but that such a person would not remain a householder, for he would at once either abandon family and home or enter nirvana (that is, die). Briefly, though the difference is one of degree, leaving home was considered conducive to total devotion to discipline and enlightenment. This is the first characteristic of the Order.

Other religions of the time shared the Buddhist belief that leaving home was important to religious cultivation and enlightenment. Few of them, however, shared the Buddhist advocation of the second significance of the act: education and guidance in faith for the ordinary masses of the people. Brahmans received instructions in the Vedas and subsidiary branches of learning but did not impart what they learned to society at large. In the other unorthodox *samana* religions, people became the disciples of leaders from whom they learned, but it seems that none of them attempted to preach to others. Only Jainism, a religion that resembles Buddhism in several points, attempts to teach people. Indeed, it acquired considerable support from its lay following. It is said that some members of the Jainist laity attained great proficiency in their religion's doctrines and creeds. Nonetheless, the missionary activities of Jainism were, and remain today, characteristically quieter and smaller in scale than those of Buddhism.

Buddhism was the first of the Indian religions to take deliberate steps for the sake of teaching and converting the ordinary masses. As I have already explained, after his enlightenment, while still meditating under the bo tree, Shakyamuni came to the decision that he must impart his unprecedented doctrine to all people in order to transform human society into a realm of peace and happiness. After attaining the correct Buddhist views of the world and human life, he felt that it was impossible for him to keep this

wonderful teaching to himself. He wanted to share it and to rejoice together with everyone, and this desire remained with him
throughout his more than forty years of enthusiastic missionary
activity. One illustration of his fervor in this connection is his immediate dispatching, on missionary work, of the five ascetics whom
he converted at Benares, and of Yasa and his more than fifty friends.
As an outcome of these efforts, Buddhism gradually grew and, within a few years, had tens of thousands of lay believers and thousands
of monks, organized into the Sangha, or the Order, which was
characterized by discipline for the sake of enlightenment and by
fervent teaching. Such teaching is the second characteristic of the
Order.

As I explained earlier, the third characteristic of the Order is the
preservation of the teachings of the Buddha. The goal of the monks
in this connection is symbolized by the motto "May the righteous
Law of the Buddha last forever!" In order that it may not perish,
the Law must be correctly transmitted for hundreds and thousands
of years. This means, of course, that the written works propounding
the Law must be handed down to succeeding generations. It further
means, however, that correct understanding of those works, discipline for realization of the ideas set forth in them, and knowledge
of the true nature of enlightenment be handed down in unmistaken
form. Only the Order is capable of preserving and propagating the
correct Law. To clarify this point, I shall make a further, detailed
explanation of the nature of the Order.

The Sangha, In the meaning of a group, the word *sangha* was used
or the Order in India before the time of Buddhism to designate
such things as unions of craftsmen and merchants. As
I have said earlier, when Buddhism first flourished, a number of
states in the middle reaches of the Ganges were actively engaged
in craft industries, as well as in agriculture. Furthermore, commerce
involving collection and dispersal of both agricultural and craft-
industry products was lively. In the vital urban centers along the
land and water transportation routes, the business establishments
of wealthy merchants and financial magnates lined the streets. The

professional unions formed by the merchants and craftsmen were known as either *sangha* or *gana* (group or union).

As the unorthodox *samana* religions grew and attained large followings, their groups too came to be known by the secular terms *sangha* or *gana*. In accordance with this practice, Buddhism referred to its group of monks as the Sangha (to be precise, *sangha* meant a group of more than four or five and *gana* a group of two or three).

Primitive Buddhist writings make it clear that the word *sangha* formerly pertained to what might be called the clerical body—that is, to the Order of men and women who had given up secular life. These early works often make mention of the Sangha of *bhikkhus* (monks) and the Sangha of *bhikkhunis* (nuns). The rock and pillar inscriptions of Emperor Asoka speak simply of the Sangha, in the sense of the Buddhist Order of monks and nuns.

The two merchants who gave Shakyamuni food after his enlightenment are considered the first lay Buddhist believers and are referred to as the *upasakas* (male lay believers) who first entrusted themselves to the Two Treasures. This means the treasures of the Buddha and the Law. At the time, the Order, the third of the Three Treasures, did not exist. The full Three Treasures became complete only when Shakyamuni had converted the five ascetics at Benares and they had become monks in the newly established Sangha. The first *upasaka* to vow to take refuge in the Buddha, the Law, and the Order was Yasa's father.

This discussion does not necessarily imply that the word *sangha* can be used only for the Buddhist clergy. Indeed, often in Japan, the Order is interpreted as the entire body of Buddhist believers, including clergy and laity. In ancient usage, however, it was employed mainly for monks and nuns and much less often for *upasakas* and *upasikas* (female lay believers).

In general, the Order of monks and nuns includes everyone— ordinary members of the clergy and advanced sages—who lives according to certain rules, among which are provisions that monks must own no more than three garments and a beggar's bowl. This tradition is alive today in such Southern Buddhist nations as Sri Lanka, Burma, and Thailand. But, if the Order is a body of people strictly abiding by the three characteristic functions—religious dis-

cipline for enlightenment, teaching of other people, and preservation of the Law—it can include only sages. Furthermore, as one of
the Three Treasures, the Order is bound to fulfill these functions,
since all Buddhist believers take refuge in it. In primitive Buddhist
classics, the Order is defined in the following way:

"The Order follows the Way [of the Buddha] well, correctly, in
the direction of truth, and justly. It signifies followers of the World-
honored One. Since it is a body of sages who have passed the four
pairs of stages—of attaining and of having attained—of the four
merits on the way to perfect enlightenment and since it is a field of
good fortune, the ordinary people must provide food for, serve, give
alms to, and pay reverence to the Order."

This definition sets forth two functions of the Order: religious
discipline for enlightenment and guidance for the masses. It further
says that the Order is a body of sages who have attained maximum
enlightenment and, as such, is a field of good fortune worthy of
merit and service. Though nothing is said about whether the Order
consists of laymen or monks, the stipulation that it be made up of
sages who have attained the highest enlightenment indicates that
the latter is more probable. People who have passed through the
four pairs of the stages of the four merits can be assumed to have
devoted themselves entirely to religion.

The development of Mahayana, or Northern, Buddhism altered
relations between the clergy and the laity in the Order. Further
changes were certainly worked by the local manners and customs
of China and Japan, both of which received Mahayana Buddhism
from India. Though a formal distinction is actually made in Japan
between the clergy and the laity, Southern Buddhists, who still
attempt to preserve the organization and strict precepts of the time
of Shakyamuni, recognize nothing like either Order or monks in
Japanese Buddhism today. Nothing resembling the rules and way
of life of the ancient Sangha is in effect, and many Japanese priests
have wives and children and live very much like ordinary lay believers. The use of the Japanese term for the Order to indicate the
whole body of believers, lay and clergy alike, results from this set
of circumstances. But does this necessarily mean that there is no
Buddhist Order in Japan?

One may give up the world physically and become a nun or a monk, or one may remain in the world while devoting oneself to religious development. In Japan, where the characteristic Mahayana flexibility finds wide application, actual physical separation from the world—which is still practiced by Theravada Buddhists—is much rarer than spiritual devotion to the religious life while remaining part of ordinary society. This attitude has long been preferred in Japan and is symbolized by the life of the ancient wealthy Indian lay householder named Vimalakirti, who remained a layman yet attained great heights of enlightenment. Vimalakirti became popular among Japanese Buddhists at an early time.

Why has Buddhism survived in one way or another in Japan, where it might be said that, in the strictest sense, there is neither clergy nor laity, when it has either died out completely or severely withered in places like India and China? It is because, no matter what may have happened in terms of formalities, in practical, substantial terms, the Japanese have preserved—even if incompletely—the three functions characteristic of the Order. Failure to fulfill even one of these functions can spell the downfall of Buddhism. All three are essential to its flourishing. And if all three are carried out, in spite of alterations in superficial form, the Order will develop and grow.

10. From Magadha to Anga

Shakyamuni's Reputation Three or four years after the enlightenment of Shakyamuni, Buddhism had spread as far as the land of the Shakyas. In ancient times, when means of communication and transportation were primitive, transmission of information was incomparably slower than it is today and relied largely on word of mouth and rumor. Ancient Buddhist writings containing the following description of Shakyamuni may be accepted as typical of the rumors that were spread about him during his lifetime.

"The following is the reputation of this Gotama: Worshipful, All Wise, Perfectly Enlightened in Conduct, Well Departed, Understander of the World, Peerless Leader, Controller, Teacher of Gods and Men, the Buddha, and the World-honored One. He has himself been enlightened and teaches his knowledge to all sentient beings, including gods, demons, and ordinary mortals, as well as *samanas* and Brahmans. He teaches the well-ordered, formally expressed Law that is excellent in the beginning, excellent in the middle, and excellent in the end. He makes clear the perfect, indispensable, pure discipline of the Buddhist way. Thus, it is very good to associate with such a noble man."

109

This paragraph deals with what are called the ten epithets of the Buddha, which I shall now briefly explain.

1. Worshipful. This pertains to the *arhat*—that is, not only to Shakyamuni but also to all of his disciples who have attained the highest enlightenment. Because such people are free of all delusions, by their very existence they make the world brighter and bring peace and hope to man. Consequently, they deserve reverence and such oblations as offerings of food, clothing, and shelter. In the time of Shakyamuni, it was believed that the person who made such offerings to *arhats* would receive many times—or many tens of times—as much merit as an outcome of his act.

2. All Wise. This pertains to a Buddha, who perceives correctly all things in the universe. The epithet makes a distinction between the total, universal understanding (enlightenment) of a Buddha and lesser degrees of enlightenment attainable by hearing the teachings of others or through self-instruction.

3. Perfectly Enlightened in Conduct. This means one who has perfect understanding of the world of humanity and engages in practical disciplines for the sake of the attainment of the ideal. In other words, it pertains to the correct theory and the correct practice of Buddhism. Even with perfect wisdom and understanding, the ideal cannot be realized without practical action. On the other hand, practical action cannot lead to the correct goal without wisdom. Action unguided by wisdom can lead into the paths of wickedness. The combination of wisdom and action leads to the perfection of the Law, and it is because it embodies this combination of elements that Buddhism is significant from the rational and ethical as well as from the religious standpoints.

4. Well Departed. In his compendious Commentary on the Perfect Wisdom Sutra (Mahaprajnaparamita-upadesha), the brilliant Mahayana scholar Nagarjuna (second or third century), who is credited with the founding of eight schools of Buddhist thought, explains this epithet as consisting of two elements. First, such a person has traveled on the great vehicle of the Buddha's wisdom and has traversed the Eightfold Noble Path to enter nirvana. Second, such a person teaches the law that there is no eternal self and that attachments to conditional phenomena must not be permitted. Fur-

thermore, a person deserving this epithet adjusts his teachings according to the abilities of his audience and guides people to conversion along the way that is most suitable for them and their condition.

5. Understander of the World. In this instance, as in the Buddhist classics, the word "world" refers not to physical space but to the sentient beings inhabiting it. Moreover, it is the minds of these beings, not their fleshly forms, that are at issue. Understanding the world means knowing the human beings that make up society and the mental attitudes they assume. In terms of this epithet, the Buddha has perfect understanding of the minds of human beings and knows what they should be like. It is knowledge of this kind that can bring ideal peace and happiness to human society.

6. Peerless Leader. Once again, according to the Mahaprajnaparamita-upadesha of Nagarjuna, the Buddha, having experienced unsurpassable nirvana, is himself unsurpassable and is in a position to guide all sentient beings. In short, nirvana is paramount among the many laws. The Buddha is paramount among all sentient beings. And, having attained the state of ultimate superiority, he is able to guide other sentient beings to it.

7. Controller. Controlling people means that, through his great mercy, compassion, and wisdom, the Buddha is able to guide and train people by conforming his methods to the capabilities of the individual and the exigencies of the situation. Sometimes he speaks gently, sometimes he scolds sharply, and sometimes he teaches in a casual fashion. The ancient Indian text and wording in the Mahaprajnaparamita-upadesha might indicate that the only people who can be the objects of the Buddha's control are men capable of conversion to Buddhism. But this is not precisely true. The buddha-nature exists in all sentient beings. For this reason, the Buddha controls, trains, and guides all sentient beings, male or female, although individual variations in speed of progress occur.

8. Teacher of Gods and Men. Shakyamuni was the teacher of all sentient beings who must migrate among the six states of existence: those of beings in hell, hungry spirits, animals, *ashuras* (demons), men, and gods. But, since the majority of his teaching was concentrated on human beings and divinities, he is here called

the teacher of gods and men. The term used for teacher in this instance is applied only to the Buddha. Different words are used for ordinary Buddhist preceptors or instructors.

9. The Buddha. It goes without saying that this term means one who has been enlightened, who works for the enlightenment of others, and whose practices are enlightened.

10. The World-honored One. The Pali original, *bhagavat,* means one who has merited all good omens. He is called the World-honored One because the world reveres a person with merits as great as his.

The ten epithets represent the merits of the Buddha, but he is sometimes described as manifesting other merits that take the form of characteristic body and facial features making his appearance incomparable. These excellences are classified as the thirty-two distinguishing marks and the eighty distinctive body marks.

In later times it became customary to combine epithets nine and ten and to add to the list the epithet Tathagata, the one who has come from the world of truth or the one who teaches the Law in absolute truth and whose actions are absolutely true. The word *tathagata,* as used in other religions before Buddhism, means one who truly brings release from the cycle of transmigration. Obviously the same meaning attaches to the word in its Buddhist usage.

The Conversion of Pukkusati Rumors describing Shakyamuni in terms like these ten epithets spread far and wide and, arousing a great deal of curiosity, naturally stimulated many people to want to meet him. A large number of members of powerful Brahman families in the Magadha region came to believe the teachings of Buddhism and to join the Order. When they actually met and talked with him, they learned that Shakyamuni was even superior to his reputation.

Not long after Shakyamuni's enlightenment, a rich householder of Magadha named Pukkusati heard of the great religious leader and, without even so much as meeting him, resolved to follow him, left the secular world, and began a life of religious discipline.

One evening, Shakyamuni, who was traveling alone in Magadha, came to the home of a potter and asked the master of the house for permission to spend the night on the earth floor of the pottery workshop. The potter, who probably did not know he was talking with Shakyamuni, replied that though he had no objections, there was already someone staying in the workshop for the night. If that person did not mind, Shakyamuni was welcome to stay there too.

The other guest turned out to be Pukkusati. Shakyamuni went to him and said, "If you don't mind, I too should like to pass the night in this workshop."

Pukkusati replied, "My friend, the workshop is spacious. There is plenty of room. Please make yourself at home."

Shakyamuni entered, spread dried grass on the floor, sat in the meditation posture, and, with correct thoughts and correct knowledge, remained meditating in this way until late at night. Pukkusati also remained in meditation until late at night. Wondering whether this monk was truly serious about his religious disciplines, Shakyamuni asked, "For whose teachings did you give up the secular life? Who is your teacher? Whose teachings have you accepted?"

"My friend, having heard the wonderful reputation of the *samana* Gotama, I took him, the World-honored One, as my teacher. In keeping with his teachings, I became a monk."

"Then have you ever met this World-honored One? If you met him, do you think you would recognize him?"

"I have never met him, and I suspect that if I did, I would not recognize the World-honored One."

Pukkusati's admission aroused in Shakyamuni a feeling of compassion, and he said, "Then I shall teach you the Law. Listen well."

"My friend, I will."

Then for Pukkusati's sake Shakyamuni preached a sophisticated sermon, probably because he perceived that this man was of intellectual capacity sufficient for him to understand difficult Buddhist theories. The sermon was a detailed, logical presentation showing that human beings have six senses—sight, hearing, smell, taste, touch, and thought—for perceiving six objects: earth, water, fire, wind, air, and knowledge. From this operation of perception are born the sixteen kinds of emotions and sensations, including pain and pleasure and joy and sorrow. Knowledge of the nature and sources of these emotions leads to understanding of the truth that there is no permanent self and that there should be no attachments to conditioned phenomena. This in turn leads to paramount wisdom and the realization that nirvana is the ultimate Noble Truth. The person realizing this can attain the highest realm of tranquillity by abandoning all things that cause delusions and by breaking with the three poisons of covetousness, anger, and delusion.

Hearing this, Pukkusati sensed that he must be listening to Shakyamuni himself and exclaimed, "Indeed I have met the World-honored One! Indeed I have met the World-honored One!" He then arose and, arranging his robe on one shoulder in sign of respect for a superior and worshipfully bowing his head to Shakyamuni's feet, said, "Not recognizing the World-honored One, I have made the great mistake of referring to him as 'friend.' Please forgive me." (The word equivalent to "friend" was used only in addressing equals and inferiors.)

Shakyamuni replied, "In our teaching, a mistake is forgiven if it is sincerely repented. You repent from your heart and are therefore forgiven."

Pukkusati requested that Shakyamuni admit him to the Order, and the request was granted. He at once set out to procure the required robes and begging bowl, which till then he had lacked, but on his way he was gored to death by a wild bull. It is said that upon hearing Shakyamuni's sermon, Pukkusati had attained the third of the four merits—that is, *anagamin*, or nonreturn into this world of desire.

The Conversion of Sona   Under the rule of King Bimbisara, who was the same age as Shakyamuni, the kingdom of Magadha grew stronger and larger. Bimbisara attacked and subjugated Anga, an independent nation to the east, and also added to Magadha's territories on the south and west until it was second in extent only to Kosala on the north.

On a certain occasion, Bimbisara called a council of the township overseers of his kingdom. The council was to be held in the capital, Rajagaha. The king sent a messenger to a wealthy family in Champa, the capital of Anga, asking that they send their son Sona to the city at the time of the meeting. It seems that hair grew on the soles of this young man's feet, and the people in the capital were eager to behold this curiosity. The son of a rich household who had never walked on the ground, Sona was carried to Rajagaha in a palanquin.

At the council of overseers, King Bimbisara discussed secular matters, including politics, economy, and law. For spiritual and religious instruction he called on the aid of Shakyamuni. A messenger from the king went to Vulture Peak outside Rajagaha, where Shakyamuni was staying at the time. When the group of overseers followed, Sagata, Shakyamuni's attendant, performed wonders that amazed them. Finally Shakyamuni appeared before them and took the seat prepared for him there. But the town overseers entertained greater reverence for Sagata than they did for Shakyamuni himself.

At this point, the Buddha ordered Sagata to perform still further wonders by means of his mystical powers. After Sagata had performed more astounding miracles than any he had accomplished before, he fell with his head at the feet of Shakyamuni and said twice, "The World-honored One is my teacher. I am the disciple of the World-honored One." Realizing at last that they were in the presence of a greater person than Sagata, the town overseers came to have profound respect for Shakyamuni and great faith in him.

Then Shakyamuni, perceiving their reaction, taught them in his customary stage-by-stage manner, beginning with almsgiving, abiding by the moral precepts, and the assurance that good acts are rewarded by rebirth in a blessed state. He went on to teach the doctrine of cause and effect, to show the error of adhering to desire, and to emphasize the merit of renouncing it. Finally, when he saw that they were purified in heart, he taught them the basic Buddhist doctrine of the Four Noble Truths. The result of this teaching was that the overseers were enlightened to the correct Buddhist views of the world and of human life, were freed of all delusions, and attained the spotless Eye of the Law. They became lay believers in Buddhism for the rest of their lives and took refuge in the Buddha, the Law, and the Order.

Sona, the rich man's son, was among the group listening to this sermon. At its conclusion, he was so deeply moved that he decided to devote himself to Buddhism entirely. He went up to Shakyamuni and asked for permission to join the Order. The permission granted, Sona began his religious discipline.

He went to stay in a place in a wild mountain forest where corpses were abandoned. Day and night he concentrated on his training. Though he had once lived so luxurious a life that he never walked upon the ground, he now underwent disciplines more rigorous than those of any of the other members of the Order. During the periods of walking with which he relieved long periods of seated meditation, his tender feet were wounded by the rough ground till the places where he trod were bathed in blood. Excessively zealous, he thought to himself, "I am a disciple of the World-honored One, a member of a group devoted to religious discipline. Yet no matter how I try, I cannot free myself of delusions and attain ultimate enlightenment. Perhaps it would be better for me to give up this training and return to secular life. There is much wealth in my house. While enjoying the good things of life, I could give alms and thereby earn merit."

When he perceived that Sona's mind was thus distracted, Shakyamuni left Vulture Peak and went at once to the place of corpses. He saw that the ground where Sona had been walking was covered with blood. Going directly to the house where Sona was, the World-honored One sat in the seat provided for him. Sona bowed before him and sat at his side. Shakyamuni then said, "Sona, just now were you not thinking these thoughts?" And Shakyamuni enumerated the distractions that had been running through Sona's mind. Sona admitted that all this was true.

Shakyamuni then asked Sona if he had played the lute when he lived at home. Sona said he had played it, and Shakyamuni asked, "If the strings are stretched too taut, will the lute produce a pleasing sound?"

"No."

"If the strings of the lute are too slack, will the instrument produce a pleasing sound?"

"No."

"But if the strings are neither too taut nor too slack, but just right, the lute will produce a pleasant sound?"

"Yes, it will."

"Well, Sona, in Buddhist discipline, if one is too eager, the mind will be shallow and unsettled. If one is too lax, the mind will become lazy. The proper way is to be neither too eager nor too lax but to make spiritual efforts and progress at a suitable pace."

When he had heard this highly appropriate metaphor of the lute, Sona acquired the ability to go on with disciplines at a suitable pace and thus to abandon illusions and hindrances and finally to attain the ultimate enlightenment of the *arhat*.

No matter how eager and assiduous a person is in religious training, achieving enlightenment depends on primary and secondary causes from previous existences. For people with the right causes, the opportunity for enlightenment will come readily; for people without them, the opportunity will probably not develop. Although it is true that the buddha-nature is inherent in all sentient beings, the speed with which enlightenment is reached depends on the causes from previous existences and the causes in the present life.

Among the disciples of Shakyamuni there was considerable variation in the speed with which enlightenment was reached. Yasa attained the first stage of enlightenment—the Eye of the Law—upon hearing Shakyamuni's customary series of sermons on the triple doctrine and the Four Noble Truths and immediately attained ultimate enlightenment and became an *arhat* when he heard the sermon Shakyamuni preached for his father. He must have had excellent roots of goodness and merit from his previous existences. The same must have been true of the five ascetics, who attained the Eye of the Law on hearing the first sermon on the Four Noble Truths and became *arhats* after a few days of religious discipline.

I have already shown how the wisest of Shakyamuni's disciples, Shariputra, attained the Eye of the Law upon hearing Assaji's single stanza about causation as the origin of all things and how he attained the enlightenment of an *arhat* two weeks later when he heard the sermon Shakyamuni preached for his skeptic uncle with the long fingernails. The other of the two great disciples, Maudgalyayana, reached *arhat* enlightenment in only one week after he attained the Eye of the Law.

Pukkusati reached the third of the four merits, *anagamin,* from hearing only one sermon by Shakyamuni. And Sona, after attaining the Eye of the Law from hearing one sermon, probably reached the *arhat* stage, the last of the four merits, a few days later. The Buddha's caution about moderation and suitability in training played an important part in Sona's final enlightenment. Still, no matter how correct the discipline, reaching the *arhat* stage is not readily possible for people without the right primary and secondary causes from previous existences.

The chief of the Buddha's followers, Ananda, attained the Eye of the Law at the first sermon he heard. Though for the next twenty-five years of active missionary life he heard Shakyamuni preach daily and was familiar with all major and minor points of his teachings, Ananda did not attain ultimate *arhat* enlightenment until three months after Shakyamuni's death. In the collection of moral teachings known as the Dhammapada it is said, "Though a fool attend on a wise man all his life, he will no more comprehend the Law than a spoon understands the taste of the soup. An intelligent man who spends only a short time with a wise man will at once comprehend the Law, as the tongue understands the taste of the soup."

In spite of the importance of causes from previous existences, however, the suitability—or lack of it—of the person's guide and the method of training and eagerness of the person himself affect the speed with which enlightenment is attained.

Unless the ear is ready to comprehend and the eye is ready to understand, no amount of listening or reading will convey the correct meaning. For a fault of some kind, at the time of his death Shakyamuni left instructions that a monk named Channa should be punished. This punishment, imposed after Shakyamuni's death, caused Channa to repent deeply. He began to train himself most enthusiastically, but he could not bring himself to assent to the formalized sermon on the five aggregates composing the minds and bodies of all sentient beings in the world of desire (that is, the ordinary world in which we live), on the impermanence of all things, and on the lack of a permanent self. He asked senior members of the Order to teach him. He questioned many people. But he could not find an answer he thought convincing. Finally, Ananda delivered to Channa a sermon that, long ago, Shakyamuni had delivered for another Order member named Kacchayana. This sermon explained how one must observe the causes of suffering and their extinction so as to avoid falling into the mistaken belief that the causes are an actual reality and that their elimination is nihility. According to the sermon, this is the way to understand the non-existence of a permanent self and the error of becoming attached to conditioned phenomena. Upon hearing this, Channa clearly perceived the meaning of the teaching of the five aggregates that constitute the individual and of the impermanence of the self, both of which doctrines had completely eluded him before.

II. Buddhism and Jainism

Early Buddhism　As noted earlier, several centuries before the time
and Jainism　of Shakyamuni, the central region of India along
　　　　　　　the upper reaches of the Ganges was the hub of
a culture controlled largely by orthodox Brahmans. Later the area
around the middle reaches of the Ganges was developed, and such
newly prospering classes as the warrior royal family and the merchants came to wield actual political and economic power. Some
members of these classes, finding the teachings of the Brahmans
insufficient, attempted to seek the truth and find solutions to the
problems of human life on their own. These unorthodox, or heretical, thinkers were called—as I have already said—*samanas*. Possibly because of their influence, many orthodox Brahmans reex-
amined their religious position and tried to find their own ways to
the truth.

India in the time of Shakyamuni was a land of great diversity.
Political and economic factions first flourished and then failed. New
and old religions were interwoven. But among all of this variety
and among the several groups of unorthodox religious thought, six
teachers—in Buddhist terms they are known as the six non-Buddhist
teachers—were especially famous and active. The only one of the
religions propounded by these six men that preserved its vitality

into later ages was Jainism, of which Nigantha-Nataputta—also called Mahavira (Great Hero)—was the leader. The word *nigantha* means freedom from bondage and indicates that the purpose of Nataputta's teaching was liberation from the suffering of the cycle of transmigration and from the bonds of evil action and delusion. Though the fundamental teaching of this school is thought to have existed two or three hundred years before Buddhism, Nataputta revised it and organized it into what is called Jainism.

The name Nataputta means that the man was a descendant of the Nata clan. (Shakyamuni could similarly be called Shakyaputta.) The Natas were aristocrats of the Vajji nation, a neighbor of Magadha on the north across the Ganges, and were associated with the Licchavis, the royal clan of Vajji. A princess of the Licchavis was a consort of Bimbisara and the mother of the future king Ajatasattu. Nataputta, the founder of Jainism, was this royal lady's cousin.

Though apparently somewhat younger, Nataputta led an early life very much like that of Shakyamuni in several respects. Married and the father of one child, he left his home in search of the answers to the problems of human life and joined the Nigantha religious order. After undergoing twelve years of ascetic practices, he became a *jina* (victor, or one who overcomes), revised the teachings of the old Nigantha order, and established Jainism as an independent religion.

Physical torture is the central aspect of Jainist discipline, though the religion possesses a highly organized body of doctrines. The leaders are serious, grave persons, and the lay believers must live and work according to strict precepts. Though it is formalized, its followers remain enthusiastic and serious, and Jainism is still alive today. In the area around Bombay, in western India, there are about one and a half million Jainists, who, largely traders and wealthy merchants, command considerable economic power.

Jainism is less philosophically abundant than Buddhism. Its quiet, unassuming founder was not as outstanding a man as Shakyamuni, and what he taught was not as excellent as Buddhism. Nonetheless, the similarities between the two religions led Westerners who first studied Jainism to regard it as a Buddhist sect.

In the lifetime of Shakyamuni, both Buddhism and Jainism spread in the area along the middle reaches of the Ganges, but the followers of the two religions lived peacefully together and did not indulge in quarrelsome competition. It is thought that Shakyamuni and Nataputta never met. There are a number of passages in Buddhist writings where we find indications that Buddhists and Jainists engaged in colloquies and that Jainists were converted to Buddhism.

Jainist scriptures claim that the royal family of Magadha, relatives of Nataputta, were Jainists, but Buddhist scriptures assert that the king, his children, and his consort were Buddhists. In all likelihood, both accounts are correct, since it was customary in India for the political leader of the land to respect and protect all religions. For instance, the famous emperor Asoka, who ruled a unified India in the third century B.C., while a devout Buddhist, extended protection to other religions as well. Probably this is an example of the magnanimity expected of monarchs in ancient India.

When Buddhism spread from Magadha to the land of the Shakyas, Shakyamuni undoubtedly made many trips back and forth between the two countries. These trips would have taken him through the land of the Vajjis, which lay between Magadha and the Shakya territory. In addition, it is likely that Shakyamuni made some trips to the land of the Vajjis specifically for the purpose of teaching and converting. Jainism, which centered in the land of the Vajjis, the homeland of the founder, spread southward to Magadha and northward to the land of the Shakyas. Obviously, the two religions encountered one another frequently.

Jainism and Buddhism in Magadha Nalanda, which is located near the Ganges, was the Jainist headquarters in Magadha. Later the great Buddhist monastery of Nalanda was to be built there and was to serve as the center of Mahayana Buddhist scholarship for centuries. Since remains of it have been excavated, it is now possible to see just how immense the monastery was in its heyday. But until the late years of the life of Shakyamuni, Nalanda was Jainist territory.

Two of the most outstanding Jainists in Magadha were the rich merchant Upali (not to be confused with the Upali who earlier became a Buddhist disciple) and the prince Abhaya. Since he was not converted to Buddhism until the final years of Shakyamuni's life, Prince Abhaya must have been an enthusiastic Jainist for a long time.

Buddhism made incursions into Jainist territory, and Nataputta was eager to do what he could to regain ground. But he lacked the self-confidence to undertake a direct discussion with Shakyamuni. He therefore encouraged Prince Abhaya, who was noted among the Jainists for his wisdom, to debate with Shakyamuni. Nataputta told the prince that his name would resound throughout the land if he managed to win Shakyamuni to Jainism. He then explained in detail how the debate should be held.

Abhaya invited Shakyamuni to his house. At the conclusion of their meal together, he began to question in the fashion in which he had been instructed. But the answers Shakyamuni made were not the ones Abhaya had been told to anticipate. The prince soon found himself unable to go on with the debate. He frankly confessed the plan in which he had been involved and apologized to Shakyamuni. The purpose of the prince's questions had been to find out whether an enlightened Tathagata would say displeasing words to other people. A further aim of this attempt was to show that Shakyamuni had acted in a way unbecoming to an enlightened Tathagata by scolding his cousin and rebellious disciple Devadatta.

Shakyamuni then turned to Prince Abhaya, who was holding a child on his lap, and said, "Prince, what would you do if that child swallowed a piece of wood?"

"I would thrust my finger in the child's mouth, bend it, and extract the wood, even if, in doing so, I should injure his throat and cause him to bleed and cry."

"In exactly the same way, when the Tathagata speaks unpleasing words to a person, it is for the sake of mercy. But the Tathagata must conform his remarks to the nature of the occasion."

Shakyamuni then explained the following six instances of the way in which advice should be given.

1. When the words are untrue and will do nothing for the good of the other party and are moreover displeasing to him, the Tathagata must under no circumstances utter them.

2. If the words are absolutely true but will do nothing for the sake of the other person and are furthermore displeasing to him, the Tathagata must under no circumstances utter them.

3. When the words are true and will do something for the sake of the other party, though they are displeasing to him, the Tathagata will know the time to utter them.

4. When the words are untrue and will do nothing for the good of the other party but are nevertheless pleasing to him, the Tathagata must under no circumstances utter them.

5. If the words are absolutely true but will do nothing for the sake of the other person and are at the same time pleasing to him, the Tathagata must under no circumstances utter them.

6. When the words are true and will do something for the sake of the other party and moreover are pleasing to him, the Tathagata will know the time to utter them.

In all six cases, the Tathagata displays an attitude of compassion.

Amazed at the precision and exactness of Shakyamuni's answers and the fluidity and pertinence with which he spoke, Prince Abhaya asked, "World-honored One, when someone puts a question to you, do you need to make advance preparations by saying, 'If I am asked this, I must answer in this way'?"

Shakyamuni replied, "I will answer with a question. Are you thoroughly familiar with the parts of a chariot?"

"I know everything about the chariot."

"Then, if someone asks you something about a chariot, do you need to prepare an answer ahead of time?"

"No, if it is about a chariot, I can answer any question on the spot without advance preparation."

"In the same way, I know all there is to know about humanity and society and can answer on the spot any question put to me on those subjects."

Deeply moved, the prince became an ardent Buddhist.

Upali, as we have noted, was a rich merchant in Nalanda and a great patron of Jainism. Once Shakyamuni visited Nalanda and was staying in a nearby mango grove. At that time, a Jainist ascetic called Dighatapassin (whose name means one who has undergone long austerities) visited him to discuss karma. Their views did not agree: Buddhist thought places emphasis on the mental motivations for good and bad actions; Jainism emphasizes physical results, the actual words and physical actions. To clarify this doctrinal difference, the Jainist ascetic returned to Nataputta and his group, to whom he explained what had taken place during his discussion with Shakyamuni. Nataputta commended the ascetic's attitude. Among those who heard the report was Upali. Assuming that Shakyamuni must be a person of no more abilities than were reflected in the words of Dighatapassin, he asked Nataputta for permission to put Shakyamuni in his place. Nataputta replied that although either he himself or Dighatapassin could easily engage in dispute with Shakyamuni, it might be a good idea for Upali to do it. Dighatapassin disagreed. He said that Shakyamuni had wondrous powers to lead people astray and that he could employ those powers in winning to his own group members of other religions.

Nataputta answered, "O ascetic, it is inconceivable that Upali should become the disciple of Gotama. On the contrary, Gotama will probably become a disciple of Upali." He then told Upali to go and debate the subject of karma with Shakyamuni.

Dighatapassin tried three times to convince the two that Upali should not undertake this task. Upali, however, refused to lend an ear to his advice and visited the World-honored One in the mango grove. After ascertaining the content of the discussion that had taken place earlier, he praised the attitude of Dighatapassin.

Shakyamuni said he was willing to engage in debate if Upali was truly serious. Upali said that he was. Shakyamuni then proceeded to prove by means of many actual examples that good or bad mental motivation is more important than actual actions and words. Moreover, he proved this from the Jainist standpoint, calling upon examples taken from Jainist teachings.

In one instance, Shakyamuni countered Upali's insistence that the physical act takes precedence in importance over the mental motivation in the following way. He asked what would happen to a Jainist who, out of respect for the minute living creatures in cool water, refused to drink it, even when suffering from a high fever, and consequently died. Upali said that attachment to the mind at the time of death would result in the man's being born again in a heaven for those who remain attached to mind. In other words, mental attachment and not the actual act of drinking or not drinking cool water produced the effect.

Jainism strictly forbids the taking of life, even that of the small creatures living in water. But, should a person unwittingly step in a puddle of water on the road and kill some of these creatures, according to Jainism his sin is not grave, since he was unaware of what he was doing. In adopting this standpoint, Jainism tacitly puts greater emphasis on mental motivation than on physical result and thus contradicts itself.

Upali found it impossible to reply to these demonstrations of Jainist inconsistencies and at once became a believer in Buddhism.

Jainism in the Lands of the Shakyas and the Vajjis Since, under the name Nigantha, Jainism was older than Buddhism, from relatively early times it spread, not only in the land of the Vajjis, but also in Magadha and the land of the Shakyas. Famous among Jainists in the Shakya clan was a man named Vappa. He and Upali of Magadha and Shiha of the Vajjis were considered the three outstanding lay patrons of the religion.

Once when Shakyamuni and his followers were visiting the land of the Shakyas and were staying in the Nigrodha Garden outside Kapilavatthu, Vappa called on Maudgalyayana and discussed karma with him in the lecture hall. In the evening of the same day, arising after meditation, Shakyamuni went to the lecture hall, where he heard part of the discussion taking place there. He said, "O Vappa, agree with the part of my doctrine that you find compatible. You need not agree with the part of which you cannot approve. If there is something in my teachings that you cannot understand, ask about it. If you do this, a correct discussion is possible."

The two of them then engaged in discussion. Shakyamuni earnestly explained the rational way to eliminate delusion and the fires of suffering. Deeply moved by what he heard, Vappa said, "World-honored One, a person who engages in the horse trade to become rich and fails to make a profit overworks and suffers greatly. Similarly, in search of merit, I became a Jainist, and when I failed to attain merit, I overworked and suffered. Now that I have heard the teaching of the World-honored One, for the first time I have attained merit. I will blow away my Jainist faith, as with a great wind, and will cast it into the rapid stream. I entrust myself to the Buddha, the Law, and the Order. Please accept me as a lifelong believer in the Buddhist faith."

At another time, when Shakyamuni was teaching in a town named Devadaha, the issue of karma was being discussed. In those times, in India, there were five explanations for the causes of present happiness and unhappiness:

1. Everything, happiness and unhappiness, is determined by karma from previous existences.

2. All fate is determined by the will of an all-powerful deity who created and controls the world.

3. Human fate is determined by the good or bad ways in which the elements—earth, water, fire, and wind—constituting the fleshly body are combined.

4. The fate of the entire life of an individual is determined by the social class and family into which he was born.

5. Human fate does not depend on any of these definite causes but is determined, from minute to minute, by completely accidental occurrences.

From the Buddhist standpoint, all of these explanations either are deterministic and fatalistic or rely purely on chance and therefore deny the significance and value of education and training and fail to take into account the importance of free will in efforts to determine and develop fate. For the sake of a correct interpretation of cosmic workings, Buddhism proposed doing away with these explanations and offered in their place the Law of Causation and the Four Noble Truths as accurate explanations of the world and of human life.

It is thought that Shakyamuni often visited Vesali, the capital of the nation of the Vajjis, in the third and fourth years after his enlightenment. In those days, a general named Shiha, a member of the royal clan and conceivably a relative of Nataputta, was a highly influential Jainist in the capital. By this time, it had become customary for Shakyamuni and his followers to cease traveling and begging during the three months of the rainy season and to take up a fixed abode where they meditated and studied Buddhism while living on offerings from the laity.

There is record of these rainy-season retreats (called *varshika*) for the forty-five years during which Shakyamuni pursued his career after his enlightenment. It is said that the first was held in Benares; the second, third, and fourth near Rajagaha; and the fifth in Vesali. This indicates that, by the fifth year, there was a large enough number of believers in Vesali to support Shakyamuni and his considerable following throughout the rainy season.

In later years, on the occasion of his final visit to the capital, Shakyamuni is said to have mentioned repeatedly the pleasantness of the many shrines he had stayed and taught in around Vesali. When he finally left the city, he is supposed to have looked back tenderly in leave-taking. Be that as it may, at first Jainists were more numerous in Vesali, but gradually the number of Buddhists grew. And the conversion of the influential general Shiha made a breach in the last Jainist wall of defense.

Once when Shakyamuni was staying in the Great Forest Monastery on the outskirts of Vesali, members of the royal clan governing the land gathered together in the town hall to discuss national affairs. During the talk, the subject of religion came up, and much was said about the wonderful nature of Buddhism. General Shiha, who heard all of this, thought to himself, "Since these distinguished Vajji aristocrats praise Gotama in this way, Buddhism must have something wonderful to offer. I think I will go to meet Gotama and investigate this myself." He then went to Nataputta and explained his wish. But Nataputta dissuaded him.

A second time, the general heard praise of Buddhism in the meeting hall and decided to visit Shakyamuni, only to be dissuaded by Nataputta again. But, on the third occasion, he took five hundred carts and went to the Great Forest Monastery, where Shakyamuni was staying. During the ensuing discussion, karma was a subject. From Shakyamuni, General Shiha heard many detailed teachings that were totally new to him. He was greatly moved and entrusted himself to the Buddhist faith.

But Shakyamuni reproved him by saying, "A person of your importance and position must not change his religious faith lightly." The general replied, "I am not being rash. I have made this decision after mature consideration. And the fact that the World-honored One gives me such advice only strengthens my resolve. If some other religion had converted a person of my authority and fame, its believers would have rejoiced wildly and would have announced it throughout the streets of Vesali with great waving of flags. But instead of this you urge me to consider my step carefully. This makes me more determined than ever to entrust myself to the Buddha, the Law, and the Order."

Then Shakyamuni said, "Believer, for a long time you have been a fount of all kinds of offerings, fulfilling all of the wishes of the followers of Nigantha. Even after you become a Buddhist, you must continue to make offerings to them cordially."

"Your admirable words, World-honored One, impress me still more deeply. Heretofore I have been told that Gotama says, 'Give alms only to me. Do not make offerings to others. Offerings to me and to my followers bring great rewards; offerings to others bring none.' Actually, the reverse is true. I shall do as you say and give offerings to the Jainists. Once again, for the third time, I entrust myself to the Buddha, the Law, and the Order and vow to be a Buddhist believer while my life lasts."

12. Reacting to Outside Criticism and Praise

Though no date is known for certain, apparently a few years after his enlightenment Shakyamuni and five hundred of his followers were on their way from Rajagaha to Nalanda when they encountered a wandering teacher and his pupil who were following the same road. The teacher's name was Suppiya; and the student's, Brahmadatta. Noticing that Shakyamuni shared their way and knowing of the increasing fame of Buddhism, the teacher and his companion were disagreeing in their estimations of this religion. Suppiya had nothing good to say about either Shakyamuni's teachings or the Order. In contrast, Brahmadatta highly praised the Three Treasures: the Buddha, the Law, and the Order.

Before long, the words of criticism and praise uttered by these men found their way to the ears of Shakyamuni's disciples. In the evening, Shakyamuni and his group, together with the teacher and his follower, settled down for the night in a mango grove belonging to the king. The grove was located about midway between Rajagaha and Nalanda. On the following morning, when his disciples, who had gathered early to discuss the evaluations of Buddhism made by Suppiya and Brahmadatta, Shakyamuni joined the group and, after hearing what they had to say, admonished them on the way they should react to outside criticism or praise of the Three Treasures.

"O brothers, you must not be disappointed or angry or harbor ill will against others who slander the Buddha, the Law, and the Order, for if you do, you will lose the calm that enables you to judge rationally whether what the person has to say is true or false.

"In instances of slander, you must remain cool so that you can distinguish between truth and error and be able to say, 'For this reason, what he says is different from the truth. In this point he fails to reach the truth. We are not as he says we are.'

"Similarly, you must not be quick to rejoice and be glad when an outsider praises the Three Treasures, for if you become carried away with being lauded, you will lose the calm that enables you to judge rationally whether the praise is true or erroneous. In cases of praise, too, you must remain cool so that you can judge facts as facts and can say, 'For this reason, what he says is a fact. In this point he has reached the truth. We do have the characteristics he attributes to us.'

"In many instances, praise of an outsider is directed toward trivial, superficial aspects and not to the basic doctrines of Buddhism. Therefore, since they do not praise the things that are truly praiseworthy, you must not rejoice or be elated by what people speaking in this way have to say."

Shakyamuni taught his disciples the nature of superficial, erroneous praise and explained in detail the correct Buddhist standpoint on such matters. Similar teachings are to be found in many places in the Buddhist sacred writings. For instance, in the Dhammapada (chapter 1, verse 3), " 'He abused me, he beat me, he defeated me, he robbed me'—in those who harbor such thoughts hatred will never cease."

In other words, as long as one forgets one's own faults and attacks only the other person, the situation will definitely not take a turn for the better. It can only worsen. But when such cases arise, calm examination of reasons why he "abused, beat, defeated, and robbed" reveals one's own faults and makes it clear that the unhappiness being experienced is no more than should have been expected under the circumstances. Reflection on one's own failings and attempts to rectify them prevent repetition of the same mistakes and make it unnecessary either to hate others or to be discouraged.

And in the Suttanipata (stanza 267) we find: "To remain unshaken by contact with the things of the secular world, to be free of anxiety, to be undefiled, and to be tranquil. This is the highest blessing."

The following eight matters are the things of the world referred to in this stanza: gain and loss, fame and disgrace, praise and slander, and pleasure and pain. We are made happy when we gain and grow wealthy; we suffer and are disappointed when we lose property and become poor. We are elated at good reputation but distressed or filled with hatred for others when we are spoken ill of or are ignored by the world. Praise lifts us to the heights of joy; slander or criticism makes us resentful or hateful. We rejoice at health and the free life, but we become despondent when we are ill or fall on hard times. These ways of being moved by the eight things of the world are common to all mankind. The person who lacks true independence is always tossed here and there by these matters and ends his life in a weak, unstable condition. Hatred, fights, bloodshed, despondency, desperation, and suicide are some of the outcomes of being swayed by the eight things of the world. Buddhism teaches that we must not be moved or suffer when we come in contact with these things but must live in tranquillity. This does not mean that we must attempt to avoid such contact. It does not mean that we must retire to remote mountainous regions to be free of the things of the world. The teaching of Buddhism is that, remaining part of society and facing the eight things of the world and all they imply directly, we must nonetheless be unmoved by them.

To do this we must maintain in our hearts something transcending these things. Doing this raises us to a position of high independence from which we must observe all things coolly, judge them accurately, and deal with them correctly. The transcendent something that enables us to live in this way is the correct Buddhist view of the world and of human life and the Buddhist understanding of the truth about all phenomena. Unbreakable faith in the Three Treasures, too, is essential. These views and this faith give human beings the ideal, rational critical attitude called right mindfulness and right knowledge. Because of this attitude, the believer is enabled to keep in mind always the basic Buddhist tenets that all things are impermanent, that nothing has an ego, and that nirvana is quiescence. This in turn makes it habitual to remain undisturbed and calm in all considerations and actions.

Everything apart from these firm, reliable truths is inconstant and untrustworthy. Distrust, doubt, emotional problems, and discord arise even between man and wife or parent and child. Doubt and distrust are even more remarkable in less intimate connections. As long as peoples' interests coincide, they can generally work together in harmony: one will usually attempt to ingratiate himself with the other. But when interests conflict, suddenly one turns on the other with hatred, antagonism, and malice. Such things happen when people are completely controlled by the things of the world and strive to satisfy only their own egoistic, narrow aims. People who understand the truth about the nature of all things neither think nor act in this egoistic way, since they see everything from a high, all-encompassing standpoint enabling them to fuse their own interests with those of everyone else. In a society composed of such people there would be no fighting, no discord, no distrust, and no suspicion because everyone would know the joy of union with his fellow human beings.

Though we must remain calm and stable in bad times as well as good, when things are going well, human beings not infrequently tend to be complacent or proud. Buddhism teaches that there are many different kinds of pride: in family background, in health, in youth and power, in good reputation, in influence, in wealth, in personal beauty, in knowledge, in strength, in technical or artistic skills, and so on. Pride in one's sense of compassion and in merciful works indicates immature faith and lack of understanding of the true nature of compassion. Although it is wrong to be proud of powers and abilities, it is still worse to be proud of powers and abilities that one does not even possess. Nonetheless, many people make this mistake.

Pride causes a person to lose modesty and the sense of sympathy with others. Buddhism has long recommended the life of poverty and suffering not for its own sake but to serve as a precaution against pride in happiness and good fortune, to stimulate a constant feeling of modesty and humility, and to awaken a feeling of compassion and protection for unfortunate people through actual knowledge of what it means to be unfortunate.

People who have known only happiness and are suddenly confronted with grave difficulties sometimes are so at a loss to know what to do that they aggravate their condition. The meaning of strife must be remembered even in times of peace. In other words, one must not give in to hard times. One must be trained in faith and in physical strength to remain stable no matter what conditions are encountered. Each new unpleasant experience resolutely faced will further strengthen faith and make it all the more unshakable.

The truth of this statement applies not only to individual human beings but to groups and nations as well. Stimulation is important. Like stagnant water, a person who lives in constant security becomes complacent and, figuratively, goes stale. Flowing water stays bright and clear because of the many obstacles it encounters. In a similar way, a human being who is frequently stimulated to find ways to solve new difficulties grows gradually stronger.

13. Buddhism in Kosala

The Founding of the Jetavana Monastery At a time when Buddhism had gained much ground and had become generally known in Magadha, Sudatta, a rich man from the kingdom of Kosala, visited the Magadha capital of Rajagaha. Though no certain evidence is available,* it seems likely that the first meeting between Shakyamuni and Sudatta occurred five or six years after the Buddha's enlightenment. A merchant with far-reaching interests throughout India, Sudatta was the wealthiest man in Savatthi, the capital of Kosala. He seems to have been a deeply compassionate person from birth, since he gave food and shelter to the orphans, the lonely old people, and the needy of Savatthi. Indeed, his good works were so great that the people called him by the name Anathapindika, which means one who gives to the needy.

*It is not unusual for ancient Buddhist texts to omit exact datings. Nor is this surprising. The people of the past were uninterested in learning historical facts: they wanted to know what sermon had been delivered on a certain occasion and to have that sermon presented to them accurately so that they could pass it on accurately to others. In thousands of ancient writings, no word is said about dating. And only in some special cases is it possible to surmise dates from remarks relating the sermon to either the Buddha's enlightenment or his entrance into nirvana.

Sudatta's visit to Rajagaha was on business, and he was staying at the home of his wealthy brother-in-law. (Sudatta's wife was from a rich Rajagaha family.) As it turned out, the brother-in-law had invited Shakyamuni and his disciples to a meal on the following day and was spending the night busily encouraging a large number of servants who were making the necessary preparations. Observing this, Sudatta turned to his brother-in-law and said, "You have put all of the servants and the whole household to work preparing a meal. Are you giving or taking in marriage? Are you going to hold a great sacrifice? Or are the king and his ministers and soldiers coming?"

The brother-in-law replied that none of these things were true but that he was to offer a meal to a Buddha and his disciples on the following day.

"Did you say a Buddha?" asked Sudatta.

When the brother-in-law answered in the affirmative, Sudatta said, "One rarely has a chance so much as to hear the name Buddha in this world. I am very surprised to learn that such a person actually exists. I should like to meet him right now."

"Now is not the time for you to visit the World-honored One," replied the brother-in-law. "You can visit him tomorrow morning."

But Sudatta was beside himself with eagerness to meet Shakyamuni. When he went to bed, he was unable to sleep. He got up several times during the night and wished that the dawn would come quickly. Unable to stand the waiting any longer, though it was still night he got up again and this time went out. Suprahuman beings opened the city gates for him. He walked toward a gloomy, deserted grove outside the city, a place where corpses were abandoned. It was dark, and the dark was so frightening that his hair stood on end. He thought of going back. But one of the suprahuman beings encouraged him: "Go on without fear. It will be to your gain." And Sudatta went on until he finally reached the deserted grove. By now, day had broken.

Shakyamuni, who had arisen at dawn and was engaging in meditation, greeted Sudatta by saying, "Welcome, Sudatta."

Sudatta was both astonished and happy to hear Shakyamuni call him by name. This aroused such warm feelings in him that at once he bowed, fell at Shakyamuni's feet, and said, "O World-honored One, I trust that you are well and at peace."

Shakyamuni replied, "The person who is unstained by desire, is refreshed and free, and has entered the ideal state of nirvana is always at peace. He is free of all attachments, he has removed all suffering from his heart, he is tranquil in his mind, and he is always at peace."

Then Shakyamuni preached a sermon for Sudatta. As was his custom, he moved gradually from the triple doctrine of almsgiving to the poor and to holy people, abiding by the moral precepts, and the assurance that good acts are rewarded by rebirth in a blessed state to the Four Noble Truths of suffering, its cause, the elimination of the cause, and the way to that elimination. As a result of this sermon, Sudatta attained the Eye of the Law and came to embrace the Buddhist interpretation of the world and human life. He then took refuge in the Buddha, the Law, and the Order and vowed to be a Buddhist believer for the rest of his life. Intending to call on his brother-in-law for help, he asked that Shakyamuni and his disciples come to him for a meal on the following day.

When his brother-in-law heard of this, he said, "You yourself are a guest. I shall provide a second meal tomorrow. You do not need to worry about it." Sudatta insisted, however, on doing it himself. It is said that King Bimbisara too offered to assume the responsibility of the meal but that Sudatta would not agree.

Sudatta was happy to serve Shakyamuni himself and, when the meal had ended, requested that the Buddha and his followers come to Savatthi, his city, and remain there throughout the rainy season. Shakyamuni promised to do so and then preached again for Sudatta, who was made very happy.

Sudatta knew many people in various regions. On his way home to Savatthi, he told all of his acquaintances that a Buddha, whom they must respect and serve, had appeared in the world. He then revealed how deeply moved he had been by his meetings with Shakyamuni.

Savatthi was not far from Shakyamuni's home city, Kapilava-tthu, but although he had returned to his own country two or three years after his enlightenment, he had not yet been in the kingdom of Kosala. Sudatta wanted him to come to teach his excellent religion to the people of this kingdom. Realizing that a monastery where Shakyamuni and his followers could spend the rainy season was necessary, as soon as he returned to the city, he began to look for a suitable piece of ground that would not be too far away from the city but would be sufficiently remote that city noise would not disturb the meditations of the monks. He found a place south of the capital that he thought was just right. It was a grove belonging to Prince Jeta, with whom Sudatta discussed the possibilities of a purchase. Unwilling to part with the land, the prince said in jest, "If you want it all that badly, cover the ground with gold. That is my price." Jeta never dreamed that Sudatta would go so far to acquire the land. But he did. So deep was his faith in the Buddha that he was willing to part with his entire wealth. To his way of thinking, wealth could always be acquired a second time, but there would be no second opportunity to hear a Buddha's teachings if this first opportunity were allowed to slip by. He therefore had gold brought from home and began to cover the grove with it.

Prince Jeta was startled. By the time he had come to himself, most of the ground of the grove was already covered with gold. He asked Sudatta why he was so determined and learned that a truly rare Buddha had appeared in this world. He then proposed that they use all of this gold to erect part of the buildings for a splendid monastery. Sudatta could then add to them as was necessary. Together the two of them would build what, in honor of the prince, came to be called the Jetavana Monastery. Though it is possible that the entire compound was not completed all at once, even during the lifetime of Shakyamuni, Jetavana became the largest of all the Buddhist monasteries in India.

Still another great monastery in Savatthi—this one in the eastern part of the city—was the Mansion of Migara's Mother—named for the rich and faithful Visakha who was known as Migara's mother and who donated the land for the monastery. Other famous Buddhist monasteries in India at this time included the Bamboo Grove Monastery in Rajagaha; the Great Forest Monastery in Vesali; and the Goshita Park Monastery in Kosambi, the capital of Vansa, in the west. Although it may be true that the Jetavana Monastery was built and that Shakyamuni and his followers visited Savatthi at a fairly early stage after his enlightenment, it was not until fourteen or fifteen years after the enlightenment that Buddhism began to spread in Kosala. Shakyamuni and his followers did not spend the rainy season at Jetavana until the fourteenth year after his enlightenment.

Early Buddhism in Kosala   It is thought that Sudatta, the wealthy merchant, spent an immense amount of money to build the huge Jetavana Monastery for Shakyamuni and his followers in the sixth or seventh year after the enlightenment. Shortly after the completion of the monastery, Shakyamuni and his disciples entered Kosala. But even with Shakyamuni's great powers, at the beginning the obstructing presence of many other orthodox and unorthodox religious sects left little room for the introduction of Buddhism. This was a very different story from the history of Buddhism in Magadha, where everything went smoothly from the outset. There, as we have seen, Shakyamuni first converted the highly influential Kashyapa brothers and their thousand followers and then, with this group, traveled to Rajagaha, where, after preaching to the people, he succeeded in converting King Bimbisara himself, many ministers, large numbers of people, and such leading Brahmans as Shariputra, Maudgalyayana, and Maha-Kashyapa. It was very fortunate for Buddhism in Magadha that the flourishing Jain sect offered no open interference.

King Bimbisara, a highly cultivated and intelligent man, was favorably disposed from his first encounters with Shakyamuni, who had then only recently left his father's home for a life of asceticism. Pasenadi, king of Kosala, was a man of much less outstanding intelligence and cultivation than Bimbisara of Magadha. The land of the Shakyas had formerly been a vassal state to Kosala. It was unlikely that the king of one of the mightiest nations in India at the time would show respect for a person who emerged from a former tributary country. And indeed, Pasenadi did not show such respect for Shakyamuni at first. Furthermore, he demonstrated no faith in Buddhism.

But the king seems to have shown no great faith in any other religion either. He probably confined himself to general formal religious tolerance of all sects and the customary tax-free land grants to Brahmans who were in charge of education and rites. As a result of this custom, landowning Brahmans were numerous and powerful. Pasenadi's consort, Queen Mallika, donated a grove in Savatthi for the use of the various religious sects that she protected.

It was under circumstances of this kind that Sudatta attempted to introduce Buddhism into Kosala. It is true that Prince Jeta, from whom Sudatta acquired the land for the Jetavana Monastery, was well disposed toward Buddhism, but he was probably only a lukewarm believer. And even if he had faith himself, his placid disposition prevented his actively promoting the religion.

Sudatta followed an entirely different course in his vigorous attempts to convert his own family and relatives and to bring the excellent teachings of Buddhism to all of the people of the nation. When Shakyamuni first visited the Jetavana Monastery, Sudatta assembled five hundred rich acquaintances and brought them to hear the Buddha's teachings. Though these men accepted Buddhism at the time, after Shakyamuni had left the city, they returned to their old faiths.

In the beginning, therefore, because of hindrances and obstacles posed by other religions, Shakyamuni and his followers seldom went to Kosala. They did not spend a rainy season there until seven or eight years later, or about the fourteenth year after the enlightenment. It was not until about twenty years after the enlightenment that Buddhism finally took root and began to win large numbers of converts in Kosala. In the late years of his life, however, Shakyamuni spent most of the rainy seasons in Savatthi, and in the latter half of his life Kosala actually became the major base of Buddhist activities.

In Kosala there lived most of the six non-Buddhist teachers. They were the leaders of sects described as heretical from the Buddhist standpoint, and among these sects the most powerful in Kosala at the time was the group of ascetics led by Makkhali-Gosala. The members of this sect, which taught improper ways of making a living, attempted to interfere with Buddhism and its founder on frequent occasions. They did not attempt to rival Buddhism in terms of debates and spiritual powers but instead cast aspersions on the reputation of Shakyamuni and claimed that he did not live according to the rules he preached. In one case they incited a young prostitute, Chincha, to try to seduce Shakyamuni. In another, they persuaded a certain woman named Sundari to spread the rumor that she had slept with Shakyamuni. Although these campaigns of slander sullied the name of Buddhism for a brief time, when it was learned that the rumors were groundless and that they had been only the results of the plotting of Makkhali-Gosala, this man's heretical sect lost both face and followers, while the good repute of Buddhism only increased. Shakyamuni had the following remarks to make about Makkhali-Gosala and his wickedness and heretical views:

"O brothers, of all woven things, those woven of human hair are the worst. They are chilly to the touch in cold weather, and since they absorb no sweat, they are wet in hot weather. They are unpleasant to the touch. Similarly, of all the teachings of the *samanas*, those of Makkhali are the worst. They do not include good and bad karma, the doctrine of the consequences of past deeds, or striving for spiritual improvement. Furthermore, O brothers, just as people put nets at the mouths of rivers to injure and harm many fish, so Makkhali-Gosala spreads his nets in the world to injure and harm many people."

King Pasenadi, who was the same age as Shakyamuni, later became a fervent believer in Buddhism. The following story about one of his trips to the Jetavana Monastery probably pertains to the time before his conversion.

After courteously greeting Shakyamuni in the monastery, King Pasenadi said, "Do you, reverend master Gotama, claim to be perfectly and supremely enlightened?"

"O king," replied Shakyamuni, "If anyone can claim perfect, supreme enlightenment, it is I. I indeed am perfectly and supremely enlightened."

Then the king said, "Reverend master, there are many Brahmans and *samanas*, such as the six non-Buddhist teachers, who are highly reputed as saviors among the people and who have large followings of disciples. None of them claims to be perfectly and supremely enlightened. Why do you, reverend master, who are younger than these men and who abandoned home and the secular world long after they did, claim supreme, perfect enlightenment?"

Shakyamuni answered, "O king, it is wrong to despise things because they are young. There are four things that must not be looked down upon because of their youth: a mighty prince, a serpent, fire, and a Buddhist monk."

Then, in lovely verses, Shakyamuni explained that a prince is not to be despised for his youth because, when he comes to the throne, he may take a despot's revenge. A snake, even a young one, can bite, and fire, though young, can destroy. Injury to a Buddhist monk can blight the heritage of the injurer.

It is said that upon hearing this explanation the king was so deeply moved that he took refuge in the Buddha, the Law, and the Order and became a Buddhist.

Legends Born **About This Time** A number of legends surround Kosala and the actions of Shakyamuni there. For instance, both Northern and Southern Buddhism preserve the legend that in the seventh year after his enlightenment he spent the rainy season in the Heaven of the Thirty-three Devas, where he preached for the sake of his mother, Maya, who had been reborn there. The probable explanation for this story is that during the three months of the rainy season of this year Shakyamuni conducted seated meditation in a place far removed from everyone who knew him. The writings of primitive Buddhism tell us that for some weeks after his enlightenment Shakyamuni sat and meditated. It is known that at various times during his life he meditated for periods ranging from two weeks to as much as three months. This does not mean that he did not eat during these times. People served him the requisite food, but they were the only persons with whom he had any contact. None of his disciples or other followers of the faith saw him throughout these periods of meditation. Long stretches of isolation from other human beings no doubt gave rise to the legend of his having gone to the Heaven of the Thirty-three Devas.

It is said that he returned to the world of men at a place called Sankassa, which is a region located well south of modern New Delhi. There is another legend—it is not preserved in the Pali texts—to the effect that when Shakyamuni returned, the nun Uppalavanna was the first to greet him. Shakyamuni realized, however, that the person greeting him was not actually Uppalavanna but the disciple Subhuti, who was reputed to understand the Buddhist doctrine of the Void (Sunyata) better than all the other disciples. At that time, however, Subhuti was at the foot of Vulture Peak near Rajagaha, where, engaged in sewing clothes, he made no attempt to go to greet the returning Shakyamuni. It seems entirely likely that this anecdote is a production of later centuries. The incident was supposed to have taken place in the seventh year after the enlightenment, but this was a time when no women had yet been allowed to enter the Order. Therefore the appearance of Uppalavanna is an anachronism. Furthermore, Subhuti, the son of the younger brother of the wealthy merchant and Buddhist patron Sudatta, is supposed to have been converted after hearing Shakyamuni's first sermon at the Jetavana Monastery, seven years after the enlightenment—that is, in the year of the alleged journey to the Heaven of the Thirty-three Devas. It is dubious that Subhuti could have mastered the doctrine of Sunyata by this time.

Another story still preserved—though not found in the Pali texts—pertains to King Udena of Vansa. This king is said to have become so lonely during the supposed sojourn in the heavens that he ordered a life-size statue of Shakyamuni carved of fragrant sandalwood and then worshiped the effigy. Though it is known that Udena became a Buddhist believer and that Buddhism was popular in Vansa, whether his conversion took place as early as the eighth year after the enlightenment is uncertain. In those days, there were four extremely powerful kingdoms in India: Kosala, Magadha, Vansa, and Avanti. Udena was the king of Vansa, and his capital city, the flourishing commercial center Kosambi, was located on the south bank of the Ganges west of Benares. Vansa became and remained for centuries an important Buddhist center. Shakyamuni stayed in Kosambi, where, as I have said, the Goshita Park Monastery was located, on several occasions and spent the rainy season there in the ninth year after the enlightenment. Buddhism was widespread in Vansa before it became popular in Kosala. King Udena was converted by hearing the teachings of Pindola-Bharadvaja, a great monk and the son of one of the local ministers of state.

But the story of the statue commissioned by King Udena does not deserve credence because it is known that no statues of Shakyamuni were made during his lifetime. In fact, there were no sculptural or pictorial representations of the Buddha in India until around the first or second century of the Christian Era. Artistic representations of other human beings and animals were employed, but even in depictions of scenes in which he should appear, Shakyamuni was always absent. Such symbols as the Buddha's footprint, the bo tree under which he attained enlightenment, the Wheel of the Law, and Buddhist reliquary towers were used in his place. All carvings and paintings of him were strictly avoided because it was considered blasphemous for imperfect human beings to represent his perfection in any form.*

*The use of images of the Buddha originated in northwestern India in the first and second centuries. This region received none of the relics that were divided up after Shakyamuni's death. To take the place of these vital objects of veneration, the people of the northwest had Buddha statues made and, as models in their production, used Greek statues of the Greek gods. The Buddha and bodhisattva statues of the Gandhara style are excellent examples of Greek-influenced Buddhist sculpture. Once the custom of religious sculpture was accepted, it spread to the central parts of India, where art in the Mathura style was produced. Such statues influenced not only Buddhism but Jainism and Brahmanism as well. After the fourth century, Buddhist sculpture was further refined and developed in the elegant Gupta style. It scarcely need be said that Indian Buddhist sculpture directly and indirectly exerted tremendous influence on the arts of China and Japan.

It is said that the statue commissioned by King Udena, after escaping the tribulations that beset Buddhism in India in the fourth century of the Christian Era, was taken to the kingdom of Kucha in Central Asia. From there, it passed ultimately into China. In the tenth century, the Japanese pilgrim Chōnen, of the great monastery Tōdai-ji, in Nara, traveled to Sung China, where he was accorded the title Great Teacher. Upon his return to Japan in 987 he brought with him a copy of the statue said to have been commissioned long ago by King Udena. (There was a tradition to the effect that the statue now in Japan is the original one, but documents recently discovered inside the statue itself definitely prove it to be a copy made in 984.) A disciple of Chōnen named Jōsan installed

From the Land of the   It is said that Shakyamuni passed the eighth
Bhaggas to Kosambi   rainy season after his enlightenment in the
country of the Bhaggas. The location of the
country is uncertain, but it was probably not far from Kosambi,
the capital of Vansa, to which it may have once been a vassal state.
The following story about Prince Bodhi of Vansa is of later date.

Prince Bodhi was the son of King Udena and, in all likelihood,
of his consort Samavati, who became a devout Buddhist but who
would never meet Shakyamuni directly herself. Instead, when she
heard he was in her neighborhood, she always sent her waiting
woman Uttara to hear his teachings and then had her report
them exactly. Called Humpback Uttara because of an infirmity,
this woman is said to have heard more of the Buddha's sermons
than any lay female believer, and it was owing to her careful
reporting that the queen Samavati attained enlightenment through
indirect means.

The Prince Bodhi who appears in the sutra known as the Discourse to Prince Bodhi was probably the son of Samavati. At the time
referred to in the sutra, he was ruling the country of the Bhaggas in
place of his father King Udena.

While Shakyamuni was spending the eighth rainy season after his
enlightenment in the deer park in the Bhakasala Grove on Mount

---

the statue in the Shakyamuni Hall of the temple Seika-ji, in Saga, north of what
is today called Kyoto. But the statue became so famous that the building in which
it was housed developed into an independent temple called the Seiryō-ji. During
the Kamakura period (1185–1336), Seiryō-ji–style statues of Shakyamuni were
often produced, and even today representatives of this style are to be found in
many parts of Japan.

As an interesting sidelight, I might comment on the relationship between the
Buddhist classics in China and the history of printing. When he returned to Japan, the pilgrim Chōnen also brought with him a full set of the Ti-pitaka, or
Buddhist canon, in more than five thousand volumes, all printed by printers of
the Sung dynasty. Although until this time such works had been copied by hand,
in the twelve years between 972 and 983 the full set was printed. This took place
nearly five centuries before Gutenberg's press was invented.

Chōnen obtained the valuable set from the Chinese imperial collection the
year after it was completed—that is, in 984—and brought it to Japan in 987. It
was stored in the sutra library of the temple Hōjō-ji, built in the eastern part of
Kyoto by the powerful regent Fujiwara no Michinaga (966–1027), but was
destroyed in a fire in 1058.

Sumsumara in the country of the Bhaggas, Prince Bodhi invited him to ceremonies to commemorate the completion of his wonderful new palace at Kokananda. Though it was customary to have Brahmans conduct ceremonies of purification on such occasions, the prince appears to have wanted this ceremony performed according to Buddhist teachings and to receive the blessings of the Buddha. In other words, it seems that the prince was already a believer in the Buddhist faith.

The prince conducted preparations for the ceremonial meal late into the night. On the following morning, when the messenger arrived to call them, Shakyamuni and his disciples departed for the palace. The prince, who was waiting to greet them outside the palace gate, followed the group in. At the bottom of the staircase, which was spread with a white cloth, Shakyamuni stopped. The prince requested three times that he mount the steps, but he would not. Finally, he turned to Ananda, who then said to the prince, "Have the white cloth removed. Only then will the World-honored One and his disciples mount the steps and enter the palace."

At the meal, the prince served the World-honored One many varieties of fine food, both hard and soft, and, when the feast was over, turned to Shakyamuni and said, "I believe that happiness is not attained through pleasure but through suffering. Do you agree?"

Then, basing his remarks on his own experiences, Shakyamuni showed the prince a point in which he was mistaken. He explained in detail how he had been unable to attain happiness as the result of the severest ascetic sufferings and how pleasure alone had brought him no true happiness.

Next the prince asked what conditions were necessary to enable an ascetic to attain his goal. Shakyamuni replied by relating what he had to say to the art of riding an elephant. Shakyamuni said that for success in elephant riding, the following things are needed: faith, good health, honesty, perseverance in striving to improve, and wisdom. In learning to ride an elephant and in learning Buddhism, absolute faith in and respect for the instructor are essential. The student cannot be frank and open unless he trusts his teacher. Health is needed because even a person with the greatest fervor is unable to carry out strenuous training if he is physically weak. Honesty is required: deceit and trickery may seem to produce good results at first, but they inevitably lead to failure. Constant striving is also important since perseverance and steadfastness are vital to any undertaking. Finally, the person must have deep and extensive experience and knowledge enabling him to view the total picture correctly.

When all of these conditions are present, a person does not require long periods to attain eminence or to become enlightened. If he is instructed in the truth in the morning, he will be able to reach his goal by the evening.

14. The Law of the Buddha and the Law of the World

True Men of Religion As I have pointed out, in the time of Shakyamuni few Brahmans and *samanas* were justly describable as men of religion in the truest sense. Though they were in charge of learning and ceremonies, the Brahmans were concerned most intently with formalities and were not the spiritual leaders of their age but merely habitual performers of empty rituals. Leading materially secure lives on land granted to them by royalty, they turned away from lofty spiritual ideals and concentrated on their own ease. Whereas some of them gained an independent livelihood by industriously tilling their land, others strove only for honor, wealth, and pleasure.

In the Sutra on the Brahman Law, Shakyamuni discussed the extent to which Brahmans of his own time had fallen from the level of their ancient forebears. He delivered this sermon to a large group of famous Brahmans from Kosala who came to hear him once when he was staying in the Jetavana Monastery. Shakyamuni was already famous by this time. And the Brahmans, probably recognizing his greatness, may have wanted to find out just what his teachings were like. They asked him if the Brahmans of their time followed the Brahman Law the way their ancestors had done. Shakyamuni replied, "The sages and ascetics of the past were self-restrained and, having abandoned sensual desires, sought only spiritual ideals. They did not have cattle, gold, and treasures the way the Brahmans of the present do. Reading the holy classics was their gold and silver. They kept guard over the treasure house of holy acts. They were themselves holy, and the Law protected them. Nothing intruded on their way of life. For this reason, the people respected and served them diligently. Some underwent solitary religious training for as long as forty-eight years. But even the Brahmans who married did nothing unethical but praised mildness, innocence, and forbearance and lived according to these. They did not keep for themselves all the food, clothing, and shelter offered to them but shared with the poor. If they were given cows at festival time, they did not kill them but loved them as friends. As long as there were Brahmans who did good and opposed evil, the people of the world were happy.

"But, observing the splendor and pleasures of the royalty and the people of the world, the Brahmans gradually came to entertain worldly desires for handsomely dressed and lovely women, swift horses drawing beautiful chariots, spacious mansions, and great fortunes. They produced written works extolling the merits to be gained from almsgiving and offerings. They told the king that he should sacrifice his great wealth in the hope of winning still greater riches in the next life. At their instigation, the king organized all kinds of festivals at which great contributions were made by the people and as a result of which the Brahmans became rich.

"Again at the instigation of the Brahmans, the king instituted the practice of slaughtering the many cows and goats given as offerings. This caused the hearts of the people to become callous and thus invited violence. Disputes arose among the castes. Wives were no longer faithful, and blood purity was spoiled. Everything was controlled solely by desire."

Since this description of degeneration accurately fitted the conditions of their times, the Brahmans who had come to listen to Shakyamuni were forced to recognize the validity of his words. They are said to have been so delighted by the Buddha's teaching of the true Brahman Law that they entrusted themselves to the Three Treasures of the faith and became Buddhists. I suspect, however, that this means only that they were interested in the teachings of Shakyamuni, since they do not appear to have abandoned everything for the sake of the Buddhist faith.

At a time about ten years after his enlightenment, Shakyamuni was staying at a place called Southern Mountain in the kingdom of Magadha. He was apparently not well known in this region then. A Brahman farmer named Bharadvaja, who lived and worked his land with the aid of laborers, was cultivating his fields with five hundred plows. One morning, having arisen, dressed, and taken his begging bowl, Shakyamuni came to the fields of Bharadvaja, who was just then distributing food to his workers. With his begging bowl in his hands, Shakyamuni approached. Displeased by the appearance of a begging priest, Bharadvaja said, "O *samana*, I till my fields, plant seed, and live on what I harvest. Instead of amusing yourself and asking others for food, you too should till, plant, and eat what you earn by the sweat of your own labor."

Although this attitude is perfectly natural from a secular viewpoint, it is surprising in the mouth of a Brahman, a member of the caste of spiritual leaders. It shows that this Brahman, like many others of his age, stressed material and economic matters above all else. Hoping to correct his mistaken attitude, Shakyamuni said, "Brahman, I too live by tilling the earth and planting seeds."

Because he failed to understand the meaning of these words, Bharadvaja said, "But, *samana*, I do not see your farming tools, your yoke, plow, plowshare, goad, or oxen. Nonetheless, you say that you live by tilling the earth and planting seeds. What can you mean?"

Then Shakyamuni answered in verse, "Faith is my seed. Right actions are the rain. Wisdom is my plow; conscience, my plow pole; the mind, my yoke; and right-mindedness, my plowshare and goad. I guard my body and speech from evil actions. I restrict the amount of food and clothing that I require. I use truth to weed out illusions, and mildness is my emancipation. Spiritual progress is my beast of burden, leading me to the serenity of nirvana, where I will have nothing to grieve about. Such tilling inevitably leads to an immortal harvest and liberation from all suffering."

Upon hearing this, the Brahman at last understood the meaning of Shakyamuni's tilling and sowing. He then filled a large bronze bowl with milk-and-rice gruel, offered it to Shakyamuni, and said, "Gotama, eat this, for you are a true tiller of the earth."

In ancient India, people were able to make a living by standing at doors of houses and reciting passages from holy writings. This practice was purely a matter of earning subsistence and had nothing to do with the true Law. Bharadvaja apparently offered Shakyamuni the gruel in the mistaken assumption that he was reciting stanzas for a living. But Shakyamuni refused, saying, "I do not eat things offered as recompense for the recitation of stanzas. Such is not the Law of people who understand the true nature of things correctly. I reject food that is offered on condition of exchange. Food acquired as an offering through mendicant practices is the true food of Buddhas of the Law. True Buddhas who have acquired all virtues and who have destroyed all illusions and have entered the realm of tranquillity should be offered food other than what is given for recitations. The Buddha gives the supreme field of good fortune to those who make offerings unconditionally."

Only when he had heard this did Bharadvaja understand Shakyamuni's meaning. He then came to respect the Buddha and took refuge in the Three Treasures of the faith. In some ancient writings it is said that he became a lay believer. In others it is said that he became a monk and ultimately attained the enlightenment of an *arhat*.

The Law of the World and the Law of the Universe As the foregoing examples indicate, in the time of Shakyamuni—the same thing is not rare today—many people who professed to be men of faith were interested in worldly desires and had lost sight of the true Law. Shakyamuni was quite different. Though born into a fortunate environment where he wanted for none of the good things of life, he was dissatisfied. He abandoned the inconstant, changing things of the world because he wanted to seek the eternal Law of the Universe. Seeing only the world of secular desire, his parents and his wife failed to understand his intentions. Even after Shakyamuni had left home for the life of an ascetic, the secular-minded Bimbisara, king of Magadha, attempted to convince him to return to ordinary affairs. But Shakyamuni refused to turn again to the glory of the world. Later he explained his pursuit of the universal Law in what is called the Discourse on the Noble Quest.

Once while staying in the Jetavana Monastery, Shakyamuni went into Savatthi to beg for food. While he was gone, a large number of his disciples came to his attendant Ananda with the request that they be permitted to hear a sermon directly from Shakyamuni. It seems that it had been a long time since they had enjoyed such intimate teaching. Ananda said, "You may hear such a sermon if you go to the hermitage of the Brahman Rammaka."

That same day, when he had finished begging and had eaten his meal, Shakyamuni said to Ananda, "For the afternoon rest, let us go to the Mansion of Migara's Mother in the Eastern Park." After the rest period, Shakyamuni engaged in seated meditation, at the conclusion of which he went to the Eastern Porch to bathe his limbs. As he stood drying his body, Ananda said, "Nearby is the hermitage of the Brahman Rammaka. It is a scenic and pleasant place. Please let us go there."*

The disciples, who had gathered at the hermitage, stopped talking as soon as Shakyamuni appeared in the doorway and asked what they had been discussing. When they replied that they had been discussing the Law, Shakyamuni said that this was good. He added that when his disciples gathered together they should either discuss the Law or maintain noble silence (that is, meditate). He then discussed the two kinds of quests in which people engage: the noble and the base.

As he explained in detail, the noble quest is the holy man's search for the truth. The base quest is the ordinary man's search for the satisfaction of worldly desire. In other words, the first quest involves the Law of the Universe; the second, the law of the world.

The law of the world and its representative elements—gain, loss,

*Since this took place after Ananda had become Shakyamuni's attendant and at a time when the Mansion of Migara's Mother was already completed, it must have been more than twenty years after the enlightenment.

fame, disrepute, praise, slander, pleasure, and suffering—are inconstant. Consequently, people controlled by this law are tossed back and forth between joy and sadness, hatred and love, gain and loss, and association and separation. Furthermore, being bound to and maddened by the law of the world ineluctably brings such kinds of suffering as birth, old age, illness, and death.

To understand these kinds of suffering in their true nature and to recognize them as the law of the world and thus spare oneself from being troubled by them requires understanding of the noble Law by the person who is freed from all illusions and delusions of the secular world. Shakyamuni explained that before his enlightenment he too had been unable to understand birth, old age, illness, and death but that, sensing his error, he had decided to embark on the noble quest for utmost tranquillity. At the time, he was young. His hair was coal black; he was in the springtime of life. Grieved by his decision, his parents wept and suffered, trying to prevent his leaving home. Still he cut his hair, shaved his beard, put on the yellow robes of the ascetic monk, and left home for a life of homelessness. Though he followed the noble quest by studying meditation with two famous sages and engaged in six years of rigorous ascetic practices, his efforts produced no results. Finally, after meditation under the bo tree, he came to understand the true nature of birth, old age, illness, and death and attained ultimate enlightenment and utmost tranquillity. His actions after his enlightenment, including the teaching of the five ascetics following the Pleading of Brahma, were all intended to help people abandon the law of the world and come to understand the Law of the Universe.

Some of Shakyamuni's sermons emphasize secular morality and everyday life. Others seem to reject the law of the world with special vigor. An example of the former is the Sutra of Good Fortune, which is especially popular in Burma, Thailand, and Sri Lanka, countries where Southern Buddhism is prevalent. This sutra offers the following definitions of the highest blessings:

"Not to associate with fools but to associate with wise men and to revere people who are worthy of reverence. This is the highest blessing.

"To live in a suitable place, to have accumulated merits and virtues in previous lives, and to have correct wishes. This is the highest blessing.

"To be learned and skillful, to be trained and to have studied much, and to speak words of good teachings. This is the highest blessing.

"To care for parents, to provide well for wife and children, and to have a way of making a living that is pure and correct. This is the highest blessing.

"To give alms, to perform correct actions, to care lovingly for and to protect relatives, and to do nothing that is blameworthy. This is the highest blessing.

"To take no pleasure in wickedness and to refrain from evil acts, to control one's own consumption of intoxicants, and to be selfless in all things. This is the highest blessing.

"To respect others, to be humble, to know what is sufficient, to be grateful for what others do, and from time to time to hear the Law taught. This is the highest blessing.

"To be forbearing, to speak gently, to meet with people of religion and occasionally to discuss the Law and teachings. This is the highest blessing.

"To make efforts, to be trained in the Buddha's way, to comprehend the Noble Truths, and to find enlightenment in nirvana. This is the highest blessing.

"To remain unshaken by contact with the things of the secular world, to be free of anxiety, to be undefiled, and to be tranquil. This is the highest blessing.

"Those who do these things are undefeated in all things, prosperous in all things, and theirs is the highest blessing."

This series of definitions represents Buddhist morality on the plane of everyday life. A person living according to these principles is not upset by contact with the law of the world. The colloquy between Shakyamuni and the herdsman Dhaniya, however, seems to reject the kind of social life discussed in the Sutra of Good Fortune.

The herdsman Dhaniya, his family, and his many assistants lived an economically secure, happy life on the banks of the Mahi

River, where they tended their cattle. The pasturage for the animals was good. His house was so well roofed that there was no need to worry about leakage of rain. Since there were no gadflies to trouble them, the cattle grazed peacefully and gave good milk. The calves were healthy and grew well. Dhaniya lived in harmony with his obedient, loving, and faithful wife. His children were strong and well. The whole household, including the people who worked for him, were enjoying an ideally happy, ordinary life when, one day, Shakyamuni came begging, inquired about Dhaniya's condition, and explained the Law of Buddhism.

When Dhaniya said that his house was well roofed and that a pleasing fire was lighted, Shakyamuni replied, "My house is uncovered, and the fire of illusion is extinguished." When Dhaniya said that he had calves, milk cows, cows in calf, heifers, and a bull to act as lord of the herd, Shakyamuni replied, "I have no bonds like calves; I have no blinding illusions like milk cows; I have no accumulations of karma like cows in calf; I have no passions like heifers; and I have no actions or occupations like the bull who is lord of the herd."

Dhaniya then said that he had strong stakes driven and a new rope stretched to keep the cattle from breaking out. To this, Shakyamuni said, "I have torn all bonds of illusion like a bull; like an elephant I have broken through the creeper vines [higher delusions] and will never enter the womb again."

After several more exchanges of this kind, Dhaniya and his wife decided to abandon secular life for earnest religious discipline. At this time, Mara, the Evil One, appeared and said, "People who have children are gladdened by them. People who have cattle are gladdened by them. Love of this kind is the highest human happiness. Without it, there is no happiness."

To this attempt to hinder Dhaniya from abandoning the secular life, Shakyamuni said, "People who have children are grieved by them. People who have cattle are grieved by them. Love of this kind is the greatest human grief. Without it, there is no grief."

Though an extreme philosophy of this kind is probably not intended for ordinary people, in the face of it, we must turn to the question of what path we must follow in relation to the law of the world and the Law of the Universe, or Buddhist truth. Buddhism does not advocate rejection of the world. It strives to ensure the peace and happiness not only of human beings, but also of animals and plants—that is, of all forms of life. Consequently, anything that pretends to be unrelated to the world and daily life cannot be called true Buddhism. True Buddhism cannot reject or claim isolation from the law of the world.

The people of the past often said that the law of the world is not the Law of the Universe (Buddhist truth), though the Law of the Universe is the law of the world. This means that, though the Law of the Universe is much more than the law of the world, it cannot exist apart from it. The Law of the Universe guides the law of the world in the way that it should follow, and only under such conditions does the law of the world have value and significance. In this sense, the Law of the Universe is not limited to Buddhism or any single religion.

15. Oneness of Theory and Practice

For forty-five years after his enlightenment, Shakyamuni never lived long in one place but traveled about the central Ganges region teaching in Magadha and Kosala until his decease at the age of eighty at a place called Kushinagara. During his mission, he delivered an immense number of sermons and lessons. Though not all of them have survived, the extant sermons attributed to him number in the thousands. Nonetheless, once when he was in a grove of *sinsapa* trees on the outskirts of Kosambi, he told his followers that his teachings were only an infinitesimal part of what he could teach if he thought they were ready to comprehend. Plucking a branch from a tree, he asked whether the leaves on it were more numerous than the leaves on all the branches in the entire grove. When his followers said that of course the leaves in the whole grove were incomparably greater in number than those on the branch, Shakyamuni said, "The things that I have taught you are like the leaves on this branch. The things that I could teach you are like the leaves on all the branches in the entire grove. I have not taught the rest because much of it is too difficult for beginners. I have told you only those things that I consider suitable to your state."

Though largely in prose, the ancient writings of primitive Buddhism include a number of teachings that are either partly or entirely in verse. Not all of the more than ten thousand verses in the classics are said to have been delivered by Shakyamuni himself. Some are attributed to his disciples, whereas others are said to be the words of demons or gods. Two of the most widely popular and beloved verses throughout both Mahayana and Theravada Buddhism are the "Verse of Impermanence" and the "Instruction of the Seven Buddhas" ("seven Buddhas" signifies all of the Buddhas of the past).

At the time of the death of Shakyamuni, in the Sala Grove near Kushinagara, the disciples and gods expressed their grief in verse. Indra, the king of the gods and a Buddhist tutelary deity, is said to have chanted the "Verse of Impermanence" at this time, though, since its contents are something taught earlier by Shakyamuni himself, Indra may have been doing no more than repeating it on this solemn and sorrowful occasion.

The verse, which says, "All things are without permanence; whatever is born will inevitably be destroyed; things are produced, and then they decay; tranquillity is the maximum joy," is found in two especially famous instances. Part of the general sorrow surrounding the death of Shakyamuni, the verse is included in the Sutra of the Great Decease. In addition, the verse plays an important part in the famous tale about an earlier existence of Shakyamuni. Once, a bodhisattva known as the Young Ascetic of the Himalayas heard the first half of the stanza from Indra, disguised as a demon. This Young Ascetic, who was Shakyamuni in a previous eixstence, then offered to give his life to the demon for the sake of hearing the second half.* Containing the truth that all things are impermanent and that total tranquillity (nirvana) is the most highly desirable state, this verse is a condensation of fundamental Buddhist theoretical philosophy. The "Verse of Impermanence" and the

---

*The story of the Young Ascetic of the Himalayas is depicted in paintings on one wall of the Asuka-period (552–646) Tamamushi Shrine in the temple Hōryū-ji, in Nara. Since, in the Chinese form in which it was introduced into Japan, the verse is difficult to understand, it was simplified in a famous poetic version of the Japanese syllabary attributed to Kūkai (774–835), one of the most famous Buddhist priests in Japanese history: "Colors [flowers] are fragrant, but they fade. Nothing in this world is permanent. Today, cross the high mountain of illusions, and there will be no more shallow dreaming, no more intoxication."

"Instruction of the Seven Buddhas" have been regarded as the most famous and most important of all the verses. The former is preached from the theoretical standpoint of the central thinking of Buddhism; the latter, from the practical viewpoint of essential teachings.

The heavy emphasis on theoretical philosophy in Buddhism— heavier than in many other religions—may result from the general Indian devotion to philosophical investigation. This and the Indian tendency to explain philosophy in terms of religious practice influenced Buddhism considerably. Shakyamuni himself was especially interested in philosophical issues and would employ nothing in his teachings that was not theoretically convincing. After having made a thorough investigation of the doctrines of the religions and philosophies of his time in order to determine which were correct and perfect, he compiled the distinctive teachings like the Law of Causation that distinguish Buddhism from other religions. Consequently, Buddhism has a rational foundation enabling it to withstand any criticism on the theoretical plane. Its rationalism is not concerned solely with abstract truth for its own sake but is a basis for actual practice of religious faith. This means that Buddhist faith is not merely unfounded enthusiasm but practical faith with a firm rational and ethical basis. Buddhist theory and practice are one. In Buddhism there is no theory that does not take practice into consideration, and there is no practice lacking theoretical substantiation.

The Buddhist sects that developed in Japan during the Kamakura period (1185–1336)—notably the Jōdo sect, the Zen sects, and the Nichiren sect—are characteristically Japanese. They manifest a lofty purity and a penetration into the true spirit of Buddhism that are difficult to find elsewhere in the history of the religion. In these sects, simple acts like chanting formulas in praise of Amida Buddha or the Lotus Sutra or like seated meditation are considered sufficient for salvation in themselves without philosophizing or theoretical inquiries. But this does not mean that these sects lack theoretical foundations. Quite to the contrary, their founders evolved direct and clear acts of practical faith—chanting and meditation—after profound and extensive scholarly research. The ordinary man is not required to perform such research for himself: he need only follow the directions of his religious leader. Indeed, in these sects, theoretical study and speculation are forbidden as hindrances to practical faith.

In Japan after the middle of the nineteenth century, when in connection with wide-sweeping reforms and a drive for Westernization the national educational level was elevated, and especially after the emphasis on democracy that developed following the conclusion of World War II, the people came to feel that they must always act independently on the basis of their own interpretations of given situations. They no longer wished to follow instructions blindly. Although complete respect for the independence of the individual has yet to be established in Japan and true democracy is still a fairly long way off, undeniably, the people of Japan will no longer agree to things that they do not find personally convincing. Consequently, unconditional belief in the efficacy of chanting formulas and engaging in Zen meditation is not as widespread as it once was. People today hesitate to chant the old formulas or meditate in the Zen fashion without understanding what relations these acts have to human life in general. Lack of religious leaders capable of convincing people of the value of such simple acts of faith aggravates the situation. Nonetheless, the sound theoretical basis of Buddhism can inspire belief in these acts even today when few people approve of trusting without questioning.

Since ordinary people are often incapable of comprehending profound doctrines, it is desirable to establish a minimum of essential theory that anyone can understand and then to help that understanding develop gradually. In his own time, Shakyamuni adjusted his teachings to the personalities of his audiences and employed expedient faith and expedient teachings centered on actual practice. It is important to remember that all of the various Buddhist doctrines are in effect examinations of the same basic issues from different viewpoints and are intimately related to practical faith.

As I have said, the "Instruction of the Seven Buddhas" is a compendium of Buddhist teachings on practical faith. To understand it accurately, it is important to take into consideration the discrepancy between the Chinese translation, which is the version that passed into Japan, and the original Pali version. In Chinese, the stanza is couched in the imperative: Commit no evil; do all that is good; purify your mind; this is the teaching of all the Buddhas. The Pali version (Dhammapada 183), on the other hand, is not in the imperative mode: To do no evil, to do all good, and to purify one's own mind are the teachings of all the Buddhas. In the Chinese reading, the teaching is no more than ordinary morality. In the Pali, however, it is a lofty teaching of free and autonomously chosen ethical morality.

Not only in Buddhism, but in all human affairs, there is a great difference between performing an act as a result of orders from somewhere else and performing even that same act on one's own initiative. Though a person may perform an act upon orders, he may not wish to perform it; and if the person who gives the order is absent, he may not perform it. There are cases in which people refuse to do as ordered even in the presence of the one who gives the order. Dislike of, dissatisfaction with, and rebellion against orders breed laziness, which means that there is no way to ensure compliance with orders.

As long as the "Instruction of the Seven Buddhas" is regarded as a commandment, Buddhism must be interpreted as only heteronomous morality. This lends credence to the opinions of those Western scholars who argue that Buddhism teaches not religion but only worldly morality.

Kant said that the highest ethical morality is free obedience to dictates of conscience. But since they too can seem to be obligatory, the dictates of conscience may be carried out unwillingly. In its ponderous gravity, Kant's attitude resembles that of the Confucians, and neither Kant nor the Confucians can be considered the pinnacle of ethical morality.

If the "Instruction of the Seven Buddhas" is interpreted not as a commandment but as a statement, then Buddhist ethical morality is seen to be one of joy and courage. Instead of following orders or unwillingly obeying dictates of conscience, the Buddhist must gradually grow to the point where perpetrating evil is impossible for him, even under conditions in which the evil act might seem seductive. The founder of the Sōtō Zen sect, Dōgen (1200–1253), said that the power of religious training is manifest in a process whereby the person wishes to do no evil, does no evil, and finally becomes incapable of evil. The process arises independently within the person and is not arbitrarily imposed from without. The Japanese Buddhist sects of the Kamakura period imposed no commandments and orders because, by becoming a truly faithful member of one of them, the person—if he was sincere, of course—was thought to be manifesting the desire to do only good. It was thought unnecessary to command such people to avoid evil.

Primitive Buddhism, in the form of the Pali version of the "Instruction of the Seven Buddhas" taught the same thing—that is, one must purify one's own mind. This instruction rests on the premise of doing no evil and perpetrating good. Purification of the mind means total entrustment to the Three Treasures—the Buddha, the Law, and the Order. A person who has entrusted himself to them is free of all trace of egoistic opinion and desire. He is selfless in relation to the Buddha and, as he perseveres in faith, becomes selfless in relation to all other people, animals, and his entire environment. Freed of personal opinions and desires, he has no egocentric ideas and does not act in an egocentric way. This means that the walls and barriers between him and other creatures, who inevitably react favorably to his attitude, collapse. He is able to become one with all beings. This is one of the major goals of Buddhism. Since it promotes the attainment of this goal, the "Instruction of the Seven Buddhas" is not only a major Buddhist teaching but also the core of Buddhist ethical practice.

16. Supernatural Powers

Miraculous powers play a part in many religions. Often religions that are most vibrant and warm-blooded depend on such powers because they appeal directly and help people find effective relief from suffering and thus deepen and broaden faith in ways that theoretical explanations cannot equal. The mystical nature of miraculous powers makes the effects of salvation directly and irrefutably apparent.

Primitive Buddhist writings attribute to Shakyamuni and his disciples what are called the three types of superior wisdom and the six powers of saving sentient beings (actually, the latter include the former). Though possessed of immense abilities in rational, theoretical thought, Shakyamuni is said to have had incomparable supernatural powers as well. Emotional people who are of an uncomplicated turn of mind and who can concentrate deeply and easily are thought to attain supernatural powers more readily than subtle intellectuals. It is part of the greatness of Shakyamuni to be peerless in both the rational and the supernatural.

I have already explained how, while still very young, Shakyamuni engaged in profound analyses of the human condition and in intense meditation. And I have told the story of the agricultural festival at which Shakyamuni entered so profound a state of meditation upon observing the cruelty of the natural world that his body gave off a brilliant light and startled everyone present.

It is said that in the early part of the night of his enlightenment Shakyamuni attained the first of the three types of superior wisdom: remembrance of one's former existences, as well as those of others. In the middle part of the night, he attained insight into the future and the eye capable of seeing everything. In the last part of the night he attained the most important wisdom: perfect freedom enabling him to overcome all passions and thus to reach supreme enlightenment. These three types of superior wisdom constitute the last of the six supernatural powers of saving sentient beings attributed to Shakyamuni and to those of his disciples who attained ultimate enlightenment in the same manner as he. Though Shakyamuni was unsurpassed in this respect, each of his disciples had his special ability. For instance, Maudgalyayana is said to have excelled in perfect freedom of activity, whereas Anuruddha was famous for eyes capable of seeing everything.

Five of the six supernatural powers are believed to be accessible to a fairly wide range of creatures; the sixth—which is the third of the three superior wisdoms—is attained only by those who are enlightened in the way that Shakyamuni was. The following are brief descriptions of the first five supernatural powers.

1. Perfect freedom of activity. The person possessed of this power can assume any multiple or single form at will, can pass through all obstacles, can dive into the earth, fly through the air, and walk on water. He can conceal or reveal himself as he sees fit. During the final trip before his death, Shakyamuni and his followers crossed the flooded Ganges from the village of Patali to reach the northern shore without the assistance of boats. The story is told in the Sutra of the Great Decease.

"At the time, the World-honored One approached the Ganges, which was then brimming full to its banks. Some people were crossing in boats, others on reed rafts. In the space of time it would take a strong man to flex or unbend his arm, Shakyamuni and the monks crossed from this side of the Ganges to the other."

(It is not explicitly stated that they flew, but this seems the only explanation.)

2. Ears capable of hearing everything. The pure ear of heaven enables the person with this power to hear all things, no matter how near or far, and to understand the voices of divinities and the utterances of birds and beasts. According to Yoga teachings, spiritual unification attained through meditation establishes a direct bond between the ear and the thing heard and makes audible even the smallest sounds at the greatest distances.

3. Insight into the minds of others. A person with such power sees directly the greed, wrath, or conceit in another's heart. He knows whether the person is mentally tranquil or disturbed and whether he has attained enlightenment and has been freed from all illusions and hindrances.

A person can acquire this ability through frequent contact with others. He can tell from a companion's facial expressions, eyes, words, and behavior something about the way that person is thinking. In general, the power of insight into the minds of others enables one to penetrate only the inner worlds of people of lower levels of understanding. Though his followers could not see into the mind of Shakyamuni, he was able to penetrate the minds of all beings.

Such ability, even in the degree allowed to ordinary mortals, is of immense importance in political and economic negotiations, education, and religious conversion.

4. Remembrance of one's former existences. This power enables the person to know former existences as far back as hundreds of former lives for himself and for others as well. He can even recall such details as names, appearances, general circumstances, and fates. The oldest Buddhist writings clearly say that Shakyamuni knew about his own former existences and those of his followers.

In the West too there are people who can accurately view the past. Most of them consider their powers innate and not the product of development through meditation. In Buddhist terms, this phenomenon is explained as manifestation of special powers in this life as the result of accumulated karma from past existences. But Westerners with this power are generally mediums who must enter a trance state and who do not act consciously and autonomously; they require the assistance of a leader. In contrast, Buddhists with the power to see into the past engage in profound meditation and speak and act freely on the basis of their own consciousness, without the help of a leader. In this respect, Buddhist and Yoga powers of seeing into the past are superior to those of Western mediums.

5. Eyes capable of seeing everything. Many people can guess something of another's future from his present circumstances, but the pure eye endowed by this power can penetrate into many lives yet to come. In the Sutra of the Great Decease occurs an incident revealing Shakyamuni's powers in this connection. Once in the village of Nadika, he was requested to foresee the future states of the monks and nuns who had recently died there. He said that more than fifty of them would never be reborn into the ordinary world of desire. Ninety would be reborn into this world once more, and five hundred had entered the stream of sanctification leading to ultimate liberation.

This power is said to enable its possessor to see clearly not only the future but also things happening in the present in distant places as well. This aspect of the power is illustrated by an interesting anecdote concerning two famous Buddhist monks living in China in the fourth and fifth centuries of the Christian Era.

Buddhabhadra, famous as a great master of meditation and a translator—one of his most notable works is a translation of the sixty-fascicle Avatamsaka-sutra—came from northern India to the Chinese city of Ch'ang-an, where the still more famous translator Kumarajiva (344–413) was translating sutras and lecturing. Soon trouble arose. Buddhabhadra, who lived strictly by the precepts set down for monks, was displeased by the lax way of life of Kumarajiva, who, though a genius in his work, broke many rules and lived surrounded by a large number of beautiful women. Disagreements among the followers of the two men aggravated the situation.

One day Buddhabhadra told his disciples, "Yesterday I saw five ships setting sail from India." This astounding remark soon became the subject of rumors and aroused the animosity of Kumarajiva's followers, who accused Buddhabhadra of attempting to mislead the people with false statements. Buddhabhadra and his disciples thereupon left Ch'ang-an and traveled to southern China. Later, however, the arrival in China of the five ships he had seen departing from India verified what Buddhabhadra had said. In spite of a royal invitation to return to Ch'ang-an, Buddhabhadra preferred to remain in the famous monasteries of Lu-shan, lecturing, guiding meditation, and translating sutras.

Shakyamuni's Super- Actions and utterances appear miraculous
natural Powers and supernatural to people whose ability to understand is inferior to that of the person acting and speaking. Shakyamuni's intelligence and wisdom were incomparably greater than those of his followers or of ordinary human beings. Consequently, his acts and words seem all the more miraculous. Because of his eloquence, believers of other religions considered him a great magician and were afraid of him. (This is illustrated by the previously related story of the Jainist Upali. See pages 125–26.)

Among the many old Buddhist writings containing frequent reference to Shakyamuni's supernatural powers, it is the Sutra of the Great Decease that relates the majority of the incidents occurring in the later years of his life. In addition to the crossing of the Ganges and the forecast of the future fates of monks and nuns who had died in Nadika, this sutra contains the following interesting stories.

The five mountains surrounding Rajagaha made the city easy to defend but difficult to get out of. Furthermore, the city was cramped, and transportation was inconvenient. For the sake of national development, the king decided to build a new capital at a place called Patali, located near the Ganges, where both land and transportation possibilities were good. In later years, this city was to become Pataliputra, the flourishing capital of India for centuries. In the closing years of Shakyamuni's life, Vassakara and Sunida, two ministers from the government in Rajagaha, were in Patali making surveys and laying out the future city. Shakyamuni passed through the area, and the ministers made offerings to him. Looking at the land with supernatural vision, Shakyamuni saw that powerful earth spirits dwelt in the plots apportioned by the ministers.

The Sutra of the Great Decease tells the story in the following way.

"Having awakened early, the World-honored One asked his attendant Ananda, 'Who is building a fortress at Patali village?'

"Ananda replied, 'World-honored One, Sunida and Vassakara, ministers of Magadha, are building a fortress there to protect the nation from the Vajjis.'

"Shakyamuni then said, 'Ananda, with my clear supernatural vision, I have seen many thousands of earth spirits occupying the land in Patali village.'"

He went on to explain that in places inhabited by powerful earth spirits, great kings and powerful ministers build their mansions; that in places where the earth spirits are mediocre, mediocre kings and ministers will dwell; and that in places where the spirits are frail, the kings and ministers will be petty.

Only with a supernatural eye could Shakyamuni have seen the earth spirits. Only with knowledge of the future could he have known that the village of Patali would become a great and thriving capital.

The second story has to do with the events occurring in the last hours of Shakyamuni's life at the foot of the twin *sala* trees in the grove just outside the town of Kushinagara. As Shakyamuni lay down, the twin trees, filled with bloom out of season, shed a rain of flowers on his body. Heavenly *mandarava* flowers and sandalwood perfume fell from the sky, and divine music played in honor of the Tathagata, the World-honored One.

Shakyamuni turned to Ananda and said that this was not the right way to pay homage to him. The right way was for the monks and nuns of the Order and all the lay believers to trust and understand the Buddha's Law correctly and to live in accordance with it. Then he exhorted all those present to understand and trust the law and follow it in daily life.

At this time, Shakyamuni said sternly to Upavana, an *arhat* who was in front fanning him, "Brother, stand aside. Do not stand in front of me." Finding this command odd, Ananda said to Shakyamuni, "World-honored One, the venerable Upavana has long been your faithful follower and attendant. Why do you order him away at this final moment?"

Then Shakyamuni said, "Ananda, many gods from the universe, the worlds of the ten directions, have gathered here to see the last hour of the Tathagata. Many great gods are gathered here for twelve leagues around the twin *sala* trees. And they murmur, 'In the last watches of this night, one of the rare Tathagatas to appear in this world must die. We have come from afar to see the last moments of the Tathagata, but a powerful monk stands in front of him blocking our view.' "*

This second story, too, reveals Shakyamuni's supernatural ability to see things—in this case, divinities—that were invisible to his followers and other ordinary human beings.

It is important to point out that Shakyamuni was completely free to employ his supernatural powers in all times, places, and conditions. People of lesser maturity cannot call on supernatural power unless they enter a deep state of meditation. As I have explained, Western mediums require something like hypnotism and, even then, do not act autonomously or consciously. A person as mature in meditation as Shakyamuni, however, can manifest supernatural powers with complete freedom. The possession of such ability may be a point shared in common by Shakyamuni and Jesus Christ.

Prohibition of the Use of Supernatural Powers Shakyamuni used supernatural powers not as an end in themselves but for the sake of teaching sentient beings, and he forbade his followers to employ them willfully for their own glory or profit, as the following story shows.

Once a wealthy man in Rajagaha obtained a piece of excellent sandalwood core and decided to have a bowl made from it. Intending to keep the chips remaining from the wood for himself and to donate the bowl to a man of religion, the rich man had the finished vessel attached to the end of a long bamboo pole set up in a public place and announced that it would become the property of the man with supernatural (*arhat*) powers who could bring

---

*Had Upavana been only an ordinary mortal, his body would not have obstructed the vision of the gods; but he was an obstacle precisely because he was a powerful *arhat*.

it down. Many followers of religions other than Buddhism tried to win the prize but failed.

One morning, Shakyamuni's disciples Maudgalyayana and Pindola-Bharadvaja were out begging for food in Rajagaha and heard about the bowl. Pindola-Bharadvaja said, "Maudgalyayana, why not use your supernatural powers to get the bowl?" But Maudgalyayana replied by urging Pindola-Bharadvaja to do so himself. Taking this advice, the *arhat* Pindola-Bharadvaja leaped into the air, took the bowl from the bamboo pole, and then flew three times around the city.

Seeing what had happened, the rich man and his family raised their hands in prayerful reverence and requested that Pindola-Bharadvaja come to their house. When he did as they asked, the rich man took the sandalwood bowl, filled it with fine foods, and returned it to Pindola-Bharadvaja, who thereupon returned to the Bamboo Grove Monastery.

Word of the event soon spread through the town, and a great crowd, talking loudly of Pindola-Bharadvaja's feat, followed him to the grove. Shakyamuni heard the clamor and asked the reason for it. When he learned what had happened, he called the Order together, questioned Pindola-Bharadvaja, and then rebuked him.

"Pindola-Bharadvaja, why have you displayed your superhuman powers before the laity for the sake of a wretched wooden bowl? This is a shameful thing to do. It will not lead the unconverted to the faith but will only increase the number of nonbelievers. A monk must not do such a thing."

Then he addressed the whole company of the monks, telling them that they should not make a show of their powers, that anyone who did so would be guilty of a minor sin, and that in the future they must not use wooden bowls. He commanded that the sandalwood bowl be crushed and the resulting powder used for eye medicine.

The most outstanding example of the misuse of supernatural powers in all Buddhist history is the case of Shakyamuni's cousin Devadatta. When Shakyamuni first visited his home country after his enlightenment, a group of young men from the Shakya clan abandoned secular life to become his followers. Among them were Ananda, who heard the Buddha's teachings so many times that he became a learned sage; Anuruddha and Bhaddiya, who attained the enlightenment of *arhats;* and Bhagu, Kimbila, and Devadatta, who did not become *arhats* but who attained the five supernatural powers. (Though the sixth and most important power is attained only by the enlightened, ordinary Buddhist believers, the faithful of other religions, and even such sly animals as foxes and badgers are thought to be able to manifest the other five.)

Attempting to devise more effective uses for his powers, Devadatta hit upon the idea of employing them to ingratiate himself with and win the confidence of the young prince Ajatasattu, who had a brilliant future. In this way, Devadatta hoped to increase his own honor and profit.

Assuming the form of a boy girdled with serpents, Devadatta appeared before Ajatasattu, who, horrified, demanded to know the identity of this alarming creature. When he received an affirmative reply to his question as to whether the prince found him frightening, Devadatta identified himself. But the prince was unconvinced. If this serpent-girdled boy was indeed the person he claimed to be, he should appear in the form that Devadatta customarily took. Devadatta then appeared before the prince in his usual monk's robes, begging bowl in hand.

The delighted prince came to trust and respect Devadatta and sent him many rich meals each day. Flattering treatment only poisoned Devadatta's mind and inspired evil desires in his heart. He vowed that he would gain control of the Buddhist Order. But because of his wicked ambitions he lost his supernatural powers. And this was the start of the series of crimes and wicked acts against Shakyamuni and the Order that finally resulted in Devadatta's destruction.

Supernatural powers are never a major goal in Buddhism. The three types of superior wisdom and six powers of saving sentient beings manifested by Shakyamuni and his *arhat* followers were always merely expedient byproducts intended for use in teaching and conversion but never for personal fame or fortune. The same thing can be said of powers that have sometimes been manifested in founders of various Buddhist sects. Even Yoga teaches that one must not make supernatural powers a primary aim and that sources of evil will vanish and profound enlightenment be attained when a person has ceased being interested in such things. From the Buddhist standpoint, the most important thing is to attain the sixth power—perfect freedom—and, after thus reaching perfect enlightenment, to work selflessly and compassionately for the good of all members of society.

17. The Great Decease

In the forty-fifth year of his teaching mission, when he had accomplished all that he was fated to do, Shakyamuni made a last, quiet journey, which is related in detail in the Theravada scripture the Sutra of the Great Decease (Maha-parinibbana-sutta). Other accounts in Mahayana texts, such as the Buddhacharita, though not all historically factual, relate much of interest about the period immediately preceding Shakyamuni's death, but they include certain extravagances. For instance, they attribute to Shakyamuni in this period sermons amounting to tens and even hundreds of pages. Delivering such instructions would have been unthinkable of a man eighty years of age, even a man of Shakyamuni's extraordinary powers. For this reason I prefer to regard the Theravada Sutra of the Great Decease as more reliable.

As he approached the age of eighty, Shakyamuni grew increasingly weak in body. It is imaginable that he must have felt sad. About a year earlier, Shariputra and Maudgalyayana, his two leading disciples, had both died. Furthermore, his home nation met with sudden disaster. King Vidudabha of Kosala overthrew his father Pasenadi, with whom Shakyamuni had been on close terms, and seized the royal power. The deposed king met an unhappy death, just as King Bimbisara of Magadha had done seven or eight years earlier at the hands of his son Ajatasattu. Having taken the throne, Vidudabha attacked the Shakyas, killing many of Shakyamuni's relatives and destroying the small nation.

No doubt grieved by the loss of many close associates and probably made more intensely aware of his own approaching end, Shakyamuni left Rajagaha with five hundred disciples and began a leisurely journey northward. Perhaps a desire to draw nearer to the place where his father's kingdom had been inspired him to take this direction.

At the same time, King Ajatasattu of Magadha, who had repented of his plottings with Devadatta and of his part in his father's death by starvation, ambitiously wanted to capture the nation of the Vajjis to the north of Magadha. The Sutra of the Great Decease opens with a passage explaining how Vassakara, one of Ajatasattu's ministers, was sent to the trusted and respected Shakyamuni to inquire about possibilities of success for such an undertaking.

The passage relates that once the World-honored One was at Vulture Peak near Rajagaha. Ajatasattu, king of Magadha and son of the queen-consort Videha, wanting to conquer the Vajjis, thought to himself, "Though they are powerful and mighty, I want to attack them. I want to destroy and root out the Vajjis." Then he said to his minister Vassakara, "Brahman, go to the World-honored One. Make obeisance at his feet and inquire about his health from me. Then say to him, 'World-honored One, Ajatasattu, the king of Magadha, wishes to conquer the Vajjis. No matter how strong and powerful they are, he wishes to destroy and root them out.' Remember the instructions the World-honored One gives you and repeat them to me when you return. Shakyamuni speaks nothing that is untrue."

The minister did as he was instructed and expressed the king's thoughts. Shakyamuni then turned to Ananda, who was standing nearby fanning him, and asked the following questions.

Have you heard that the Vajjis hold frequent public assemblies?

Have you heard that the Vajjis meet in concord, rise in concord, and act as they are supposed to do in concord?

Have you heard that the Vajjis enact nothing new, break no

enacted rules, and act according to the Vajji laws long ago established?

Have you heard that the Vajjis respect, honor, and support their elders?

Have you heard that the Vajjis never forcefully carry away or abduct women and girls?

Have you heard that the Vajjis esteem and honor the shrines in their territory and observe the customary offerings and rites?

Have you heard that the Vajjis offer proper protection and support for *arhats* and permit future *arhats* from other countries to live safely within their territory?

Ananda replied in the affirmative to all these questions. Shakyamuni next said that as long as the Vajjis continued to behave in this good way they could be expected to prosper and not to be destroyed.

Shakyamuni then explained to the minister that while he had lived at the Sarandada temple in Vesali, the Vajji capital, he had taught the local people the seven rules for security implicit in the questions he had asked Ananda. He added that the Vajjis would continue to prosper as long as they abided by these rules. Vassakara replied that abiding by one such rule would be sufficient to security and that a nation abiding by them all would certainly flourish. The king of Magadha would be unable to conquer the Vajjis in war or in any kind of diplomacy short of breaking alliances. Finally, pleading press of business, he excused himself and departed.

The seven rules Shakyamuni taught are as applicable today as they were then and represent a truly democratic approach. For the sake of successful government, people must meet and exchange opinions; act correctly and in concord; respect good traditions; esteem and support elders, people of religion, and religious institutions; and show proper respect for women. Any society following these rules is likely to prosper and remain peaceful.

After the minister had gone, Shakyamuni instructed Ananda to assemble the monks from the Rajagaha area in the hall on Vulture Peak. When all were gathered, he taught them seven rules for the welfare of the Order. These rules are slightly different from the ones he taught the Vajjis and the minister of the king of Magadha.

1. The monks should meet for democratic mutual exchanges of opinion.

2. They should manage the Order correctly and in cooperation and concord.

3. They should abide by correct established precepts and rules.

4. They should respect and heed the words of elders.

5. They should not indulge in the kind of sensual pleasure that keeps human beings bound to the cycle of transmigrations.

6. They should prefer a life of solitude in remote places.

7. They should be the kind of people whom good men of religion are happy to meet and should provide men of religion with pleasant places to live in.

Shakyamuni earnestly taught the monks that as long as they abided by these rules the Order would thrive.

Moral Conduct and the Mirror of the Law As he continued at an unhurried rate of about three or four kilometers a day, Shakyamuni delivered many splendid sermons for monks and lay believers at the various places he passed through. Since it is impossible to discuss them all here, I shall limit myself to the ones I consider most outstanding.

From Vulture Peak, Shakyamuni and his group went to the mango grove near Rajagaha and from there passed through Nalanda and entered the village of Patali, where the lay believers greeted them and led them to a resting place. After washing their feet, the group entered the resting place, where Shakyamuni taught a sermon on the misfortune of breaking moral rules and the merits of abiding by them.

He explained that a person who does wrong by breaking the rules of moral conduct suffers five kinds of misfortunes: through sloth, he loses much property; his evil conduct gains him an evil reputation; he lacks self-confidence and is embarrassed in any society, whether it be that of kings, Brahmans, lay believers, or *samanas;* he ends his life in psychological anxiety and ignorance; and, after a fearful death, he is reborn into one of the four temporary evil states. A person who does good and abides by moral precepts, on the other hand, enjoys fivefold merits: through diligence he gains great wealth; his good actions win him a good reputation; he has self-confidence and is unembarrassed in any society; he is free of psychological anxiety at death; and, after death, he is reborn into a blessed state.

Shakyamuni taught, delighted, and inspired the villagers of Patali until late at night, when he told them to go to do what they thought suitable. They departed, and Shakyamuni and his disciples went to their private quarters.

As I have shown before, Shakyamuni's teaching method was to move gradually from the worldly and easy to the abstract and difficult. His standard practice of beginning instruction with the triple doctrine of almsgiving to the poor and holy people, abiding by moral precepts, and the assurance that good acts are rewarded by rebirth in a blessed state and this instance of teaching beginner lay believers in terms of secular misfortune and merit are examples of my meaning. There are many instances in the Sutra of the Great Decease in which Shakyamuni uses simple illustrations to express sophisticated doctrines. In other instances he attempted to make his meaning clearer by means of the simple device of repetition. For example, the following teachings, always in this same conventionalized form, turn up several times throughout the sutra.

"The World-honored One held extensive discussions on the Law with the monks. He discussed good conduct, meditation, and wisdom and said that there is great fruit and great merit in contemplation if it is governed by upright conduct and great fruit and merit in intellect if it is governed by earnest contemplation. The intellect governed by contemplation is completely free of the great evils: craving for sensual pleasure, craving for continued existence, delusion, and ignorance."

I have already discussed the dinner and sermon in the presence of the ministers of the king of Magadha and the miraculous crossing of the Ganges (see pages 115, 164). Later at the village of Koti, he taught the monks that it was by failing to understand the Four Noble Truths that both he and they had been forced to live so long in the cycle of birth, death, and rebirth but that it was through understanding of the Four Noble Truths that they were now free of delusion and liberated from that cycle. He expressed the same teaching in the following stanza:

"When the veracity of the Four Noble Truths is unseen,
Each life is long tied to the cycle of rebirths.
A vision of the Four Noble Truths roots out delusion.
The causes of suffering are destroyed,
And there is no more rebirth."

As I have said, at the village of Nadika, Shakyamuni complied with requests to predict the future fates of local lay believers and monks who had recently died. But since it would be troublesome to answer each such request, Shakyamuni taught what is called the Mirror of the Law, by means of which an elect disciple can say for certain whether for him the worlds of hell, animals, hungry spirits, suffering, and evil are destroyed and whether he has entered the stream leading unfailingly to final salvation. The Mirror of the Law consists of four elements: faith in the Buddha, faith in the Law, faith in the Order, and faith in the sacred precepts. Possessed of these four faiths, the disciple knows that he will never backslide. Faith in the Three Treasures leads to the state where violations of the sacred precepts or other evil acts are impossible. Since the disciple is unable to do ill, such evil states as hell, animals, hungry spirits, and others, which are the effects of evil causes, cease to exist for him. Living only in the good, he is liable only to good karma, and this means that he has joined the company of the elect who are assured of ultimate salvation.

From the village of Nadika, Shakyamuni traveled to Vesali, the Vajji capital, where he stayed in the Ambapali grove and taught the monks about being mindful and thoughtful. He took this occasion to fortify them morally, since not far from the grove lived the luxurious courtesan Ambapali and her many lovely waiting women, who might tempt the members of the Order.

The monks were instructed to be mindful—that is, while in this world, they must be strenuously earnest and thoughtful in regard to the body, the sensations, the mind, and objects of observation so as to eliminate the grief and cravings arising from these things. They were further instructed to be thoughtful. By this is meant that they must be in full presence of mind in all actions: advancing or returning; looking forward or backward; bending or stretching the body; wearing and using robes, other clothing, and the beggar's bowl; eating; chewing; tasting; evacuating; walking or remaining seated; sleeping or waking; speaking or remaining silent; and carrying out all other motions or states of being.

The courtesan Ambapali visited Shakyamuni, who instructed her in the Buddha's Law and then accepted an invitation to take the morning meal with her on the following day. On the way home, Ambapali's carriage collided with another carrying a number of Vajji aristocrats about to pay Shakyamuni a visit themselves. When they learned that the courtesan had invited Shakyamuni to a meal the next morning, they attempted to persuade her to let them give the meal in her stead. She refused. Later, Shakyamuni satisfied the aristocrats by teaching and instructing them.

On the following morning, Ambapali offered Shakyamuni and his following a fine meal of delicacies of all kinds. As her faith deepened, she came to give the grove to the Order and ultimately abandoned secular life to become a nun.

The Rainy Season and the Buddha's Illness When the rainy season came—the forty-fifth and last after the enlightenment—Shakyamuni and Ananda decided to sojourn in Beluva. Since this small village could not house and feed all of them, the remaining monks spent the rainy season with friends and acquaintances in and around Vesali.

During this period, Shakyamuni fell gravely ill but, thinking it wrong for him to die without giving his followers final instructions, resolved to overcome the sickness by strong effort and by being mindful and thoughtful. He did so and thus prolonged his life for a while.

When Shakyamuni had recovered, Ananda said to him, "World-honored One, I have seen you in good health and fine condition. But when you were sick, I did not know what to do. Everything before my eyes went dark; my faculties were upset. But I took some small comfort from the idea that you would not leave the world without parting from the monks."

Shakyamuni replied, "Ananda, what can the monks expect of me? I have taught them everything, both the esoteric and the exoteric, for the Tathagata is not the kind of teacher who conceals things from his followers. If I felt that I should lead the Order or that the Order was dependent on me, I would have something to say. But I do not feel that way. Why then should I make pronouncements?

"Moreover, Ananda, I am old and frail. I am eighty. Like an old cart that can only be kept in operation by the help of leather thongs, the body of the Tathagata can only be kept going with much help. Only when I am in the deep state of meditation where I am free of all suffering and entertain no thoughts about anything is my body at rest. Therefore, Ananda, you must all be lamps unto yourselves. You must rely on yourselves and on no one else. You must make the Law your light and your support and rely on nothing else."

This was Shakyamuni's way of saying that the most important things for Buddhists are these: (1) To meditate mindfully and thoughtfully on the four insights that the body is impure, perception leads to suffering, the mind is impermanent, and the world is transient and in this way to eliminate the suffering and craving arising from these four things. This teaching is known as the four insights.* (2) To be a lamp unto oneself by first raising one's spiritual level through relying on the lamp of the Law in the form of these basic teachings (that the body is impure, that perception leads to suffering, that the mind is impermanent, and that the world is transient) and then relying on oneself in further deepening and elevating one's level of understanding and religious practice.

Shakyamuni concluded his teaching on this point in this way: "Ananda, now or after my death, of all those who are willing to study, the people who are a lamp and support to themselves, who

*Practicing these four insights is considered vitally important to all people in all stages of development from that of the beginner to that of the *arhat* and the Buddha.

rely on no one else, who employ the Law as a lamp and a support and call on nothing else shall reach the ultimate height."

Shakyamuni remained for some time in Vesali, enjoying the many gardens and places he had visited in the past and recalling the impressions they had made on him. He already knew that his death was only three months away.

Mara, the Evil One, approached Shakyamuni at this time and told him that it was time for him to leave the world. The sutras say that Mara had made a similar statement shortly after the enlightenment. At that time, Shakyamuni had said that he would die when the members of the Order and the lay believers had matured in knowledge of the Law, practiced it well, taught it to the people around them, used it to confound other teachings, and proclaimed it freely. Mara said that all these things had come to pass and that it was therefore time for Shakyamuni to die. Shakyamuni replied that he would not die until his religion had become perfected, widespread, and known to many people and until many people had found liberation through it. Once again, Mara said that all this had come to pass.

Finally, Shakyamuni said, "Mara, be at ease. The Tathagata's death is not far away. In three months the Tathagata will die." In saying this, Shakyamuni rejected the remainder of the span of life allotted to him. When this happened, a great tremor shook the earth, and thunder roared, as the Buddha recited this stanza:

> "The sage has abandoned all actions
> Causing life, equal or unequal.
> Inwardly rejoicing and deep in meditation,
> He broke his own life like a mirror."

The Four Great Teachings and the Final Meal Shakyamuni and Ananda went to the Great Forest Monastery on the outskirts of Vesali. Shakyamuni instructed Ananda to have all the monks in the vicinity gather at the hall. When they had done so, Shakyamuni came forth, took the seat prepared for him, and told them that they must abide by his teachings for the sake of the preservation of his righteous Law, the well-being of mankind, the pity of the world, and the good and gain of man and gods. He next listed the truths he had taught (thirty-seven in all): the Four Insights, the Four Kinds of Right Effort, the Four Bases of Supernatural Power, the Five Moral Powers, the Five Organs of Good Conduct, the Seven Qualities of Wisdom, and the Eightfold Noble Path.* People who have abandoned the secular life and become members of the Order must practice these truths if Buddhism is to prosper.

Then Shakyamuni said: "O brothers, I have taught you that all things are fated to decline and destruction. You must diligently strive to reach your goal. Before long, the Tathagata will die. In three months, the Tathagata will die. My age is fulfilled. Little of my life remains. I leave you. I have made my own source of reliance. Brothers, be earnest. Abide by the truths and the good precepts. Be thoughtful in meditation and keep guard over your own minds. Those who are earnest and live in the Law and the precepts will escape the cycle of transmigrations and put an end to suffering."

At this time and once again immediately before his death, Shakyamuni gave the paramount instruction that, since all things

*Since they are a compendium of basic Buddhist teachings, it will be helpful to expand slightly on the truths that Shakyamuni listed for his followers on this important occasion.

1. The Four Insights. The insights that the world is transient, the body is impure, perception leads to suffering, and the mind is impermanent.

2. The Four Kinds of Right Effort. These are the effort to prevent evil from arising, to abandon evil when arisen, to produce good, and to increase good when produced.

3. The Four Bases of Supernatural Power. These are will, exertion, thought, and investigation. All of these must be accompanied by insight and right effort.

4. The Five Moral Powers. These are belief, endeavor, memory, meditation, and wisdom.

5. The Five Organs of Good Conduct. These are the organs that lead man to good conduct: the sense of belief, the sense of endeavor, the sense of memory, the sense of meditation, and the sense of wisdom.

6. The Seven Qualities of Wisdom. These are the requisites for attaining enlightenment: investigation of the Law, endeavor, the joy of practicing the true teachings, tranquillity, the cessation of clinging, contemplation, and mindfulness.

7. The Eightfold Noble Path: right view, right thinking, right speech, right action, right living, right effort, right memory, and right meditation.

are impermanent, the Buddhist must use all of his time in earnest
effort to reach the final goal.

After a stay in Vesali, Shakyamuni and Ananda went northward
to the village of Bhanda, then to Hatthi, Amba, Jambu, and then
out of the kingdom of the Vajjis to Bhoga, in the land of the Mallas,
where, at the Ananda shrine, Shakyamuni preached on the topic of
the Four Great References. According to this sermon, the members
of the Order are instructed to be critical of all reported teachings;
to examine them diligently; to compare them with the scriptures
and the genuine teachings; and, on the basis of such comparison,
to decide whether they are true. Four kinds of reports to be
subjected to such inquiry are cited: words reported as having been
heard directly from Shakyamuni himself, words reported as having been heard from a group of elders, words reported as having
been heard from several elders, and words reported as having been
heard from a single elder. Monks must not accept blindly what has
been said but must examine it on the basis outlined above. Today,
too, it is important to investigate what is offered as truth in the
light of the counsel of trustworthy leaders and authoritative scriptures before accepting it as true. Buddhists are taught to compare
an opinion with teachings, reason, and actuality to determine
whether it is true.

Then Shakyamuni and his followers went to Pava, where they
stayed in the grove of a smith named Chunda, who, upon hearing
of the arrival of the group, the next morning offered them a meal of
fine foods. This was to be the last meal that Shakyamuni ever ate.
He was fatigued by age and the heat, and the food diligently prepared by Chunda caused a severe gastric upset and a diarrhetic
attack.

Nonetheless, after the meal and before retiring, Shakyamuni
gladdened the heart of Chunda with teachings and sermons. Parting from their host, Shakyamuni and his group left for Kushinagara.
On the way, under a roadside tree, Shakyamuni asked Ananda to
fold a robe in four and spread it on the ground, since he was tired
and wanted to sit down. He then asked Ananda to bring him
water, since he was thirsty. Ananda told him that the five hundred

carts that had just passed had stirred up the water in the nearby stream, making it shallow and muddy. He went on to say that the river Kakuttha was not far away. Its waters were pure and clear, and the bank was a pleasant place. Ananda suggested that the World-honored One wait to drink until they reached the river. But Shakyamuni insisted on water at once. This exchange having been repeated three times, Ananda decided that there was nothing to do but obey, took up his begging bowl, and walked toward the nearby stream. To his astonishment, as he approached, he discovered that the muddied waters were clean and pure.

Upon returning, Ananda praised the immense powers and might of the Tathagata and told him of the cleansing of the water, some of which he offered Shakyamuni. After drinking, Shakyamuni rested quietly. A caravan leader named Pukkusa, who happened to be passing by, approached, made a respectful greeting, and asked the World-honored One many questions about meditation. Shakyamuni told Pukkusa that in a truly unified state of meditation a person could be fully aware of five hundred passing wagons or of thunder overhead without actually hearing or seeing either. This astonished Pukkusa and won him to the Buddhist faith. In the sutra, his confession of faith is couched in the following conventional form: "It is wonderful and marvelous. It is as if a fallen man had been lifted up, as if what was concealed had been revealed, as if a lost man had found the way, as if a light had shone in the dark enabling those who have eyes to see. In all of these many ways, the World-honored One has made the truth clear to me. World-honored One, I take refuge in the Buddha, the Law, and the Order and wish to be accepted as a lifelong believer."

Pukkusa gave two robes of soft, gold-colored silk to Shakyamuni, who said that he would accept one but that the other should be given to Ananda. Ananda refused and put the robe on Shakyamuni instead. As he did this, he was amazed to see that the clear, bright effulgence of Shakyamuni's skin dulled the luster of the gold-colored cloth. Shakyamuni then explained to him that on two occasions the body of a Tathagata gives off a radiant light: when he has attained ultimate enlightenment and when he is about to enter nirvana. Shakyamuni said, "The Tathagata will die in the

late watch of this night in the Sala Grove of the Mallas at Upavatta-
na. Let us now go to the Kakuttha River."

After Shakyamuni and his followers had bathed in the river and
had drunk some water, Shakyamuni said to Chundaka, the younger
brother of Shariputra, "Fold a robe in four and spread it on the
ground. I am tired and wish to lie down." So the World-honored
One lay on his right side, with one leg resting on the other, like a
lion, and meditated in a thoughtful and mindful fashion.

Even in his last hours of pain and old age, Shakyamuni was
concerned about the feelings of the faithful. He said to Ananda,
"It is possible that someone will cause Chunda the smith to feel
remorse by telling him he has incurred evil and loss by giving me
the meal that has caused my death. But you must relieve Chunda of
remorse by telling him that you have heard it from the very mouth
of the Tathagata that, through this meal, he has incurred great
good and gain. There are two meals of equal merit and fruit and
of greater merit and fruit than any other: the meal offered to a
Tathagata at the time of his perfect enlightenment and the meal
offered a Tathagata at the time of his passing into nirvana. By giving
me this meal, Chunda the smith has laid up great good karma
leading to long life, fame, heavenly fortune, and sovereign power."

This incident is concluded with the following stanza:

"Good fortune increases for him who gives.
Malice does not accumulate for the person who controls his mind.
The good person abandons all evil
And, by destroying lust, wrath, and ignorance, becomes com-
    pletely tranquil."

The Twin Sala Trees   Then Shakyamuni told Ananda that they
                must go to the *sala* grove at Upavattana of
Kushinagara, on the opposite bank of the Hiranyavati River. When
they reached the place, he told Ananda to make a bed for him
between two *sala* trees, the head of the bed to the north. Being
tired, Shakyamuni lay down on the couch Ananda prepared.
Again, he is described as lying on his right side, with one leg rest-

ing on the other, like a lion. And he was mindful and thoughtful.

As has already been mentioned (page 168), at this time, the *sala* trees burst into bloom out of season, and heavenly music and fragrances filled the air in homage to the Tathagata, who said, however, that this was not the way to do him honor, for he could best be honored by reverence for the Law and living in accordance with it.

Some of the multitude of gods who came to witness the final hours of the Tathagata and for whose sake Shakyamuni had the venerable Upavana step aside tore their hair, stretched out their arms, and rolled about while crying that it was too soon for the World-honored One to die and for the good light of the world to go out. But those gods who were already enlightened and free of all desires were mindful and thoughtful and said, "All things are impermanent. How can there be anything that does not pass away?"

Ananda then complained that after the death of the Tathagata the Order would be deprived of the opportunities its members had enjoyed of meeting with and paying respect to the many enlightened monks who had gathered around him during his lifetime. Shakyamuni told Ananda that after his death believers should revere four places: the place of his birth (Lumbini), the place where he attained enlightenment (Bodh Gaya), the place where he preached the first sermon (Deer Park in Benares), and the place of his death (Kushinagara). Good, faithful believers would gather in these places, he said, and if any one of them should die while making such a pilgrimage, he would be reborn in a blessed state.

After advice on other things that were thought likely to happen after the death of Shakyamuni, Ananda asked for instructions about the funeral. Shakyamuni replied that the monks should not trouble themselves about it but should diligently and enthusiastically apply themselves for the sake of the highest good. Faithful believers among the nobles and Brahmans would take care of the Tathagata's funeral. Ananda nonetheless asked how the ceremony should be carried out. Shakyamuni replied that it should be the kind of funeral afforded to a wheel-rolling king and then explained in detail.

Unable to bear the thought that the World-honored One, whom

he had served for more than twenty years, was leaving him while he had not himself attained the stage of *arhat* enlightenment, Ananda went to his quarters, closed the door, and wept.

After a while, Shakyamuni summoned Ananda, who, after a slight delay, finally came. Shakyamuni told him not to grieve and weep. "After all, I have taught you that we must be parted from those who are close and dear to us. It is unreasonable to think that anything that has come into being will escape dissolution. For a long time, you have cared for the Tathagata with compassion and love, undivided and immeasurable, in actions, words, and thoughts. You have done many good things. Now strive to make progress. If you do, you too will soon be freed of all illusions."

After thanking and encouraging Ananda in this way, Shakyamuni said to the assembly of monks, "Ananda is a wise man, for he knows the right time for members of the Order of both sexes, lay believers of both sexes, kings, ministers, leaders of other religions, and their followers to come to see the Tathagata. And four miraculous things shall be true of him: the four classes of believers— male and female members of the Order and male and female lay believers—shall be gladdened and made happy by meeting him or hearing him preach."

So that they would not be grieved at having missed the final hours, the Mallas were invited to the *sala* grove. And people of all ages and both sexes were sorrowful and wept. When they had made their farewells, an old wandering ascetic named Subhadda came to observe the death of a Buddha, a rarity in this world. At first, Ananda refused to allow him to approach; but, hearing the talk between the two, Shakyamuni summoned Subhadda to his side and gave him religious instruction. Subhadda at once asked to be admitted to the Order, gained ultimate enlightenment, and died slightly before Shakyamuni. This was the last person converted to Buddhism by Shakyamuni himself.*

*This account contains a verse that is the oldest reference to chronology in Shakyamuni's life: "At twenty-nine, I gave up the secular life in search of what is good, Subhadda, and fifty-one years have passed since then." Seven years passed from the time that he left his father's house until his enlightenment at the age of thirty-five, and he was active as a Buddha for forty-five years.

Since he had taught monks around him many things so far, there were no more questions to be asked. Shakyamuni then made his final pronouncement: "Now, brothers, I exhort you. It is the Law that all component things must decline and decay. Attain your goal through diligence."

He then entered successive stages of deeper and deeper meditation and, in the last part of the night, died and entered the state of total tranquillity.

According to the sutra, stanzas were uttered at this time by the gods Brahma and Indra and by Anuruddha, Ananda, and others. The one uttered by Indra is the famous Verse of Impermanence cited earlier in this book.

The Mallas paid homage to the body of Shakyamuni with garlands of fragrant flowers and with music for one week. Deciding that the time for cremation had come, they took the body from the *sala* grove, entered the city through the north gate, turned from the center to the east gate, and finally carried it to the Makuta-bandhana Shrine farther eastward. Following Ananda's instructions, the Mallas made a handsome coffin and treated the body of Shakyamuni with the respect and attention owing to that of a wheel-rolling king. They built a pyre, but when they tried to ignite it, the wood refused to burn. Maha-Kashyapa had not yet returned.

Maha-Kashyapa was regarded as the chief disciple after the deaths of Shariputra and Maudgalyayana. Away on a trip to the Southern Mountain in Magadha, he sensed that the death of Shakyamuni was near and, with his five hundred companions, set out at once on the return journey. On the road between Pava and Kushinagara, they encountered a believer of another religious sect carrying a *mandarava* blossom. Their questions as to the whereabouts of Shakyamuni were greeted with the news that the World-honored One had died about a week ago and that the *mandarava* flower had been part of the funeral decorations.

This was a sudden and great shock. The monks who had not yet been enlightened wept, beat their breasts, and prostrated themselves, saying, "Too soon has the World-honored One passed away.

Too soon has the Blessed One died. Too soon has the eye of the world closed." But the monks who were enlightened and free of desires and delusions were mindful and thoughtful and said, "All things are impermanent. It is impossible that anything created should escape destruction."

Maha-Kashyapa, however, overheard one old monk saying that the death of Shakyamuni was cause for rejoicing, not sorrow, since, with him gone, they would all be free to do precisely what they wanted without being advised and reprimanded by him at every turn. Maha-Kashyapa thought that if shameless monks of this kind, willing to break the moral precepts, were to increase in the Order, Buddhism would soon lose its laws and would eventually decline and fail. He saw at once that to prevent this it was essential to collect the true doctrines and thereupon decided to produce a compendium of the sutras and other basic Buddhist teachings.

When he reached Kushinagara, Maha-Kashyapa ignited the pyre, and the cremation ceremonies were concluded. The relics of the Buddha's body were distributed equally among eight nations and regions professing the Buddhist faith, and stupas were built to house them in each place. It is said that Emperor Asoka further subdivided them and that eighty-four thousand stupas were constructed in and beyond India.

The First Council   When the funeral ceremonies for the World-honored One were over, Maha-Kashyapa called together the monks gathered in that place from various parts of the nation and suggested that a council be held to collect all of the teachings of the Buddha. This was essential if the true Law was to survive and if false laws and precepts were to be prevented from springing up. The assembly agreed to the suggestion and at once chose five hundred *arhats* to participate in the task. The teachings were divided into two categories: first, sermons and precepts and, second, ordinances governing all aspects of the daily lives of members of the Order. Since, in those days in India, writing was highly uncommon and convenient writing materials did not exist, reliance had to be placed on the memories of *arhats* who had actually heard the words of Shakyamuni. The council to collect all of these teachings was held during the three-month rainy season three months after the death of Shakyamuni. It took place in the Cave of the Seven Leaves at the foot of Mount Vebhara on the outskirts of Rajagaha, the capital of Magadha. King Ajatasattu made all the necessary preparations for it before the rainy season set in.

I have said that five hundred *arhats* were selected to collect the teachings. This is not precisely accurate. Four hundred and ninety-nine were *arhats,* but Ananda had not yet reached the final stage of enlightenment when the selection was made. Nonetheless, Maha-Kashyapa and many of the other monks agreed that it would be impossible to exclude him. For the last twenty-five years of Shakyamuni's life, Ananda had been in constant attendance on his master. He had heard more of Shakyamuni's sermons than anyone else and had remembered all of them accurately. Furthermore, he had heard and learned from Shakyamuni and other monks all of the sermons delivered before he himself had entered the religious life.

Ananda wanted desperately to become totally enlightened before the great work started. But on the night before the council he still had not attained his goal. He stayed up until late without success. Then, according to tradition, when he went to bed, his feet refused to stay down, and his head rose from the pillow. Suddenly, in that instant, he was enlightened and finally qualified to participate in the council.

Maha-Kashyapa led the meeting. Upali, the former slave and barber, known for his deep knowledge of the subject, recited all the ordinances, and Ananda recited all the sermons. Upali first sat in the seat of the Buddha and recited all of the ordinances, one by one. The assembly listened, checked to make sure that everything Upali said was correct, and in this way evolved a collection of rules for daily monastic life. Then Ananda took the seat of the Buddha and recited all of the sermons. Deeply moved, the assembly approved what they heard, and the first collection of the sermons was compiled. It is thought that the phrase "Thus have

I heard," which occurs at the opening of all of the sutras, was repeated by Ananda each time he started a sermon. All of the sermons and rules pronounced by the Buddha during his lifetime were recited and orally corrected at the First Council, but it was not for another four or five centuries that the Buddhist canon was given written form.*

---

*In the hundreds of years that passed from the end of the First Council to the time when the canon was written down, undoubtedly amplifications and losses and other changes occurred. Nonetheless, the versions of these works that exist today as the primitive Buddhist canon are invaluable for the light they shed on Shakyamuni as a historical being.

The Pali canon consists of three parts called Ti-pitaka, or the Three Baskets: the Sutra Basket (Sutta-pitaka), containing the sermons; the Ordinance Basket (Vinaya-pitaka), containing the rules for monastic life; and the Treatise Basket (Abhidhamma-pitaka), which contains doctrinal commentaries and is of a later date than the other two.

Teachings delivered by Shakyamuni in his lifetime must have reached an immense number, for in the primitive Pali canon there are more than ten thousand sutras. It is true that some of them are short, but some of them run to considerable length. The Sutra Basket is divided into five major groups; the Long Sayings (Digha-nikaya); the Middle-length Sayings (Majjhima-nikaya); the Kindred Sayings (Samyutta-nikaya), in which sutras are categorized according to content; the Gradual Sayings (Anguttara-nikaya), in which sutras are categorized according to the number of topics occurring in each; and the Minor Sayings (Khuddaka-nikaya) of fifteen fascicles, containing miscellaneous short works and including some sutras that are late and others that are older than all the others.

In the Second Council, held one hundred years after the death of the Buddha, seven hundred *arhats* participated. According to tradition in the Pali texts, a third council, during the reign of Emperor Asoka, was held in Pataliputra some two hundred and thirty years after the Buddha's death. In this meeting, one thousand *arhats* took part. In the later history of the religion, additional councils were held by the adherents of both Northern (Mahayana) and Southern (Theravada) Buddhism, as stated in the documents of these religions.

18. A Buddhist Guide for Living

Having given an outline of the life of Shakyamuni and having sketched the lofty religious philosophy that he presented to mankind, I should like to conclude this book with three examples of the kind of practical guidance the Buddha's teachings offer. The first instance shows the principles of thrift and conservation deemed suitable for members of the Order.

At the conclusion of the First Council, Maha-Kashyapa instructed Ananda to carry out the wish expressed by Shakyamuni before his death that the audacious and disobedient monk Channa be strictly ostracized by all the members of the Order. With five hundred monks, Ananda traveled up the Ganges to Kosambi, the capital of the state of Vansa, where Channa was living at the time. When he arrived there, he went to a royal park in the city and sat under a tree. At the time, King Udena was strolling in the park with some courtesans. Upon hearing that the holy teacher Ananda was in the vicinity, the ladies informed their royal master and requested permission to hear what the sage had to say. The permission granted, they hurried to Ananda, whose sermons delighted them so much that they made him a present of five hundred upper garments. Happy and pleased, the ladies returned to the king, who asked them about Ananda. They told him of the wonderful sermons they had heard and of the five hundred upper garments they had presented to Ananda. The surprised Udena jokingly asked if Ananda was going into the garment trade and then went himself to Ananda, asked whether he had received the garments from the courtesans, and inquired what he intended to do with them.

Ananda said, "O king, I intend to give them to five hundred monks whose upper garments are tattered."

"What, then, will you do with the five hundred tattered garments?" asked the king.

"We will make bedspreads of them."

"And what will you do with the five hundred old bedspreads?"

"We will make pillowcases of them."

"And what will you do with the five hundred old pillowcases?"

"We will make floor mats of them."

"And what will you do with the five hundred old floor mats?"

"We will make foot towels of them."

"And what will you do with the five hundred old foot towels?"

"We will make cleaning rags of them."

"And what will you do with the five hundred old cleaning rags?"

"We will shred them, combine them with mud, and use them for flooring."

From this, Udena saw that monks waste nothing and use all things carefully and to the fullest extent. He was so delighted that he presented Ananda with five hundred additional upper garments. This was the first time that Ananda had ever received such a donation.

Ananda then proceeded to the famous Goshita Park Monastery in the city of Kosambi—the enthusiastic Buddhist layman Goshita had donated a park for the creation of the monastery—to meet Channa, who was staying there. Upon learning that Ananda and five hundred monks had arrived, Channa came out to greet them.

When Ananda announced that the elders of the Order were ostracizing him for his past disobedience, Channa, crying that such punishment was tantamount to the death sentence, fell to the ground in a faint. Later he repented for what he had done and lived apart in great humility and striving for spiritual progress until he ultimately attained the enlightenment of an *arhat*. At that time, Ananda revoked the punishment of ostracism.

The second example of practical guidance occurs in the Sutra of Good Fortune, which explains the maximum happinesses to which men can attain and suggests practical ways they can be achieved. This sutra is recited daily by the faithful in lands where Southern (Theravada) Buddhism prevails.

Once when Shakyamuni was in the Jetavana Monastery, a deity of surpassing beauty approached him and said, "Many gods and men have longed for various blessings and have sought the highest blessing. World-honored One, tell me what is the highest blessing."

And Shakyamuni answered with the following precepts:

1. Not to associate with fools but to associate with wise men and to revere people who are worthy of reverence. This is the highest blessing.

2. To live in a suitable place, to have accumulated merits and virtues in previous lives, and to have correct wishes. This is the highest blessing.

3. To be learned and skillful, to be trained and to have studied much, and to speak words of good teachings. This is the highest blessing.

4. To care for parents, to provide well for wife and children, and to have a way of making a living that is pure and correct. This is the highest blessing.

5. To give alms, to perform correct actions, to care lovingly for and to protect relatives, and to do nothing that is blameworthy. This is the highest blessing.

6. To take no pleasure in wickedness and to refrain from evil acts, to control one's own consumption of intoxicants, and to be selfless in all things. This is the highest blessing.

7. To respect others, to be humble, to know what is sufficient, to be grateful for what others do, and from time to time to hear the Law taught. This is the highest blessing.

8. To be forbearing, to speak gently, to meet with people of religion and occasionally to discuss the Law and teachings. This is the highest blessing.

9. To make efforts, to be trained in the Buddha's way, to comprehend the Noble Truths, and to find enlightenment in nirvana.
This is the highest blessing.

10. To remain unshaken by contact with the things of the secular
world, to be free of anxiety, to be undefiled, and to be tranquil.
This is the highest blessing.

11. Those who do these things are undefeated in all things,
prosperous in all things, and theirs is the highest blessing.

The third and final example, the Sutra of Reverence to the Six
Directions, is a more detailed explanation of the ways human beings
ought to conduct relations with all classes of associates.

Once when the World-honored One had left the Bamboo Grove
Monastery near Rajagaha early in the morning and was going into
the city to beg for alms, he saw a young householder named
Singala, who, having washed his body and hair, was making worshipful reverences to the six directions (north, south, east, west, zenith, and nadir), as was his daily custom. Shakyamuni approached
the young man and asked why he was doing this. The young man
replied that it had been his father's dying wish that he do so, though
he himself did not understand the reason behind the practice. Shakyamuni said that such was not the noble way to worship the six directions and, in response to the young man's request, explained the
proper way. He first said that one must remain free of the fourteen
evils: 1–4. freedom from the four vices, which are killing, stealing,
sexual misconduct, and lying. 5–8. freedom from the reasons for
committing evil: desire, anger, ignorance, and fear. 9–14. Avoid-
ance of the six ways of dissipating wealth: indulgence in intoxicants,
wandering the streets at late hours, infatuation with holiday theatricals, infatuation with gambling, association with evil companions,
and laziness.

He then explained the six kinds of loss accruing to each of the
six ways of dissipating wealth.

1. Indulgence in intoxicants leads to these things: (a) Loss of
wealth, (b) Quarreling, (c) All kinds of disease, (d) Bad reputation,
(e) Exposure of parts of the body that should remain concealed,
(f) Decline of the intellect.

2. Wandering the streets late at night leads to the following

things: (a) Danger and lack of protection for the person himself, (b) Lack of protection for his wife and children, (c) Lack of protection for his property, (d) Liability to suspicion and all manner of evils, (e) Liability to false rumors, (f) Occurrence of much suffering and trouble.

3. Infatuation with holiday theatricals leads to the following constant preoccupations: (a) Where is the dancing? (b) Where is the singing? (c) Where is the music? (d) Where are the jokesters and storytellers? (e) Where are the cymbal players? (f) Where are the drummers?

4. Infatuation with gambling leads to the following things: (a) The winner is hated by the loser, (b) The loser wails and suffers, (c) The gambler loses his property, (d) Assemblies of people refuse to trust the gambler's word, (e) The gambler is despised by friends and acquaintances, (f) The gambler is not desired as a matrimonial partner.

5. Association with evil companions means that the following kinds of people become one's associates: (a) Wicked people, (b) Drunkards, (c) Alcoholics, (d) Swindlers, (e) Deceivers, (f) Rowdies.

6. Laziness means that the person refuses to work under the following conditions: (a) When it is too cold, (b) When it is too hot, (c) When it is too late, (d) When it is too early, (e) When he is hungry, (f) When he is thirsty.

Using all these excuses, the lazy person does not work, fails to acquire additional wealth, and loses whatever wealth he may have.

In connection with associating with evil companions, Shakyamuni described the following kinds of people as enemies disguised as friends:

1. The person who takes things, because he later takes what he earlier gave, wants much for little, does things for his friends only out of fear or out of inescapable necessity, and is friendly only for his own benefit.

2. The person who is amiable in words, because he is friendly in relation to the past, friendly in relation to the future, meaninglessly affable, and unreliable when true need arises.

3. The flatterer, because he approves of one's evil deeds, dis-

approves of one's good deeds, praises one to one's face, and speaks evil of one behind one's back.

4. The person who is a friend in amusements only, because he is a companion in excessive indulgence in and addiction to alcohol, in wandering the streets at late hours, in infatuation with holiday theatricals, and in enthusiastic gambling.

The following four kinds of people are described as true friends:

1. The helpful person, because he protects the prodigal, protects the prodigal's property, protects the fearful, and offers twice what is needed when work must be done.

2. The person who is the same in suffering and happiness, because he tells his secrets to his friend, keeps his friend's secrets, does not forsake his friend in time of danger, and is willing to give his life for his friend.

3. The one who speaks to one's benefit, because he prevents one from doing evil, encourages one to do good, tells his friend what his friend does not know, and points out the way to be reborn in a heaven.

4. The sympathetic person, because he does not rejoice at his friend's sorrow, does rejoice at his friend's prosperity, prevents his friend from criticizing others, and encourages his friend to speak highly of others.

Shakyamuni then explained that the true Buddhist must worship the six directions with the intention of ministering to the people of those directions: parents (east), teachers (south), wife (west), friends and acquaintances (north), servants and other employees (nadir), and men of religion (zenith). There are five ways in which a person ought to minister to each of these groups and five ways in which members of the groups must show compassion in return for such ministrations.

Parents

Children should minister to their parents in the following ways: (1) Caring for parents as they cared for one when one was a child, (2) Fulfilling their duties, (3) Maintaining the family line, (4) Carrying on the family inheritance, (5) Respecting and making offerings to the family ancestors.

Parents show compassion for these services in the following ways: (1) Restraining their children from evil, (2) Encouraging them to do good, (3) Teaching them arts and sciences, (4) Arranging suitable marriages for them, (5) Giving them their inheritance when the proper time comes.

Teachers

Students should minister to teachers in the following ways: (1) Standing in sign of respectful greeting, (2) Attendance on them, (3) Obedience, (4) Careful service, (5) Reverence and affection for learning.

In return, teachers show compassion to their students in the following ways: (1) Training them well, (2) Instructing them well, (3) Teaching them all arts and sciences, (4) Introducing them to their own friends and acquaintances, (5) Protecting them in all things.

Wife

A man should minister to his wife in the following ways: (1) Respecting her, (2) Not despising her, (3) Being sexually faithful to her, (4) Giving her authority, (5) Giving her clothes and ornaments.

In return, the wife should show compassion for her husband in the following ways: (1) Performing her duties well, (2) Treating employees kindly, (3) Being sexually faithful to him, (4) Protecting and guarding his property, (5) Being skillful and industrious in all her work.

Friends

One should minister to one's friends in the following five ways: (1) Being generous, (2) Speaking affectionately to them, (3) Working for their good, (4) Regarding them as a unity with oneself, (5) Telling them no lies, never deceiving them, and never treating them unjustly.

Friends should respond to these ministrations by showing compassion in the following ways: (1) Protecting the friend when he is prodigal, (2) Protecting his property when he is prodigal, (3)

Protecting him when he is afraid, (4) Staying with him when he is in trouble or danger, (5) Respecting and serving his relatives.

Servants and Employees

A master should minister to servants and employees in the following ways: (1) Assigning duties according to their abilities, (2) Providing them with food and wages, (3) Caring for them well when they are ill, (4) Sharing delicacies with them, (5) Allowing them to rest when suitable.

Servants and employees should show compassion to their masters in the following ways: (1) Arising before the master does, (2) Going to bed after he does, (3) Taking only what is given, (4) Performing their duties conscientiously, (5) Upholding the master's good name.

Men of Religion

People should minister to men of religion in the following ways: (1) Performing deeds filled with love, (2) Speaking words filled with love, (3) Having thoughts filled with love, (4) Keeping the door always open to them, (5) Providing them with food.

Men of religion should respond to such ministrations by being compassionate in the following ways: (1) Restraining people from evil, (2) Encouraging them to do good, (3) Being compassionate and sympathetic with good thoughts, (4) Teaching them what they have not heard, (5) Clarifying what they have already heard and thus showing them the way to rebirth in a heaven.

When he heard this sermon, Singala was deeply moved and became a devout Buddhist for the rest of his life, entrusting himself to the Three Treasures: the Buddha, the Law, and the Order.

Glossary

Where the transliteration of Sanskrit or Pali words used in the text differs from the original form, the latter is given in parentheses with correct diacritical markings. In the abbreviations used here, S stands for Sanskrit and P for Pali. It should be noted that a number of the terms included here are not common to both languages, hence only one original spelling is given.

Abhaya (P, S) A prince of Magadha in the time of Shakyamuni who was a devout Jain and later became a follower of Shakyamuni. Among the Jains he was noted for his wisdom.

Abhidhamma-pitaka *See* Ti-pitaka.

Agama (Āgama, P, S) sutras One of the oldest extant Buddhist scriptures, existing in two slightly different forms. The Agama sutras of the Pali canon consist of the complete Sutta-pitaka (Digha-nikaya, Majjhima-nikaya, Samyutta-nikaya, Anguttara-nikaya, and Khuddaka-nikaya), while the Agama sutras of the Chinese Mahayana canon consist of the first four collections of the Sutta-pitaka, as well as fragments and independent sutras drawn from other sources. These sutras contain fairly detailed accounts of Shakyamuni's activities during the first two or three years after he attained enlightenment and during the year preceding his entrance into nirvana.

Ajatasattu (Ajātasattu, P; Ajātaśatru, S) King of Magadha and son of King Bimbisara.

Alara-Kalama (Āḷāra-Kālāma, P; Ārāḍa-Kālāma, S) A hermit-sage under whom Shakyamuni studied.

Ambapali (Ambapālī, P; Āmrapālī, S) A courtesan and follower of Shakyamuni.

anagamin *See* four merits.

Ananda (Ānanda, P, S) A cousin of Shakyamuni and one of the Buddha's ten great disciples. He was famous for his excellent memory and is supposed to have memorized the Buddha's sermons, which were later recorded as sutras.

Anathapindika (Anāthapiṇḍika, P; Anāthapiṇḍada, S) "One who gives to the needy," a name given to Sudatta.

Anga (Aṅga, P, S) One of the sixteen major kingdoms of India in Shakyamuni's time.

Anguttara-nikaya (Aṅguttara-nikāya, P) The "Gradual Sayings," one of the five major sutra collections of the Sutta-pitaka of the Pali canon.

Anuruddha (P; Aniruddha, S) A cousin of Shakyamuni and one of the Buddha's ten great disciples.

Aranyaka (Āraṇyaka, S; Āraññaka, P) The "Forest Treatises," compiled around 600 B.C., one of the four types of literature included in the Veda.

arhat (S; *arahat*, P) Literally, "man of worth, honorable one." (1) One who is free from all cravings and thus from rebirth. (2) One of the titles of the Buddha. (3) The highest stage attained by a Theravada Buddhist.

artha (S) Material gain, one of the four ideals for mankind, according to ancient Indian philosophy.

ashura (S; *asura*, P, S) A titan or spirit that may be either good or evil. The *ashuras* are the enemies of the *devas*, celestial or heavenly deities, and are the mightiest of all demons.

Asita (P, S) The seer who prophesied that if Shakyamuni remained at home he would become a great wheel-rolling king and that if he left home he would become a Buddha.

Asoka (P; Aśoka, S) A devout Buddhist monarch of the third century B.C., the third emperor of the Maurya dynasty, who unified most of India under his rule and fostered the dissemination of Buddhism.

Assaji (P; Aśvajit, S) One of the five fellow seekers who practiced ascetic disciplines with Shakyamuni and became one of his earliest disciples.

Assaka (Assakā, P; Aśmakā, S) One of the sixteen major kingdoms of India in Shakyamuni's time.

atman (*ātman*, S) The individual self or the soul in Brahmanic thought.

Avanti (P, S) One of the sixteen major kingdoms of India in Shakyamuni's time.

Avatamsaka-sutra (S) The Flower Garland Sutra, a lengthy sutra that sets forth the practices of a bodhisattva.

Bamboo Grove Monastery (Veḷuvana, P; Veṇuvana, S)   The first monastery of the Buddhist Order, built by King Bimbisara.

Benares (Bārāṇasī, P, S)   A city on the Ganges; the capital of the ancient kingdom of Kasi.

Bhaddakapilani (Bhaddakapilānī, P; Bhadra-Kapilānī, S)   A follower of Shakyamuni; the wife of Maha-Kashyapa.

Bhaddiya (P; Bhadrika, S)   One of the five fellow seekers who practiced ascetic disciplines with Shakyamuni and became one of his earliest disciples.

bhagavat (P, S)   World-honored One, an epithet of a Buddha.

bhikkhu (P; *bhikṣu,* S)   Literally, "beggar." A religious mendicant who has left home and renounced all possessions in order to follow the way of the Buddha and who has become a fully ordained monk.

bhikkhuni (*bhikkhunī,* P; *bhikṣuṇī,* S)   A Buddhist nun observing the same rules as a *bhikkhu.*

Bimbisara (Bimbisāra, P, S)   King of Magadha and a follower of Shakyamuni.

Bodh Gaya (Buddhagayā, P, S)   The place where Shakyamuni Buddha attained enlightenment, near present-day Gaya.

Bodhi (P, S)   Prince of Vansa and son of King Udena who is known through his appearance in the Discourse to Prince Bodhi Sutra.

Bodhi (P, S)   Wisdom, enlightenment, buddhahood. (1) The wisdom of Shakyamuni Buddha's enlightenment. (2) Nirvana. (3) The way to nirvana. (4) The Buddhist Way.

bodhisattva (S; *bodhisatta,* P)   *Bodhi,* buddhahood; *sattva,* living being. (1) A being in the final stage prior to attaining buddhahood. (2) One who devotes himself to attaining enlightenment not only for himself but also for all sentient beings.

Brahma (Brahmā, P, S)   One of the three major deities of Hinduism, along with Viṣṇu (Vishnu) and Śiva (Shiva). Adopted as one of the protective deities of Buddhism.

brahma-charin (*brahma-cārin,* P, S)   Studenthood; the first of the traditional Brahmanic four periods of life.

brahma-chariya (*brahma-cariyā,* P; *brahma-caryā,* S)   Both the studenthood period (see *brahma-charin*) and the life of purity and celibacy enforced during it.

Brahman (*brāhmaṇa,* P, S)   A member of the priestly caste, highest of the four major castes of India.

Brahmana (*Brāhmaṇa,* S)   The portion of the Veda that deals with ceremony and ritual.

Buddha (P, S)   A title meaning "one who is enlightened," or "enlightened one."

Buddhabhadra (S)   A monk born in northern India who was well versed in the Zen rules of discipline. He went to China in A.D. 406

and was a friend of Kumarajiva. Buddhabhadra translated thirteen sutras, including the Avataṃsaka-sūtra, into Chinese.

Buddhacharita (Buddhacarita, S)　A biographical account of the life and teachings of Shakyamuni Buddha composed by the second-century A.D. Buddhist poet Aśvaghoṣa, a native of Savatthi.

buddha-nature　The potential for attaining buddhahood, or potential for enlightenment, innate in every sentient being.

Cave of the Seven Leaves (Saptaparṇa-guhā, S; Sattapaṇṇa-guhā, P)　The site of the First Buddhist Council, near Rajagaha.

chakravarti-raja　*See* wheel-rolling king.

Champa (Champā, P, S)　The capital of the kingdom of Anga.

Channa (P; Chandaka or Chanda, S)　A servant of Prince Siddhattha (Shakyamuni). He led the white horse Kanthaka, on whose back the prince was riding on the night of his renunciation of the world. Channa later became a disciple of the Buddha.

Cheti (Ceti, P, S)　One of the sixteen major kingdoms of India in Shakyamuni's time.

Chunda (Cunda, P, S)　A blacksmith and follower of Shakyamuni. He prepared the last meal that the Buddha ate before his death.

Chundaka (Cundaka, P. S)　Shariputra's younger brother.

Deer Park　*See* Migadaya.

deva (P, S)　A celestial or heavenly deity.

Devadaha (P, S)　The capital city of the Koliya tribe.

Devadatta (P, S)　A cousin of Shakyamuni. At first he was a follower of the Buddha but later left him and even attempted to kill him.

Dhammapada (P; Dharmapada, S)　A sutra consisting of two sections and divided into thirty-nine chapters, composed by Dharmatrāta in the fourth or third century B.C. A collection of moral teachings, it stresses good conduct stabilized by concentration and strengthened by perfect wisdom.

Dhaniya (P, S)　A prosperous herdsman whose dialogue with Shakyamuni Buddha (see pages 154–55) is recorded as the Dhaniya Sutra in the Suttanipata.

dharma (S; *dhamma*, P)　(1) In ancient Indian philosophy, morality and religion, the most important of the four ideals for mankind. (2) *D-* In its literal meaning, a reference to something that maintains a certain character constantly and becomes a standard of things. In Buddhist teaching it signifies the universal norms or laws that govern human existence and is variously translated as "Law" or "Truth." (3) *D-* The teaching of the Buddha.

dhuta (*dhūta*, P, S)　An ascetic practice or precept. There are twelve *dhutas*, or mendicant's duties: (1) living in a forest, (2) taking whatever seat may be offered, (3) living on alms, (4) using only one seat for both meditation and eating, (5) wearing coarse garments, (6) not eating at unregulated times, (7) wearing clothes made of discarded rags, (8) having only three robes, (9) living in or near a cemetery, (10) living under a tree, (11) living in the open air, (12) sleeping in a seated posture.

Digha-nikaya (Dīgha-nikāya, P)   The "Long Sayings," one of the five major sutra collections of the Sutta-pitaka of the Pali canon.

Dighatapassin (Dīghatapassin, P; Dīrghatapasvin, S)   A Jain ascetic whose name means "one who has undergone long austerities."

Eightfold Noble Path   Right view, right thinking, right speech, right action, right living, right effort, right memory, right meditation.

eight sufferings   (1) The suffering of birth, (2) the suffering of old age, (3) the suffering of illness, (4) the suffering of death, (5) the suffering that comes from being apart from those whom one loves, (6) the suffering that comes from being with those whom one hates, (7) the suffering that comes from the fact that one cannot have what one wants, and (8) the suffering that comes from the fact that one is attached to the five aggregates of which one's body, mind, and environment are composed.

eighty distinctive body marks   Unique distinguishing characteristics of the body of a Buddha, which include some of the thirty-two distinguishing marks. *See also* thirty-two distinguishing marks.

Eye of the Law   Initial enlightenment. The theoretical understanding of the truth of the Buddha's teachings and the first stage toward ultimate enlightenment, which is attained only after this understanding has been perfected through practice.

First Council   The first assembly of Buddhist monks—in this case five hundred of the Buddha's leading disciples—which gathered some three months after the Buddha's death to compile the Buddhist sutras.

five aggregates   The elements or attributes of which every human being is composed: (1) form, or the body; (2) receptivity, sensation, feeling; (3) mental conceptions and ideas; (4) volition, or various mental activities; (5) consciousness. The union of these five aggregates dates from the moment of birth and constitutes the individual.

five ascetics   The five men whom King Suddhodana ordered to accompany Siddhattha (Shakyamuni) when he renounced his worldly life: Ājñāta-Kauṇḍinya (Aññāta-Koṇḍañña), Aśvajit (Assaji), Bhadrika (Bhaddiya), Mahānāman, and Vāśpa (Vappa). They practiced asceticism with Shakyamuni but left him when he abandoned such practices. Later, when Shakyamuni attained Buddhahood, his first sermon was preached in Migadaya to these men, who became his first disciples.

five moral powers   (1) Belief, (2) endeavor, (3) memory, (4) meditation, and (5) wisdom.

five organs of good conduct   The organs that lead man to good conduct: (1) the sense of belief, (2) the sense of endeavor, (3) the sense of memory, (4) the sense of meditation, and (5) the sense of wisdom.

five precepts   The five basic Buddhist precepts: (1) not to take life, (2) not to steal, (3) to refrain from wrong sexual activity, (4) not to lie, and (5) not to drink intoxicants.

five senses   (1) Sight, (2) hearing, (3) smell, (4) taste, and (5) touch.

four bases of supernatural power   Will, exertion, thought, and investigation.

four insights   The insights that (1) the world is transient, (2) the body is impure, (3) perception leads to suffering, and (4) the mind is impermanent.

four kinds of right effort   These are the effort (1) to prevent evil from arising, (2) to abandon evil when arisen, (3) to produce good, and (4) to increase good when produced.

four merits   Also called the "four fruits" or "four rewards." (1) *Sotapanna (sotāpanna*, P; *srota āpanna*, S), one who has entered the stream (leading to nirvana); (2) *sakadagamin (sakadāgāmin*, P; *sakṛdāgāmin*, S), returning, or being reborn only once more; (3) *anagamin (anāgāmin*, P, S), not returning, or not being reborn again; (4) *arhat.* See also *arhat.*

Four Noble Truths   (1) All existence entails suffering (the Truth of Suffering). (2) Suffering is caused by ignorance, which gives rise to craving and illusion (the Truth of Cause). (3) There is an end to suffering, and this state of no suffering is called nirvana (the Truth of Extinction). (4) Nirvana is attained through the practice of the Eightfold Noble Path (the Truth of the Path). This is one of the fundamental doctrines of all forms of Buddhism and was the content of the first sermon preached by the Buddha. *See also* Eightfold Noble Path.

four sufferings   The first four of the eight sufferings, q.v.

gana (gaṇa, P, S)   A group of two or three people.

Gandhara (Gandhāra, S)   One of the sixteen major kingdoms of India in Shakyamuni's time.

Gaya-Kashyapa   *See* Kashyapa brothers.

Gotama (P; Gautama, S)   The surname of the Shakya clan into which Shakyamuni was born. Another name for Shakyamuni. *See also* Shakyamuni.

grihastha (gṛhastha, S; *gahaṭṭha*, P)   Householder; the second of the traditional Brahmanic four periods of life.

Ikshvaku (Ikṣvāku, S; Okkāka, P)   "Sugar-Cane King," legendary ancestor of the Pūru tribe, of King Pasenadi, and of Shakyamuni. Also one of the surnames of the Shakya clan.

Indra (S; Inda, P)   In Hinduism, the deity controlling thunder, lightning, wind, and rain. He is the enemy of Mara and the *ashuras*. Adopted as one of the protective deities of Buddhism.

Jeta (P, S)   Crown prince of Kosala and owner of the land on which the Jetavana Monastery was built.

Jetavana (P, S) Monastery   A monastery for Shakyamuni and his followers built by Sudatta and Prince Jeta at Savatthi.

Kacchayana (Kaccāyana or Kaccāna, P; Kātyāyana, S)   One of the ten great disciples of Shakyamuni.

kalpa (S; *kappa*, P)   The period of time required for a celestial woman to wear away a ten-mile-cubic stone if she brushes it with her garments once every three years—that is, an infinitely long period of time.

kama (*kāma*, P, S)   Love of pleasure, one of the four ideals for mankind, according to ancient Indian philosophy.

Kanthaka (Kaṇṭhaka, P, S)   Prince Siddhattha's (Shakyamuni's) horse.

Kapilavatthu (P; Kapilavastu, S)   Capital of the Shakya kingdom; present-day Kapilavastu, in Nepal.

karma (*karman*, S; *kamma*, P)   The results of actions, which produce effects that may be either good or bad; conforming to the law or principle of cause and effect, or causality.

Kasi (Kāsī, P; Kāśī, S)   One of the sixteen major kingdoms of India in Shakyamuni's time. Its capital was at Benares.

Kashyapa (Kāśyapa, S; Kassapa, P) brothers   Three brothers from a Brahman family. The eldest brother, Uruvilva (Uruvilvā, S; Uruvelā, P) Kashyapa, had five hundred disciples; the second brother, Nadi (Nadī, P, S) Kashyapa, had three hundred disciples; and the youngest brother, Gaya (Gayā, P, S) Kashyapa, had two hundred disciples. Together with their disciples, the three brothers became followers of Shakyamuni.

Khuddaka-nikaya (Khuddaka-nikāya, P)   The "Minor Sayings," one of the five major sutra collections of the Sutta-pitaka of the Pali canon.

Koliya (S; Koḷiya, P)   The country of the Koliya tribe.

Kosala (Kosalā, P; Kauśalā, S)   The most powerful of the sixteen major kingdoms of India in Shakyamuni's time.

Kosambi (Kosambī, P; Kauśāmbī, S)   The capital of the kingdom of Vansa.

Kshatriya (*kṣatriya*, S; *khattiya*, P)   The warrior caste, second highest of the four major castes of India. Kings and other members of the ruling class, as well as warriors, were traditionally of this caste.

Kumarajiva (Kumārajīva, S)   344–413. Born in Kucha in Central Asia to an Indian father and the sister of the king of Kucha, Kumarajiva went to China in 401 as a Buddhist missionary. From that time until his death he was responsible for the translation of a large number of important sutras, including the Lotus Sutra, and is known as one of the greatest translators into Chinese.

Kushinagara (Kuśinagara, S; Kusinārā, P)   The village where Shakyamuni died, and the capital of the kingdom of Malla.

Law of Causation   The central doctrine of Buddhism, that all phenomena in the universe are produced by causation. According to this doctrine, since all phenomena arise from causes coming into contact with conditions, all things in the universe exist in interrelationship with one another ("Nothing has an ego") and all things and phenomena in this world constantly change ("All things are impermanent"). It was to this law that Shakyamuni was awakened when he attained enlightenment, and it is this doctrine that all his other teachings elucidate.

law of cause and effect   Normally subsumed under the Law of Causation, the law of cause and effect treats of the Law of Causation as it relates to an individual.

Licchavi (Licchavī, P, S)   One of the major tribes of ancient India, members of the Vajji confederation.

Lotus Sutra   The popular name of the Sutra of the Lotus Flower of the Wonderful Law, or Saddharma-puṇḍarīka-sūtra (S), which consists of a series of sermons delivered by Shakyamuni toward the end of his forty-five-year teaching ministry. One of the most important documents of Mahayana Buddhism, the Lotus Sutra teaches: that all sentient beings can attain Perfect Enlightenment—that is, buddhahood—and nothing less than this is the appropriate final goal of believers; that the Buddha is eternal, having existed from the infinite past and appearing in many forms to guide and succor beings through the teaching of the Wonderful Law; and that the noblest form of Buddhist practice is the way of the bodhisattva.

Lumbini (Lumbinī, P, S)   The birthplace of Shakyamuni.

Magadha (P, S)   One of the sixteen major kingdoms of India in Shakyamuni's time.

Maha-Kashyapa (Mahā-Kāśyapa, S; Mahā-Kassapa, P)   One of the ten great disciples of Shakyamuni.

Mahapajapati (Mahāpajāpatī, P; Mahāprajāpatī, S)   The younger sister of Maya, who married King Suddhodana after Maya's death and raised Shakyamuni. The mother of Nanda, and the first *bhikkhuni* in Buddhism.

Maha-parinibbana-sutta (Mahā-parinibbāna-sutta, P; Mahā-parinirvāṇa-sūtra, S) The Sutra of the Great Decease, in which are recorded the final sermon, the death, and the funeral of Shakyamuni.

Mahaprajnaparamita-upadesha (Mahāprajñāpāramitā-upadeśa, S) The one-hundred-fascicle commentary on the Mahāprajñāpāramitā-sūtra (the Perfect Wisdom Sutra) attributed to Nagarjuna and translated into Chinese by Kumarajiva.

Mahavira *See* Nigantha-Nataputta.

Mahayana (Mahāyāna, S) Literally, "Great Vehicle." The northern of the two main branches of Buddhism. The southern branch, Theravada (Theravāda, P, the "Teaching of the Elders"), which is also known as Hīnayāna (S, literally, "Small Vehicle" or "Lesser Vehicle"), spread from India to Sri Lanka, Burma, Thailand, and Cambodia. In Theravada Buddhism one strives to become an *arhat*. The Mahayana branch of Buddhism spread from India to Central Asia, Tibet, Mongolia, China, Korea, and Japan. In contrast to Theravada Buddhism, which tended to remain conservative and rigid, Mahayana Buddhism adapted itself to the needs of peoples of diverse racial and cultural backgrounds and varying levels of understanding. Its ideal is the bodhisattva. The Theravada school is based on the Pali canon, while the Mahayana scriptures are written in Sanskrit, Tibetan, and Chinese.

Majjhima-nikaya (Majjhima-nikāya, P) The "Middle-length Sayings," one of the five major sutra collections of the Sutta-pitaka of the Pali canon.

Makkhali-Gosala (Makkhali-Gosāla, P; Maskali-Gośāla, S) One of the six non-Buddhist teachers.

Malla (P, S) One of the sixteen major kingdoms of India in Shakyamuni's time.

Mallika (Mallikā, P, S) The consort of King Pasenadi and a follower of Shakyamuni.

mandarava (*mandārava*, P, S) flower One kind of heavenly flower, said to be red in color.

Mara (Māra, P, S) The Evil One (literally, "murderer"), so called because he takes away the wisdom-life of all living beings.

Maudgalyayana (Maudgalyāyana, S; Moggallāna, P) One of the ten great disciples of Shakyamuni. He is said to have possessed supernatural powers.

Maya (Māyā, P, S) The mother of Shakyamuni, thought to be a princess of the royal house of Koliya. She is also called Mahamaya.

Middle Path One of the most basic teachings of Buddhism, this is the doctrine of the middle path between two extremes, such as self-indulgence and self-mortification.

Migadaya (Migadāya, P; Mṛgadāva, S) Deer Park, in Benares, where shortly after his enlightenment Shakyamuni preached his first sermon to five fellow ascetics: Ājñāta-Kauṇḍinya (Aññāta-Koṇḍañña), Aśvajit (Assaji), Bhadrika (Bhaddiya), Mahānāman, and Vāśpa (Vappa).

moksha (*mokṣa*, S) Devotion to spiritual pursuits, one of the four ideals for mankind, according to ancient Indian philosophy.

Nadi-Kashyapa *See* Kashyapa brothers.

naga (*nāga*, P, S) A dragon-king.

Nagarjuna (Nāgārjuna, S) Born into a Brahman family in India in the second century A.D., he became one of the chief philosophers of Mahayana Buddhism and is considered to be the fourteenth Indian patriarch in the lineage of the transmission of the Law.

Nanda (P, S) The younger half brother of Shakyamuni and one of the ten great disciples of the Buddha.

Nataputta *See* Nigantha-Nataputta.

Nigantha-Nataputta (Nigaṇṭha-Nātaputta, P; Nirgrantha-Jñātiputra, S) One of the six non-Buddhist teachers and founder of the Jain religion.

nirvana (*nirvāṇa*, S; *nibbāna*, P) Literally, "extinction." (1) The state of enlightenment attained by the Buddha. (2) The highest state of enlightenment. (3) Emancipation from all forms of existence.

Pandava (Paṇḍava, P; Pāṇḍava, S) A mountain near Rajagaha in the kingdom of Magadha.

Pasenadi (P; Prasenajit, S) King of Kosala, he was the same age as the Buddha and ascended the throne the same year that Shakyamuni attained enlightenment. Together with his wife and son, he became a devout follower of the Buddha.

Pataliputta (Pāṭaliputta, P; Pāṭaliputra, S) Present-day Patna, in the state of Bihar.

Pava (Pāvā, P, S) The village where Shakyamuni ate the meal that led to his final illness.

Pindola-Bharadvaja (Piṇḍola-Bhāradvāja, P, S) An *arhat*, originally a subject of the king of Vansa.

Piprahwa The Indian village some thirteen kilometers southeast of Kapilavatthu near which an urn containing the relics of Shakyamuni was excavated from an ancient tomb in 1898.

Pukkusa (P; Pukkuśa, S) A caravan leader who became a follower of Shakyamuni.

Pukkusati (Pukkusāti, P) A rich householder of Magadha and a follower of Shakyamuni.

Rahula (Rāhula, P, S) The son of the Buddha, born before Shakyamuni's renunciation of the world. He is one of the ten great disciples of Shakyamuni.

Rajagaha (Rājagaha, P; Rājagṛha, S)   Present-day Rajgir, in the state of Bihar; the capital of the ancient kingdom of Magadha.

sakadagamin   See four merits.

Sala (*sāla*, P; *śāla*, S) Grove   The stand of twin-trunked *sala* (or possibly teak) trees near Kushinagara where Shakyamuni died.

samana (samaṇa, P; *śramaṇa,* S)   One who practices austerities; an ascetic.

samnyasin (saṃnyāsin, S)   Homeless wanderer; the last of the traditional Brahmanic four periods of life.

samsara (saṃsāra, P, S)   Transmigration; the realm of birth and death.

Samyutta-nikaya (Saṃyutta-nikāya, P)   The "Kindred Sayings," one of the five major sutra collections of the Sutta-pitaka of the Pali canon.

Sangha (*saṃgha,* P, S)   The monastic community of *bhikkhus* or *bhikkhunis* (Buddhist monks or nuns); more generally, the community of Buddhist believers.

Sanjaya (Sañjaya-Belaṭṭhiputta, P; Sañjaya-Vairaṭīputra, S)   One of the six non-Buddhist teachers.

Sankhya (*Sāṃkhya,* S)   A major system of Hindu philosophy, involving two ultimate, completely distinct, principles of matter and spirit.

Savatthi (Sāvatthī, P; Śrāvastī, S)   The capital of the kingdom of Kosala.

Seal of the Three Laws   The three great truths taught by Shakyamuni in order to eliminate ignorance, the fundamental cause of human suffering: (1) All things and phenomena in this world constantly change ("All things are impermanent"). (2) All things in the universe exist in interrelationship with one another ("Nothing has an ego"). (3) The ultimate freedom is to be rid of greed, aggression, and self-delusion ("Nirvana is quiescence").

seven qualities of wisdom   The seven requisites for attaining enlightenment: (1) investigation of the Law, (2) endeavor, (3) the joy of practicing the true teachings, (4) tranquillity, (5) the cessation of clinging, (6) contemplation, and (7) mindfulness.

Shakya (Śākya, S; Sākiya, P)   The tribe to which Shakyamuni belonged.

Shakyamuni (Śākyamuni, S)   Literally, "Sage of the Shakya Clan." The usual Mahayana Buddhist appellation of the historical Buddha.

Shariputra (Śāriputra, S; Sāriputta, P)   The foremost of the ten great disciples of Shakyamuni.

Siddhattha (P; Siddhārtha, S)   Literally, "he who has accomplished his aim." The personal name of the historical Buddha before his renunciation of the world.

six powers of saving sentient beings   (1) Perfect freedom of activity,

(2) ears capable of hearing everything, (3) insight into the minds of others, (4) remembrance of one's former existences, (5) eyes capable of seeing everything, and (6) perfect freedom.

sotapanna *See* four merits.

Subhadda (P; Subhadra, S)   A man who became Shakyamuni's disciple shortly before the latter's death and is therefore known as the Buddha's last disciple. Subhadda realized arhathood immediately after hearing the Buddha's last sermon.

Subhuti (Subhūti, P, S)   One of the ten great disciples of Shakyamuni.

Sudatta (P, S)   A wealthy man of Savatthi and a disciple of Shakyamuni. *See also* Anathapindika.

Suddhodana (P; Śuddhodana, S)   King of the Shakyas and father of Shakyamuni, whose disciple he became.

Sudra (*śūdra*, S; *sudda,* P)   The lowest of the four major castes of India.

Sundari (Sundarī, P, S)   (1) The wife of Nanda. (2) A prostitute who was persuaded to slander Shakyamuni.

Sutra of Good Fortune   The Mahāmaṅgala-sutta (P), a very short sutra (see pages 194–95) in which Shakyamuni defines the highest blessing. Included in the Suttanipata, it is recited daily by Theravada Buddhists.

Sutra of the Great Decease   *See* Maha-parinibbana-sutta.

Suttanipata (Suttanipāta, P)   A Theravada Buddhist text, the "Collection of Discourses," consisting of five fascicles. Composed after the third century B.C., it contains the oldest known sutras and is included in the Khuddaka-nikaya.

Sutta-pitaka   *See* Ti-pitaka.

Tathagata (Tathāgata, P, S)   Literally, "one who has thus gone"—that is, one who has reached the truth and come to declare it; the highest epithet of a Buddha.

Theravada   *See* Mahayana.

thirty-two distinguishing marks   The body of a Buddha is said to be marked by the following distinctive features: (1) flat soles, (2) the Wheel of the Law on the soles, (3) slender fingers, (4) supple limbs, (5) webbed fingers and toes, (6) rounded heels, (7) long legs, (8) slender legs like those of a deer, (9) arms extending below the knees, (10) a concealed penis, (11) an arm span equal to the height of the body, (12) light radiating from the pores, (13) curly body hair, (14) a golden-hued body, (15) light radiating from the body ten feet in each direction, (16) supple shins, (17) legs, palms, shoulders, and neck harmoniously proportioned, (18) swollen armpits, (19) a dignified body like that of a lion, (20) an erect body, (21) full shoulders, (22) forty teeth, (23) firm white teeth, (24) four white canine teeth, (25) full cheeks like those of a lion, (26) flavored saliva, (27) a long slender tongue, (28) a beautiful voice, (29) blue eyes, (30) eyes shaped like those of a bull, (31) a circle of white hair between the eyebrows, and (32) a bump on the top of the head.

three cravings   Cravings for gratification of the desires, for continued existence, and for annihilation.

three poisons   (1) Greed, covetousness, or sensual desire; (2) wrath, anger, or ill will; and (3) ignorance, foolishness, or delusion.

Three Treasures   (1) The Buddha; (2) the Law, or Teaching, of the Buddha; and (3) the Sangha, or community of believers.

three types of superior wisdom   The fourth, fifth, and sixth of the six powers of saving sentient beings, q.v.

Ti-pitaka (Ti-piṭaka, P; Tri-piṭaka, S)   The three parts of the Pali canon, consisting of: (1) Sutta-pitaka (Sutta-piṭaka, P; Sutra-piṭaka, S), or the Sutra Basket, containing the Digha-nikaya, Majjhima-nikaya, Samyutta-nikaya, Anguttara-nikaya, and Khuddaka-nikaya; (2) Vinaya-pitaka (Vinaya-piṭaka, P, S), or the Ordinance Basket, containing the rules for monastic life; and (3) Abhidhamma-pitaka (Abhidhamma-piṭaka, P; Abhidharma-piṭaka, S), or the Treatise Basket, containing doctrinal commentaries.

triple doctrine   (1) Giving alms to the poor and to people of religion; (2) abstaining from destroying life, stealing, lying, and wrong sexual activity; and (3) the assurance of a happy rebirth in Brahma heaven if one leads a life in which such alms are given and these moral precepts are observed.

Udayin (Udāyin, P, S)   A childhood friend of Shakyamuni who became one of his disciples.

Uddaka-Ramaputta (Uddaka-Rāmaputta, P; Udraka-Rāmaputra, S)   A hermit-sage under whom Shakyamuni studied.

Udena (P; Udyana, S)   King of Vansa and a follower of Shakyamuni.

Upali (Upāli, P, S)   (1) One of the ten great disciples of the Buddha. A former slave, he became a monk and was very strict in his observance of the precepts. (2) A rich merchant and Jain who became a follower of Shakyamuni.

upasaka (upāsaka, P, S)   A male lay believer of Buddhism.

upasika (upāsikā, P, S)   A female lay believer of Buddhism.

Upanishads (Upaniṣads, S)   Brahmanic philosophical texts.

Uruvilva-Kashyapa   See Kashyapa brothers.

Vaishya (vaiśya, S)   The merchant caste, third of the four major castes of India.

Vajji (Vajjī, P; Vṛjjī, S)   A major tribal confederation of India in Shakyamuni's time.

vanaprastha (*vānaprastha*, S) Hermit; the third of the traditional Brahmanic four periods of life.

Vansa (Vaṃsa, P; Vatsā, S) One of the sixteen major kingdoms of India in Shakyamuni's time.

Vedas (*veda*, S) The basic scriptures of Hinduism, composed between 2000 and 500 B.C. They consist of the Ṛg-veda, Sāma-veda, Yajur-veda, and Atharva-veda.

Veluvana *See* Bamboo Grove Monastery.

Vesali (Vesālī, P; Vaiśālī, S) The chief city of the Vajji tribes.

Videha (P, S) The wife of King Bimbisara and the mother of King Ajatasattu.

Vinaya-pitaka *See* Ti-pitaka.

Vidudabha (Viḍūḍabha, P, S) King of Kosala and son of King Pasenadi.

Vulture Peak (Gijjhakūṭa, P; Gṛdhrakūṭa, S) A mountain near present-day Rajgir, Bihar; its name is said to derive from the fact that its peak is shaped like a vulture, and also that many vultures are supposed to have lived on the mountain.

wheel-rolling king (*cakkavatti-rāja*, P; *cakravarti-rāja*, S) (1) In Indian mythology, the ideal ruler. (2) In Buddhist terms there are four such kings, each with a precious wheel of gold, silver, copper, or iron. The kings reign over the four great regions, north, south, east, and west. The king of the gold wheel rules the entire world; the king of the silver wheel the east, west, and south regions; the king of the copper wheel the east and south; and the king of the iron wheel the south alone. The coming of the king of the gold wheel in order to unify the world is one of the prophecies of the Buddha and is one of the strongest beliefs of some Buddhists.

Yasa (P; Yaśas, S) An early convert of Shakyamuni.

Yasodhara (Yasodharā, P; Yaśodharā, S) The wife of Shakyamuni before he left home and the mother of Rahula; she later became a *bhikkhuni*.

Index

Abhaya, prince and Jainist, 123–24
advice, six instances of way to give, 124
Agama sutras, ix
Ajatasattu, prince, king, 121, 171, 174, 190
Alara-Kalama, ascetic, 23–24, 31
all things are impermanent, 97, 133
All Wise (epithet of a Buddha), 110
Ambapali, courtesan, 178, 179
anagamin (state in which no return to this world is necessary), 103, 114, 118
Ananda, disciple of Shakyamuni, 97, 118, 152, 168–69, 170–71, 174–75, 179–80, 181, 183–85, 186–87, 190–91, 192–94; enlightenment of, 190
Anathapindika, *see* Sudatta
anatman (non-self), 29
Anuruddha, disciple of Shakyamuni, 97, 164, 171
Aranyaka, *see* Forest Treatises
arhat, 35, 38, 39, 40, 46, 53–54, 103–4, 110, 117–18; definition of, 35
artha (material gain), 102
Aryans, 3–4
asceticism, ascetic austerities, 6, 24–

26; practiced by Shakyamuni, 24–26
Asita, seer, 15
Asoka, emperor, 11, 14, 122, 189
Assaji, ascetic, 68, 85–86
atman (individual self), 6, 29
Avanti, major Indian state, 10

Bamboo Grove Monastery, 67–68, 138
base quest, 152
beggar, begging, 87, 91, 102
Bhaddiya, disciple of Shakyamuni, 97, 171
bhagavat (one who has merited all good omens, World-honored One), 112
Bhaggas, country of the, 145, 146
Bhagu, disciple of Shakyamuni, 171
Bharadvaja, 150–51
bhikkhu (beggar, monk), 102, 106
bhikkhuni (nun), 106
Bimbisara, king of Magadha, 20–22, 65–67, 114–15, 121, 137, 139, 152, 173–74
biographies of Shakyamuni, ix–x
birth as suffering, 47

bo tree, 27, 27n
Bodh Gaya, 27n, 186
Bodhi, prince, 145–46
Brahma, chief among Hindu gods, 30; Pleading of, 30
brahma-charin (student), 100
brahma-chariya (studentship and life of purity and celibacy), 101
Brahmadatta, student, 130
Brahman (universal Self), 6
Brahmanas (commentaries on sacred rituals), 4
Brahmanic religion, 4–5
Brahmans (priests), 4, 5, 103, 104, 148–51; and Brahmanic Law, 148–51
Buddha, the (epithet of a Buddha), 112; ten epithets of, 110–12; *see also* Shakyamuni
Buddha, Buddhas, as generic and specific terms, x–xi
Buddhabhadra, master of meditation, translator, 166–67
Buddhacarita, Mahayana text, 11, 173
buddha-nature, 111, 117
Buddhism, Northern, *see* Northern Buddhism
Buddhism, Southern, *see* Southern Buddhism
Buddhism and Jainism, 120–29
Buddhism and Upanishadic philosophy, 6
Buddhist canon, formation of, 189–91, 191n
Buddhist Order (Sangha), *see* Order

castes, caste system, 4
causation, *see* Law of Causation
cause and effect, *see* law of cause and effect
chakravarti-raja, see wheel-rolling king
Channa, retainer and monk, 18, 19, 118–19, 192, 193–94
Chincha, prostitute, 141
Chunda, smith, 183, 185
Chundaka, brother of Shariputra, 185
Commentary on the Perfect Wisdom Sutra (Mahaprajnaparamita-upadesha), 110, 111
Controller (epithet of a Buddha), 111

dating of events in Buddhism, 135n
death as suffering, 47, 48
Deer Park (Migadaya), 26, 36, 38, 39, 186
Devadaha, 15
Devadatta, cousin and disciple of Shakyamuni, 97, 123, 170–71
devotion to spiritual pursuits (*moksha*), 102
Dhammapada, collection of moral teachings, 118, 131
dharma (morality and religion, righteous duty), 102
Dhaniya, herdsman, 154–55
dhuta (ascetic precepts), 89
Dighatapassin, Jainist ascetic, 125
Discourse on the Analysis of the Truths, 47
Discourse on the Noble Quest, 152
Discourse to Prince Bodhi, 145
Dravidians, 3, 4

ears capable of hearing everything, 165
earth spirits, 168
Eightfold Noble Path, 34, 46, 52–58, 182
eight sufferings, 47–48
eight things of the world, 132–33
elephant riding, analogy of, 146–47
eleven categories of merit, 64
enlightenment, 26–27, 34–35, 38, 41–42, 103–4, 117–18, 164; of Shakyamuni, 26–27, 34, 164
epithets of a Buddha, 109, 110–12
ethical morality, *see* morality and religion
evils, *see* fourteen evils
Eye of the Law, Eye of Wisdom (initial enlightenment), 34, 38, 41–42, 117, 118
eyes capable of seeing everything, 166

female lay believers, see *upasika*

First Council, 189–91
five aggregates, 47, 48
five ascetics, 31–32, 34–35, 105, 117
five moral powers, 182
five organs of good conduct, 182
five precepts, 38–39
Forest Treatises (Aranyaka), 100
four bases of supernatural power, 182
Four Great References, 183
Four Great Teachings, 181–83
four ideals of ancient Indian philosophy, 102
four infinite virtues, 64
four insights, 57, 180, 182
four kinds of right effort, 56, 182
four merits, *see* four stages of enlightenment
Four Noble Truths, 33–34, 43, 45–54, 177–78; and principle of healing, 44–46
four places to be revered after Shakyamuni's death, 186
four stages of enlightenment (four merits), 103–4
four stages of life, 100–103
four sufferings, *see* eight sufferings
four things not to be despised because of their youth, 142

gana (group, union), 106
Gaya-Kashyapa, ascetic and disciple of Shakyamuni, 61
Goshita Park Monastery, 138, 193
Gotama Buddha, xi
Great Decease, 173–89
Great Forest Monastery, 128, 129, 138
grihastha (householder) stage of life, 101

heart of benevolence, 64–65
Heaven of the Thirty-three Devas, 92, 142
heretical teachers and sects, *see* non-Buddhist teachers and sects
hermit (*vanaprastha*) stage of life, 101–2
highest blessings, 153–54, 194–95

homeless-wanderer (*samnyasin*) stage of life, 102
householder (*grihastha*) stage of life, 101

illness as suffering, 47, 48
impermanence, 97, 133, 158–59, 158n
India, culture of, in ancient times, 3–5; political conditions in, in Shakyamuni's time, 9–11
Indian philosophy at time of Shakyamuni's birth, 5–8
individual self (atman), 6
Indra, Hindu god and Buddhist tutelary deity, 158
insight into the minds of others, 165
"Instruction of the Seven Buddhas," 158, 159, 160–62

Jainism, 25, 104, 120–29; and Buddhism, 120–29; and early Buddhism, 120–22; and Buddhism in Magadha, 122–26; in lands of Shakyas and Vajjis, 126–29
Jeta, prince, 138, 140
Jetavana Monastery, 138–39, 140
jina (victor), 121
Jōdo sect of Buddhism, 159

kama (love of pleasure), 102
karma (results of actions), 6, 7, 37, 127
Kapilavatthu, Buddhism in, 90–98
Kashyapa brothers, 61–63, 66, 139
Kimbila, disciple of Shakyamuni, 97, 171
Kosala, major Indian state, 10; Buddhism in, 135–42
Kshatriyas (warriors and members of ruling class), 4
Kumarajiva, translator of sutras, 166
Kushinagara, site of Shakyamuni's death, 185, 186

Law, 60, 105, 148–56
Law of Causation, 28, 29–30, 41, 43, 46–47, 86, 96, 97
law of cause and effect, 6, 28, 37, 95–96

Law of the Universe, 152–56
law of the world, 152–56
Licchavis, 121
Long-nailed Itinerant Ascetic, skeptic and uncle of Shariputra, 88–89
love of pleasure (*kama*), 102
Lumbini Garden, 14, 15, 186
lute, analogy of, 116–17

Magadha, major Indian state, 10; Buddhism in, 60–68, 85–89, 112–19, 122–26, 139
Maha-Kashyapa, disciple of Shakyamuni, 89, 139, 188–89, 190, 192
Mahapajapati, foster mother of Shakyamuni, 16
Mahaprajnaparamita-upadesha, the (Commentary on the Perfect Wisdom Sutra), 110, 111
Mahavira, *see* Nataputta
Mahayana, *see* Northern Buddhism
Makkhali-Gosala, ascetic, 140, 141
male lay believers, see *upasaka*
Mallika, queen, 140
Mansion of Migara's Mother, monastery, 138
Mara, the Evil One, 155, 181
material gain (*artha*), 102
Maudgalyayana, disciple of Shakyamuni, 68, 85–89, 117–18, 126, 139, 164, 170, 173
Maya, mother of Shakyamuni, 15, 16, 142
meditation, 22–24, 57–58, 159–60
meditation practice of Shakyamuni, 22–24
Middle Path, 33, 52
Migadaya, *see* Deer Park
miraculous powers, *see* supernatural powers
Mirror of the Law, 178
moksha (devotion to spiritual pursuits), 102
monasteries, 138–39
morality and religion (*dharma*), 102, 161–62, 176–77

Nadi-Kashyapa, ascetic, 61

Nagarjuna, Mahayana scholar, 110, 111
nagas (dragon-kings), 15
Nalanda, monastery at, 122–23
Nanda, half brother and disciple of Shakyamuni, 91–93, 94–95, 96; and Sundari, 92–93; and female monkey, 92; and nymphs, 92–93
Nata clan, 121
Nataputta, founder of Jainism, 121, 122, 123, 125, 128
Nichiren sect of Buddhism, 159
nigantha (freedom from bondage), 121
Nigantha as name for Jainism, 121, 126
Nigantha-Nataputta, *see* Nataputta
nirvana, 6, 97, 111, 133, 158
nirvana is quiescence, 97, 133
noble quest, 152, 153
non-Buddhist (heretical, unorthodox) teachers and sects, 7, 106, 120–21, 140–41
non-self, 29, 34
Northern (Mahayana) Buddhism, xi, 107, 108
nothing has an ego, 97, 133

old age as suffering, 47, 48
Order (Sangha), growth of, 59–68, 85–89; early missionary activities of, 59–60; functions of, 59–60; in Uruvela, 60–64; in Rajagaha, 65–68, 85–89; joining of, 99; characteristics and value of, 103–5; formation of, 105–6; definition and functions of, 107–8; rules for welfare of, 175–76

Pali, xi
Pali canon, 191n
Pasenadi, king of Kosala, 20, 139–40, 141–42, 173
Peerless Leader (epithet of a Buddha), 111
perfect freedom, 40
perfect freedom of activity, 164
Perfectly Enlightened in Conduct (epithet of a Buddha), 110

philosophical emphasis in Buddhism, 159
Pindola-Bharadvaja, disciple of Shakyamuni, 170
Piprahwa, 14
Pleading of Brahma, 30
political conditions in Shakyamuni's time, 9–11
precepts (morality), 53
pride, 133–34
psychological suffering, 48–51
Pukkusa, caravan leader, 184
Pukkusati, conversion of, 112–14, 118
purification of the mind, 162

Rahula, son of Shakyamuni, 18, 91
rainy-season retreats (*varshika*), 128
rationalism of Buddhism, 159
religion, 49, 93–97; reasons for turning to, 93–97
remembrance of one's former existences, 165–66
right action, 56
right effort, 56–57
right living, 56
right meditation, 57–58
right memory, 57
right speech, 55–56
right thinking, 55
right view, 54–55
Rolling of the Wheel of the Law, 33
rules for welfare of the Order, 175–76

Sagata, attendant of Shakyamuni, 115
sakadagamin (state in which one will be born once again into this world), 103
samana (monk, ascetic), 7, 102, 103, 104
Samana Gotama, xi
Samavati, queen, 145
samnyasin (homeless wanderer) stage of life, 102
Sangha (Order), explanation of origin of, 105–6; *see also* Order
sangha (group, union), 105–6
Sanjaya, skeptic, 85, 86

Sankhya, 25
Sanskrit, xi, 98
Seal of the Three Laws, 97
Second Council, 191n
secular morality, 153–54
self, soul, 29
Sermon on Burning, 63–64
seven qualities of wisdom, 182
seven rules for security of the Vajjis, 174–75
seven rules for welfare of the Order, 175–76
Shakyamuni, biographies of, ix–x; as historical figure, ix–x; origin and use of name of, x–xi; birth of, 9, 11, 14–15; birthday of, 11, 14; day of enlightenment of, 14; day of death of 14; childhood and young manhood of, 16–19; at agricultural festival, 16; in Magadha, 20–24, 60–68, 115, 123–26; and King Bimbisara, 20–22, 65–67, 114–15; meditation practices of, 22–24; and Alara-Kalama, 23–24; and Uddaka-Ramaputta, 24; ascetic austerities of, 24–26; enlightenment of, 26–27, 164; and Law of Causation, 28–30; and Pleading of Brahma, 30; and the five ascetics, 31–32; first sermon of, 33–35; in Benares, 36–60; and Yasa, 36–39; teaching mission of disciples of, 40; and the Kashyapa brothers, 61–63; in Rajagaha, 65–68, 85–89; and disciples Shariputra and Maudgalyayana, 87–89; and Long-nailed Itinerant Ascetic, 88–89; and Maha-Kashyapa, 89; and Suddhodana, 90–91; in Kapilavatthu, 90–98; and Nanda, 91–93; and Upali (disciple), 97–98; reputation of, 109–12; and Pukkusati, 112–14; and council of overseers in Rajagaha, 114–15; and Sona, 116–17; and Prince Abhaya, 123–24; and Upali (merchant), 125–26; and Vappa, 126–27; in Vesali, 128–29, 178–79, 181–83; and General Shiha, 128–29; on

criticism and praise of the Three Treasures, 131; and Sudatta, 136–37; in Kosala, 139–44; and six non-Buddhist teachers, 140–41; and King Pasenadi, 141–42; in Heaven of the Thirty-three Devas, 142; in legends surrounding Kosala, 142–44; and King Udena, 143–44; in Kosambi, 143–44; symbols of, 144; in images and statues, 144–45n; in the country of the Bhaggas, 145–46; and Prince Bodhi, 145–47; and the Brahmans, 148–51; and Bharadvaja, 150–51; on food, 151; on the law of the world and the Law of the Universe, 152–56; on secular morality, 153–54; and Dhaniya, 154–55; sermons and teachings of, 157–58; as the Young Ascetic of the Himalayas, 158; supernatural powers of, 163–64, 167–69; and the earth spirits, 168; and the twin *sala* trees and Upavana, 168–69; and the sandalwood bowl, 169–70; prohibits use of supernatural powers for show, 169, 170; last activities of, 173–85; and seven rules for security of the Vajjis, 174–75; and rules for welfare of the Order, 175–76; and Mirror of the Law, 178; and the courtesan Ambapali, 179; and Mara, 181; final teachings of, 181–83; and Chunda, 183; and Pukkusa, 184; final hours and death of, 185–89; and Subhadda, 187; on character of Ananda, 187; funeral of, 188–89; and deity at Jetavana monastery, 194–95; and Singala, 195–99

Shakya tribe and state, 9–11, 14, 90–91, 126–27; conversion of, 91

Shariputra, disciple of Shakyamuni, 68, 85–89, 117, 139, 173

Shiha, general and Jainist, 126, 128–29

Siddhattha, original name of Shakyamuni, 15

Singala, householder, 195, 199

six non-Buddhist (heretical) teachers, 7, 120–21, 140–41

six powers of saving sentient beings, *see* six supernatural powers

six states of existence, 111

six supernatural powers, 40, 164–66, 171

Sona, 115, 116–17; conversion of, 116–17, 118

sotapanna (entrance into the stream of sanctification), 103

soul, self, 29

Southern (Theravada) Buddhism, x, xi, 107, 108

Stanza on Production by Causation, 86

student (*brahma-charin*) stage of life, 100–101

Subhadda, ascetic, 187

Subhuti, disciple of Shakyamuni, 143

Sudatta, merchant and disciple of Shakyamuni, 135–38, 139, 140, 143

Suddhodana, king (father of Shakyamuni), 10, 15, 26, 90–91

Sudras (slaves), 4

suffering, 33–34, 44–46, 47–52, 153

Sundari, fiancée of Nanda, 92–93

Sundari, rumored prostitute, 141

Sunida, minister of Magadha, 167, 168

Sunyata (Void), 143

supernatural powers, 163–72; of Shakyamuni, 163–64, 167–69; prohibition of use of for show, 169–72

Suppiya, wandering teacher, 130

Sutra of the First Rolling of the Wheel of the Law, 33, 47

Sutra of Good Fortune, 153–54, 194

Sutra of the Great Decease, 158, 164, 166, 167–68, 173, 174, 177

Sutra of Reverence to the Six Directions, 195

Sutra on the Brahman Law, 148–49

Suttanipata, 132

Tathagata, term for a Buddha, 30, 112, 123–24; *see also* Shakyamuni

Teacher of Gods and Men (epithet of a Buddha), 111–12

teaching by due course (or in due order), 36–37

teaching the masses, 104–5

ten epithets of a Buddha, 110–12

theoretical and rational foundations of Buddhism, 159–60

therapy and healing, 43–44, 52

Theravada, *see* Southern Buddhism

three cravings, 50–51

Three Treasures, 39, 42, 106

three types of learning, 53–54

three types of superior wisdom, 39–40, 164

Ti-pitaka, Buddhist canon, 145n, 191n

trance state of nonthinking, 23

transmigration, 6

triple doctrine, 37

Truth of Cause, 45

Truth of Extinction, 45–46

Truth of the Path, 46

Truth of Suffering, 45

twin *sala* trees, 168–69, 185–86

Two Treasures, 106

Udayin, disciple of Shakyamuni, 90

Uddaka-Ramaputta, ascetic, 24, 31

Udena, king of Vansa, 143–44, 192–93

Understander of the World (epithet of a Buddha), 111

universal Self (Brahman), 6

unorthodox teachers and sects, *see* non-Buddhist teachers and sects

Upaka, 15, 31

Upali, disciple of Shakyamuni, 97–98, 190

Upali, merchant and Jainist, 123, 125–26

Upanishads, Upanishadic philosophy, 6–7, 23; adopted by Buddhism, 6

upasaka (male lay believer), 106

upasika (female lay believer), 106

Upavana, disciple of Shakyamuni, 168–69

Uppalavanna, nun, 143

Uruvilva-Kashyapa, ascetic, 61, 62–63, 66

Uttara, waiting woman, 145

Vaishyas (farmers, shepherds, people of commerce), 4

Vajjis, 121, 122, 174–75

vanaprastha (hermit), 101

Vansa, major Indian state, 10

Vappa, Jainist, 126–27

varshika, see rainy-season retreats

Vassakara, minister of Magadha, 167, 168, 174, 175

Vedas, Vedic doctrines, Vedic religion, 3–4, 68, 101

"Verse of Impermanence," 158–59, 158n

Vesakha Festival, 14

Vidudabha, king, 173, 174

Vimalakirti, layman, 108

Vinaya-pitaka, ix

Visakha, mother of Migara, 138

Void, *see* Sunyata

Vulture Peak, 115

Well Departed (epithet of a Buddha), 110–11

wheel-rolling king (*chakravarti-raja*), 9, 33

World-honored One (epithet of a Buddha), 112

Worshipful (epithet of a Buddha), 110

Yasa, disciple of Shakyamuni, 36–39, 105, 117

Yasodhara, wife of Shakyamuni, 15, 16

Yoga, 22–24, 25, 171–72

Young Ascetic of the Himalayas, 158, 158n